To
peace and mutual understanding
between the Muslims and al-Ahl al-Kitab—
allathina amanu bi-rabbihim.

R. HRAIR DEKMEJIAN is Professor of Political Science, State University of New York at Binghamton. He is also Lecturer on Middle Eastern affairs, Foreign Service Institute, U.S. Department of State. A graduate of Columbia University, he has served as consultant to the Agency for International Development, the Department of State, and the United States Information Agency. He is the author of many articles and books, including *Patterns of Political Leadership* and *Egypt under Nasir.*

Islam in Revolution

Contemporary Issues in the Middle East

ISLAM IN REVOLUTION

Fundamentalism in the Arab World

R. HRAIR DEKMEJIAN

State University of New York at Binghamton

SYRACUSE UNIVERSITY PRESS   1985

This study was supported and monitored by the Defense Intelligence Agency of the Department of Defense under Contract No. MDA908-83-C-06023. The views contained in this document are those of the author and should not be interpreted as necessarily representing the official policy, either expressed or implied, of the Defense Intelligence Agency, the Department of Defense, or the U.S. Government.

Library of Congress Cataloging in Publication Data

Dekmejian, R. Hrair, 1933–
  Islam in revolution.

  Bibliography: p.
  Includes index.
  1. Islam—Arab countries—History.   2. Islam—20th
century.   I. Title.
BP63.A4D45   1985   322'.1'09174927   84-26766
ISBN 0-8156-2329-1
ISBN 0-8156-2330-5 (pbk.)

Manufactured in the United States of America

Contents

Figures

Tables

Preface

THE LAST DECADE has witnessed the heightening and deepening of Islamic consciousness in Muslim communities throughout the world. The resurgence of the Islamic ethos is at once spiritual, social, economic, and political in its manifestations. As in centuries past, the hallmark of the contemporary resurgence is a return to Islamic roots—the fundamentals of the faith as revealed and practiced by the Prophet Muhammad.

The primary concern of this book is to examine the historical roots and patterns of Islamic resurgence and the forms of its manifestation in the crisis milieu of present-day Muslim society. This work does not purport to be a comprehensive study of Islam or its fundamentalist expression. It focuses on political Islam and its revolutionary implications in the Arab world.

To the extent possible, the study relies on original Arabic sources, including many underground publications, pamphlets, and tracts. It provides some empirical evidence on the fundamentalist movement through the analysis of ninety-one Islamic societies and groups. The compilation of data was accomplished by the staff of the Center for Research and Development, Inc. Originally begun as a report for the United States government, this study has been revised and significantly expanded to include a comprehensive analytical framework and new data on recent developments in the Arab sphere.

I wish to gratefully acknowledge the invaluable assistance of many colleagues and co-workers including Professors Matti Moosa of Gannon University, Eliz Sanasarian of the University of Southern Cali-

ix

fornia, Safia Mohsen and Don Peretz of SUNY Binghamton, and G. R. Bassiry of Indiana University of Pennsylvania. Equally significant was the assistance of Beth Ann Binns in performing the statistical analysis with the help of my colleague Professor David Cingranelli of SUNY Binghamton. In addition, I profited immensely from two conferences held under the aegis of SUNY Binghamton's Southwest Asian and North African Studies Program on Islamic Resurgence (1981) and Comparative Religious Fundamentalism (1983). I owe a particular debt for the insights expressed at these conferences by Professors Ali Hillal Dessouki, Leonard Binder, Eric Davis, Richard Antoun, Khalil Semaan, John Voll, Charles Adams, Akbar Muhammad, Ismail al-Faruqi, Richard Moench, Norman Stillman, and Archbishop Tiran Nersoyan. I am also grateful to Dr. Peter Bechtold of the Foreign Service Institute and Dr. Pamela Johnson of USAID for their suggestions and encouragement. Special thanks are due to Professor Hermann Eilts of Boston University, for taking the time to read and comment on the entire manuscript.

Throughout the exciting but painful process of research and analysis, I was fortunate to have the devoted support of Dr. John Bezazian, without whose wholehearted efforts this volume would not have been possible. Nor should I fail to mention the spiritual reinforcement and research efforts of my wife Anoush and of our children Gregory, Armen, and Haig. Armen's virtuosity on the word processor along with the computer skills of Beth Ann Binns and Wayne Baggett were instrumental in producing the five extensive revisions of this study. I am equally thankful to my mother, sister, brother-in-law and the Kassabian clan of California for their forbearance and moral support during the trying days of last summer spent in the final revision of the manuscript.

My list would be incomplete without mentioning the wise counsel of Colonel Alfred B. Prados and his colleagues who were kind enough to share with me their unrivalled expertise on Middle Eastern affairs. I also wish to thank the SUNY Binghamton administration, particularly Professor Arthur Banks, my department chairman, for a sabbatical leave in Fall 1983 to complete this project. Finally, I must mention the inestimable help accorded by my graduate students and the several dozen individuals who have asked to remain anonymous.

As an Armenian Christian born and raised in a predominantly Muslim society, I have endeavored to capture as much as possible the Islamic perspective on the fundamentalist phenomenon. In view of the enormity of the task, I have labored in humble realization of the Quranic maxim:

Al-ruhu min amri rabbi,
wa ma utitum min al-ilmi illa qalilan.

The Spirit is by command of my Lord, and
of knowledge only little has been imparted to you.

With all of its shortcomings, this book constitutes the modest product of the concerted *ijtihad* of the author and his many helpers.

Binghamton, New York   R. HRAIR DEKMEJIAN
Autumn 1984

Obey God and obey the
Messenger and those
charged with authority
amongst you.

The Quran

You are the best
community ever
brought forth to men.

The Quran

A strong Muslim is
better than a weak one.

Hadith

Part I   Islamic Fundamentalism

Catalysts, Indices, and Responses

1 Islamic Resurgence in Modern Society

$\mathcal{D}$URING THE LAST THREE CENTURIES, the world of Islam has been buffeted by internal and external crises of major proportions. The progressive decline of Ottoman and Persian power in the face of European imperial might prompted an ongoing quest to reexamine the basic tenets of Islam. As in centuries past, the Islamic community generated its own culturally nativist response to crisis—a return to Islam and its fundamental precepts. At the onset of Islam's fourteenth century (A.D. 1980), the movement back to Islamic roots has assumed a powerful self-propelling dynamic with significant political, economic, and strategic implications. In its militant form, Islamic fundamentalism has manifested itself in diverse national settings during the last half-decade:

- The Islamic Revolution in Iran.
- The takeover of the Grand Mosque in Mecca.
- Disturbances in the Eastern Province of Saudi Arabia.
- Resistance to the Soviet occupation of Afghanistan.
- Rebellion against the Syrian Baath regime.
- Armed opposition to Iraq's Baath regime.
- The assassination of President Sadat.
- Suicide attacks and armed struggle against Israeli, American, and French forces in Lebanon.
- Disturbances in Bahrain and bombings in Kuwait.
- Rioting and demonstrations in Algeria, Tunisia, and Morocco.

3

Both in its militant and passive forms, contemporary Islamic fundamentalism possesses three general attributes: pervasiveness, polycentrism, and persistence. It is pervasive since Islamic groups and movements have sprung up in virtually every Muslim community regardless of size or political, economic, and cultural setting. Nor is Islamic revival limited to particular social and economic classes. While much of its grassroots support is based on the lower, lower-middle, and middle classes, there is increasing evidence of widespread emulation of Islamic lifeways among the upper-middle and upper strata. The Islamic rebirth movement is also polycentric since it possesses no single revolutionary leadership or organizational epicenter. To a significant degree, the return to Islamic roots has had a local character as a response to particular crisis conditions existing in various national environments. Yet to the extent that crisis situations in different societies are similar, the Islamic movement could eventually assume a truly transnational character. Finally, Islamic fundamentalism has shown an unusual degree of persistence during the last century and in previous eras, with a cyclical propensity to intrude upon the sociopolitial process to shape its evolution.[1]

The heightening of Islamic consciousness has been variously characterized as revivalism, rebirth, puritanism, fundamentalism, reassertion, awakening, reformism, resurgence, renewal, renaissance, revitalization, militancy, activism, millenarianism, messianism, return to Islam, and the march of Islam. Collectively, these terms are useful in describing the complexity of the Islamic phenomenon; yet they impute a certain dormancy to Islam, which does not conform to reality. In point of fact, Islam has successfully resisted the encapsulation imposed upon Christianity in the West—a resistance that is at the core of the ongoing conflict between state and religion in the Islamic world. Thus, it is instructive to review terms and constructs in the original Arabic usage regarding the Islamic phenomenon. Proponents and sympathizers frequently use the following expressions: *baath al-Islami* (Islamic renaissance), *sahwah al-Islamiyyah* (Islamic awakening), *ihya al-Din* (Religious revival), *usuliyyah al-Islamiyyah* (Islamic fundamentalism).[2]

The most appropriate term is *al-usuliyyah al-Islamiyyah* since it connotes a search for the fundamentals of the faith, the foundations of the Islamic polity *(ummah),* and the bases of legitimate authority *(al-shariyyah al-hukm).* Such a formulation emphasizes the political dimension of the Islamic movement, more than its religious aspect. In terms of general usage in the vocabulary of Islam, the concept of *tajdid* refers to the periodic renewal of the faith, while *islah* means restoration or reform. Another group of important terms include the specific appellations used in Arabic to describe fundamentalist individuals and groups. Usually the proponents of Islamic fundamentalism refer to themselves as *Islamiyyin*—Islamists, or as *asliyyin*—the original or authentic ones. Also used is the term *mutadayyin* (pl. *mutadayyinin*)—the pious or the devout, in sharp contrast to *mutaassib* (pl. *mutaassibin*)—meaning zealot or fanatic. The word *mutaassib* is often used by non-fundamentalists to describe the Islamic militants who are predisposed to the use of violence; a related label is *mutatarrif* or radical. The term *mutadayyin* is given two distinct meanings: as a general reference to characterize the faithful Muslim and as a specific appellation used by the fundamentalists about themselves, as distinct from other Muslims. The terms "fundamentalist" and "Islamist" are used interchangeably in this study.

Analytical Objectives

The present study seeks to synthesize the Muslim, Western, and other perspectives on Islamic fundamentalism to achieve a balanced understanding of its manifestations in the Arab sphere. To this end, the inquiry is cast in a broad framework that combines historical, theological, psychological, political, and socioeconomic factors affecting the fundamentalist phenomenon. The analysis will focus on the examination of eleven salient topics:

    1. historical and theological anchors of Islamic fundamentalism and its cyclical patterns,
    2. catalysts of contemporary Islamic fundamentalism,
    3. the social-psychological makeup of the fundamentalist individual,
    4. elements of Islamic fundamentalist ideology,
    5. techniques and targets of Islamist ideological propagation,
    6. indices of Islamist behavior,
    7. taxonomy of ninety-one Islamic fundamentalist societies,
    8. leadership of Islamist movements,
    9. state responses to fundamentalism,
    10. prognosis of fundamentalist movements in Arab conflictual milieux,
    11. Islamic fundamentalism as a challenge to American interests.

Figure 1
Conceptual Framework

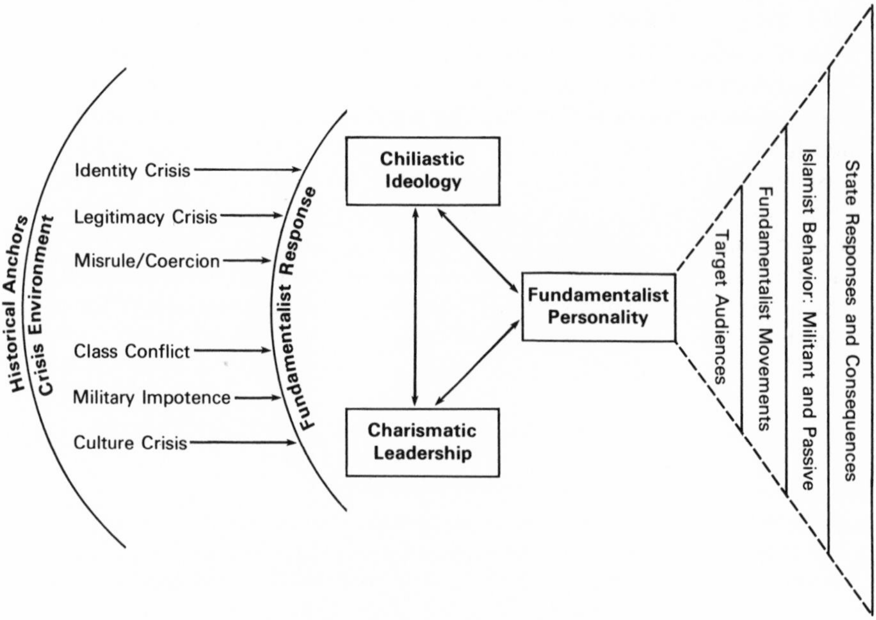

Conceptual Framework

The foregoing categories of inquiry necessitate the employment of an eclectic conceptual approach that combines theories of crisis, leadership, personality, class conflict, and dialectical causality. The conceptual linkages between the components of the theoretical framework depicted in Figure 1 may be summarized in several propositions:

1. *Social crisis*—Islamic fundamentalism is perceived as a cyclical phenomenon which occurs as a response to acute and pervasive social crisis.

2. *Attributes of crisis milieux*—The scope and intensity of the fundamentalist reaction, ranging from spiritual reawakening to revolutionary violence, depends on the depth and pervasiveness of the crisis environment characterized by six attributes:
   a. Identity crisis

    b. Legitimacy crisis
    c. Misrule/coercion
    d. Class conflict
    e. Military impotence
    f. Culture crisis

3. *Fundamentalist responses*—As a reaction to social crisis, religio-political fundamentalism manifests itself through
    a. Charismatic leadership committed to a spiritual and/or revolutionary transformation of society.
    b. Chiliastic ideology containing a salvational prescription of primordial values, beliefs, and practices that are to shape the new fundamentalist order.
    c. Fundamentalist personality formed under the impact of the crisis environment and the counter-influences of fundamentalist ideology.
    d. Social groups and classes particularly susceptible to the fundamentalist call by virtue of their psychocultural orientations and specific socioeconomic positions in society and the world economic order.
    e. Fundamentalist movements and groups typically led by charismatic personalities and manifesting behavioral patterns ranging from spiritual fervor to revolutionary activism.

4. *State responses and consequences*—The political manifestations of fundamentalism and its propensity for violence induce state policy responses ranging from violent repression to accommodation and cooptation. The future resurgence or decline of fundamentalism is dependent on the nature of state policies, external stimuli, and the quality of leadership of fundamentalist movements.

The regeneration of the Islamic ethos in the contemporary setting is a complex phenomenon which is at once spiritual, social, economic, and political in nature. The Western practice of placing Islamic fundamentalism under the rubric of "fanaticism" is singularly dysfunctional to a balanced and dispassionate analysis of the subject. Indeed, to a Western world preoccupied with growing economic problems and security concerns, the Islamic challenge was unexpected and ominous. Few in the non-Islamic sphere were able to anticipate an Islamic resurgence in the modern context.[3] The conceptual myopia induced by Western and Marxist materialism had effectively blindfolded both scholars and statesmen, who tended to dismiss or underestimate the regenerative capacity of Islam. Any intellectually valid approach to the subject requires a culturally indigenous perspective based on Islamic theology and history and the writings of Islamist theorists. Thus, the present study seeks to focus on the nativist perspective, while augmenting it with relevant insights from Western social theory, including Erikson's contributions on personality and religious leadership and Weber's concept of charisma and prophetic authority, as derived from the writings of St. Paul.

A plethora of Western theorists, including Marx, Weber, Durkheim, and Berger, have persuasively argued that social and economic deprivation produces an increase in religious commitment.[4] Without denying the salience of socioeconomic causality, this study proposes to adopt a more comprehensive and multidimensional framework to analyze the contemporary Islamic crisis setting. Hence, the emphasis on the crisis of the spirit—the crisis of identity and culture—and the crisis of legitimacy—the erosion of the moral basis of authority and its dysfunctional concomitants—elite misrule, military impotence, and class conflict. This eclectic conceptualization has the advantage of combining Western theories of crisis with the Islamists' own diagnosis of their crisis milieu. The subsequent chapters are structured according to the components of the conceptual framework schematically depicted in Figure 1.

2 History of Islamist Movements

A Cyclical Pattern

$\overline{\bigwedge}$N OUTSTANDING CHARACTERISTIC of religious fundamentalist movements is their cyclical propensity, consisting of successive periods of dormancy and resurgence. A causal pattern can be discerned whereby manifestations of religious resurgence correspond to periods of intense spiritual, social, and political crisis. Islamic fundamentalism is no exception to this historical pattern.[1] Indeed, throughout Islamic history, the incidence of fundamentalist resurgence has been closely associated with periods of great turmoil when the very existence of the Islamic polity and/or its moral integrity were under threat.

The present phase of Islamic resurgence can be viewed as conforming to the cyclical appearance in times of crisis of revivalist movements reaching back to the Prophet's era. Such a dialectical approach, reminiscent of Ibn Khaldun, is dictated not only by historical reality but also by the self-view and worldview of today's Islamist movements. Indeed, contemporary Islamic fundamentalists view themselves as the direct successors and emulators of past leaders and movements of resurgence and renewal.

Cycles of Crisis and Fundamentalist Responses

The practice of present-day fundamentalists to view Islamic history in terms of cycles of decline and resurgence possesses considerable his-

9

Figure 2
Stages of Social Crisis and Islamist Response

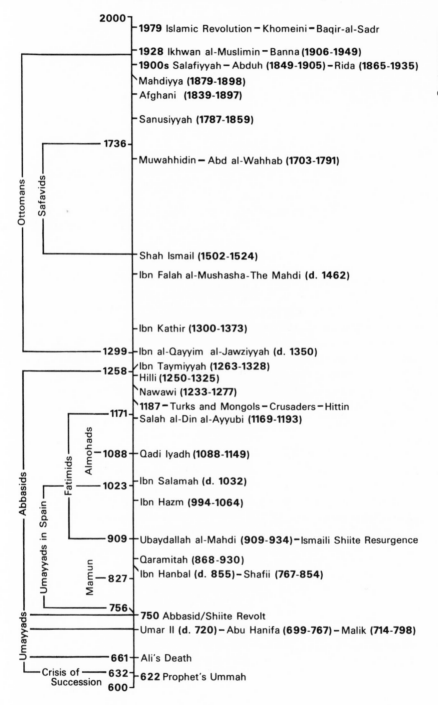

2000

1979 Islamic Revolution – Khomeini – Baqir-al-Sadr

1928 Ikhwan al-Muslimin – Banna **(1906-1949)**
1900s Salafiyyah – Abduh **(1849-1905)** – Rida **(1865-1935)**
Mahdiyya **(1879-1898)**
Afghani **(1839-1897)**

Sanusiyyah **(1787-1859)**

1736

Muwahhidin – Abd al-Wahhab **(1703-1791)**

Shah Ismail **(1502-1524)**
Ibn Falah al-Mushasha-The Mahdi **(d. 1462)**

Ibn Kathir **(1300-1373)**
1299 Ibn al-Qayyim al-Jawziyyah **(d. 1350)**
1258 Ibn Taymiyyah **(1263-1328)**
Hilli **(1250-1325)**
Nawawi **(1233-1277)**
1171 **1187** – Turks and Mongols – Crusaders – Hittin
Salah al-Din al-Ayyubi **(1169-1193)**

1088 Qadi Iyadh **(1088-1149)**

1023 Ibn Salamah **(d. 1032)**

Ibn Hazm **(994-1064)**

909 Ubaydallah al-Mahdi **(909-934)** – Ismaili Shiite Resurgence
Qaramitah **(868-930)**
827 Ibn Hanbal **(d. 855)** – Shafii **(767-854)**

756
750 Abbasid/Shiite Revolt
Umar II **(d. 720)** – Abu Hanifa **(699-767)** – Malik **(714-798)**

661 Ali's Death

Crisis of 632
Succession 622 Prophet's Ummah
600

Ottomans

Safavids

Abbasids

Umayyads in Spain

Fatimids

Almohads

Mamun

Umayyads

Crisis of Succession

Contemporary Islamic Resurgence

torical validity. Indeed, the causal relationship between spiritual-social-political turmoil and fundamentalist ascendance has been a recurrent pattern in Islamic history as depicted in the chronological diagram in Figure 2. This cyclical dynamic of crisis and resurgence is discernible in various historial periods:

1. Umayyad decline—Umar ibn Abd al-Aziz (d. 720)
   Abu Hanifa (699–767)
   Malik (714–798)
   Shiite/Abbasid Revolt (750)
2. Abbasid degeneration—Ibn Hanbal (780–855)
   al-Shafii (767–854)
   Ismaili Shiite resurgence:
   Qaramitah (c. 890)
   Ubaydallah al-Mahdi (909)
3. Umayyad decline in Spain—Ibn Hazm (d. 1064)
4. Fatimid decline and Crusaders—Salah al-Din (1171–1187)
5. Abbasid demise/Turkish and Mongolian conquests—
   Nawawi (d. 1277)
   Ibn Taymiyyah (d. 1328)
   Ibn al-Qayyim (d. 1350)
   Ibn Kathir (d. 1373)
6. Mongol/Turkic Invasions and chaos—
   Shiite resurgence: Hilli (d. 1325)
   Mushasha (d. 1462)
   Shah Ismail (d. 1524)
7. Ottoman decline—Abd al-Wahhab (d. 1791)
   Sanusiyyah (1800s)
   Mahdiyyah (1880s)
   Salafiyyah (1890s): Afghani (d. 1879)
   Abduh (d. 1905)
   Rida (d. 1935)
8. Contemporary Islamic crisis milieux—
   Muslim Brotherhood (1930s)
   Banna
   Sibai
   Qutb
   Mawdudi
   The Islamic Revolution and Shiite resurgence
   Khomeini
   Baqir al-Sadr
   Shariati
   Sunni Resurgence (1970s)
   Utaybi

Faraj
Hawwa
Turabi
Tilmisani
Sadiq al-Mahdi

Each phase of decline would trigger a revivalist response—a movement back to Islamic roots led by charismatic individuals (see Figure 2). Some of these leaders would assume the role of *mujaddid*—renewer of the faith, while others would seek to effect a radical sociopolitical transformation through militant messianic movements as *mahdi*—a savior sent by God. In their ideological formulations and political actions these leaders would legitimize themselves by invoking the Quran, the Prophet's Traditions *(sunnah),* and historical precedents reaching back to the early Islamic community.

The Prophet's Ummah (A.D.622–632)

The first Islamic community founded by the Prophet Muhammad constitutes for Muslims the perfect expression of social existence. Muhammad's epicentric role embodied both prophethood and leadership, whereby divine revelation was translated into political community. Thus, during his lifetime the Prophet combined theory and practice—a precedent which has exercised a profound influence on Muslim communities throughout the ages.

There are two main sources of emulation for later generations of Muslims. The first is the Quran—God's revealed word through his Messenger, the Prophet Muhammad. The second source is the *sunnah*—the exemplary behavior of the Prophet consisting of his statements, deeds, and judgments, as embodied in narrative traditions *(hadith).* In the fundamentalist view, deviation from the original Islamic model constitutes a return to *jahiliyyah,* the pre-Islamic society of ignorance and conflict.

The Crisis of Succession (A.D. 632–660)

The first major crisis of Islamic history was the struggle for succession after the Prophet's death. In the absence of a clearly designated heir, Abu Bakr was chosen as successor or *khalifah* (caliph) through the consensus of community leaders. He was succeeded by Umar, under whom the Islamic state began its vast conquests. The third caliph, Uthman, faced tribal opposition to the dominance of his Umayyad kinsmen and to the materialism engendered by imperial conquest. Uthman was killed during a mutiny in A.D. 656 and was succeeded by Ali, a cousin and son-in-law of Muhammad. Since he was the father of the Prophet's grandsons, Hasan and Husayn, Ali's supporters *(shiat Ali)* had asserted his right to the succession over the previous three caliphs. Upon Ali's accession to the caliphate in 656, he was opposed by some companions of the Prophet and his wife Aishah, the Kharijites, and Muawiyah, the Umayyad leader. While Ali succeeded in defeating the Prophet's companions, he faced the defection of Kharijite militants who opposed Ali's willingness to compromise with Muawiyah. The Kharijites preached an egalitarian doctrine, asserting that any strict follower of Allah's rules is worthy of becoming caliph. Thus, the Kharijites opposed the legitimacy of keeping the succession in the Prophet's tribe (Quraysh), while the Shiites insisted on the sanctity of the "seed" or lineage of Muhammad through Ali and Fatimah, the Prophet's daughter. After Ali's assassination by a Kharijite (661), Muawiyah emerged victorious, ushering in the age of dynastic Islam. The split in the *ummah* between Ali's partisans (Shii) and the rest of the community (Sunni) persists to the present day.

The precedents established by the Prophet and his four successors have been regarded with great reverence by subsequent generations of Muslims. However, in the quest to return to Islamic roots, present-day Sunni and Shiite fundamentalists exhibit significant differences regarding the early Islamic community. While the Sunni revere the Prophet and the four "Rightly Guided" Caliphs *(Rashidin),* the Shiites venerate Muhammad, Ali, and his descendants. Despite recent attempts at mutual accommodation, the problem has persisted and has become magnified in the context of the Iran-Iraq war. Nevertheless, there has been substantial reciprocal sympathy between Shiite and Sunni fundamentalists, particularly since the victory of the Islamic cause in Iran.

Early Dynastic Phase: Umayyad Decline (A.D. 660–750)

The dynastic phase of Islamic history occupies a special place in shaping the content of fundamentalist thought. The monopolization of

the Caliphate by the Umayyads (660–750) is perceived by many fundamentalists as a major disaster for the Islamic community. This act
signified dynastic rule which is rejected by most contemporary Sunni
fundamentalists. More vehement is the Shiite rejection of the Umayyads, who are regarded as usurpers of the rightful succession through
Ali and Husayn. The other Islamist objection to the Umayyads concerns their policies of progressive secularization of society. Indeed,
many Muslims have never accepted Umayyad legitimacy because Abu
Sufyan, Muawiyah's father, had fought Muhammad; and Abu Sufyan's
descendants had converted to Islam for convenience rather than conviction in order to secure power.

It was significant that the first reaction to the Umayyads' moral
decline came from an *Umawi*—the Caliph Umar II. After his assumption of the Umayyad throne at the age of thirty-seven, Umar initiated a
comprehensive reform of the government along Islamic principles,
while presiding over a powerful revivalist movement which earned him
the distinction as the first *mujaddid* (renewer) of Islam. Umar's work
was cut short when the young caliph was killed by poisoning (d. 720).
However, his legacy was perpetuated by the Imams Abu Hanifa and
Malik who assumed the role of *mujaddid* despite their persecution by
those in authority.[2]

A major crisis engulfed Islam in A.D. 750, culminating in the
bloody overthrow of the Umayyad Caliphate by a revolutionary coalition under Abu al-Abbas, a descendant of the Prophet's uncle. The
Abbasid takeover originated from a Shiite-backed millenarian movement which advocated a return to Islamic origins.[3]

Abbasid Degeneration (A.D. 813–909)

At the height of its power and wealth, the Abbasid theocracy
renounced its radical fundamentalist ideology together with its Shiite
supporters, and transformed itself into a Sunni cosmopolitan empire.
Under Caliph al-Mamun, the Mutazilah doctrine became the state
ideology (827). The Mutazilah had evolved into a rationalist creed
claiming the supremacy of reason over Quranic revelation. To insure
obedience to Mutazilite official dogma, Mamun instituted an inquisitional tribunal *(mihnah)*. This generated popular opposition and a new
fundamentalist wave led by Ahmad ibn Hanbal. Despite his trial and
imprisonment, Ibn Hanbal stubbornly refused to recant his uncompromising adherence to Islamic orthodoxy. Consequently, Ibn Hanbal

is regarded as the first "patron saint" of Sunni fundamentalism.[4] The Hanbali School of Law constitutes the foundation of Wahhabi fundamentalism—the ideology of the Saudi Kingdom. Meanwhile, Imam al-Shafii (b. 767) had emerged in Egypt as another exponent of Islamic renewal (Figure 2).

The crisis of faith at the zenith of Abbasid power under Mamun was transformed into a larger crisis of legitimacy engulfing the dynasty during the tenth century. The brutal Abbasid persecution of their former Shiite allies engendered growing resistance which culminated in Shiite-Persian penetration of imperial institutions and ultimately open rebellion. One manifestation of opposition was the widespread Qaramitah insurrectionary movement based on esoteric *(batini)* and communistic precepts (877–951). The Qaramitah set the stage for the rise of Fatimid power in Tunisia under Ubaydallah al-Mahdi (909) and its implantation in Egypt. This was an expression of Ismaili Shiite fundamentalist revolt against Sunni Abbasid rule. Meanwhile, the call to fundamentalism was being sounded in the East by Abu al-Qasim ibn Salamah (d. 1032), who provided a militant interpretation of *jihad* (holy struggle) against unbelievers during the Abbasid decline.[5] Also relevant were the notable theological contributions of Abu Hamid al-Ghazali (b. 1058), who struggled to institutionalize the anti-Mutazilah orthodoxy of Abu al-Hasan al-Ashari (d. 935) as the universal creed of Sunni Islam; one of Ghazali's twentieth-century disciples was Hasan al-Banna, the founder of the Muslim Brotherhood.[6]

Umayyad Decline in Spain (A.D. 1002–31)

The reign of Abd al-Rahman III marked the apogee of Muslim rule in Spain. Soon after 1002, anarchy gripped Spain, leading to the Umayyad collapse despite the efforts of the brilliant philosopher and vizir Ibn Hazm al-Andalusi (b. 994). This crisis prompted a new call to Islamic traditions by Ibn Hazm. This zealous Muslim son of Christian forebears serves as an important source of inspiration for contemporary fundamentalists.

Fatimid Decline and the Crusaders (A.D. 996–1171)

The decline of the Fatimid Caliphate began under al-Hakim (d. 1021) and continued until its extinction in 1171 by Salah al-Din al-

Ayyubi (Saladin). During this period, the Islamic world faced the challenge of the Crusaders. The response was another wave of Islamic resurgence led by Salah al-Din, who defeated the Crusaders at Hittin (1187). However, it proved impossible to reverse the decline of the Abbasid Caliphate, which soon fell prey to Turkic warlords only to be destroyed by the Mongols under Hulaghu (1258).

Abbasid Demise and Islamic Revival (A.D. 1258–1500)

The destruction of the Abbasid state by the "infidel" Mongols is considered an important turning point by fundamentalist writers, who discern parallels between the thirteenth century and the contemporary phase of Islamic decline. Equally significant is the militant content of Islamic political thought produced in the wake of the Mongolian conquest. The massive ravages inflicted by Hulaghu, coupled with the anarchy after his sudden departure, had created a political vacuum and spiritual crisis of major proportions. The enormity of crisis produced an Islamic response of radical militancy in the hands of the puritan conservative Taqi al-Din Ahmad ibn Taymiyyah (1263–1328) and his contemporaries.[7] His militant message was perpetuated by his student, Ibn al-Qayyim al-Jawziyyah (d. 1350) and Imad al-Din ibn Kathir (d. 1373)—both of whom are considered important pillars of Sunni fundamentalism.[8]

Shiite Fundamentalism (A.D. 1300–1500)

New manifestations of Twelver Shiite fundamentalism appeared in Iraq and Iran after the fall of the Fatimids, beginning in the late thirteenth century. This was a response to the chaotic political and social conditions of the region as well as the Shiites' tenuous position with respect to the Sunni majority. One illustrious exponent of Shiism was the Allama Ibn Mutahhar al-Hilli (b. 1250) who produced the most authentic exposition of Twelver dogma and practice. The fifteenth century saw the emergency of the Mushashain, a movement in Ahwaz led by Muhammad ibn Falah al-Mushasha (d. 1462) who declared himself the *Mahdi* (Messiah) and leader of the Arabs in Khuzistan.[9] These manifestations of Shiite resurgence prepared the groundwork for the implantation of Twelver Shiism as the state religion of Persia by Shah Ismail (d. 1524). The Shah belonged to the Safavid family which had led the *Qizilbash* (redheads) Shiites of Eastern Anatolia.[10]

Ottoman Decline (A.D. 1699–1922)

The rise of the Ottomans marked the transfer of Islamic power from Arabs to Turks. Despite the absence of a geneological connection between the Ottoman Sultans and the Prophet, Sultan Selim I assumed the title of caliph after his conquest of Egypt (1517). While several subsequent sultans styled themselves as caliphs, their use of the title was not always recognized outside the Ottoman domain. The progressive decline of Ottoman power after the seventeenth century, coupled with sultanic profligacy and harsh rule, precipitated new movements of Islamic resurgence among the Arab subjects of the empire. All these movements were centered on charismatic personalities who preached a salvational message to engrave their own vision of Islam on society.

Wahhabis, Sanusis, and Mahdists

The three revivalists movements of the late Ottoman era—al-Wahhabiyyah, al-Mahdiyyah and al-Sanusiyyah—arose in the periphery of the empire. The remoteness of Ottoman power, reinforced by the militant solidarity *(asabiyyah)* of the tribes led by religious charismatics, were responsible for the significant success of these movements. In retrospect, the most dynamic was Ibn Abd al-Wahhab's Muwahhidin (Unitarians), who became a potent force in the hands of Muhammad ibn Saud and his descendants. Ibn Abd al-Wahhab drew his inspiration from Ibn Hanbal as interpreted by Ibn Taymiyyah; he was determined to purge Islam from its deviations and innovations by strict adherence to the Quran and *sunnah*. After their defeat by Muhammad Ali of Egypt in 1819, the Muwahhidin (Wahhabi) reappeared in the early 1900s as the Ikhwan movement in support of Saudi rule. Meanwhile, revivalist movements began to emerge outside the Ottoman and Persian realms. One such movement arose in India under Shah Waliullah of Delhi (d. 1763).

In contrast to Wahhabi militancy, the Sanusiyyah movement began as a missionary effort among the semi-Islamized Bedouins of Cyranaica. Under Muhammad ibn Ali al-Sanusi (1787–1859) and his missionaries, the movement blossomed throughout the eastern Sahara through *baraka*—the divinely bestowed blessings of its saintly founder. Of Maghribi origin, al-Sanusi was a mystic and reformer, not a revolutionary. He did not establish a state but rather a spiritual *(sufi)* movement which accommodated itself to tribal cultures and beliefs. The Sanusiyyah became militant only in its third generation, when *jihad* was imposed upon it by imperialism.[11]

The Mahdiyyah differed from the Wahhabiyyah and Sanusiyyah in important respects. While its militancy matched the Wahhabi zeal, the Mahdiyyah was a millenarian and messianic movement combining religious, political, and military authority in the hands of one person—Muhammad Ahmad ibn Abdallah—who declared himself "The Expected One" in accordance with the Sunni criteria of mahdiship.[12] As an ascetic turned warrior, the Sudanese *Mahdi* defeated the British-led Egyptians under General Gordon, established an Islamic state, and aspired to conquer the Ottoman realm. The Mahdiyyah survived its founder well into the late 1890s, when it was overwhelmed by superior British fire power.

Despite the geographic marginality of these tribal movements, they were instrumental in providing a bridge to the Islamic fundamentalists of the twentieth century. In view of their primitivism, however, none of them could become an adequate model for the urban modernist milieu. This task was left to the Salafiyyah movement.

Islamic Reform (Salafiyyah)

Ottoman misrule and decline in the face of European imperialism engendered reformist reactions during the nineteenth and early twentieth centuries. The outstanding catalyst of this intellectual movement was Jamal al-Din al-Afghani (1838–97) who preached Pan-Islamic solidarity and resistance to European imperialism though a return to Islam in a scientifically modernized setting. His disciple, Muhammad Abduh of Egypt, emphasized the inherent rationality of the Islamic tradition to illustrate the viability of its modernism. This was the essence of the Salafiyyah movement led by Abduh and his Syrian disciple, Rashid Rida. After Abduh's death in 1905, the Salafiyyah became increasingly conservative although it continued to modernize Islamic law on the basis of the Quran and the *sunnah*. In the interwar years, the Salafiyyah reformists in Egypt and Algeria became involved in political activism of a non-revolutionary nature. The most militant of these was Rida, who justified defensive *jihad* when the Muslims were being persecuted. As a Hanbali, Rida supported the pristine revivalism of the Wahhabis.[13] In the mid-1930s, Rida's moderate activism was replaced by the radicalism of the Muslim Brotherhood under Hasan al-Banna. In a period of acute crisis induced by political turmoil, ineffective leadership, socioeconomic conflict, and European imperialism, the quest for the militant Islamic alternative appeared inevitable.

The Contemporary Crisis Environment (A.D. 1930–80)

The fundamentalist response to the crisis situation in the Arab world found its most vocal expression in the Egyptian Muslim Brotherhood and its affiliates in Syria and Jordan. After its suppression by Nasser, the Brotherhood reemerged during the Sadat era as part of a new fundamentalist wave. The new resurgence transcended the Brotherhood to include several of its militant offshoots, along with a plethora of other Islamic societies. Meanwhile, both spiritual and militant manifestations of resurgence could be seen throughout the Islamic world. The establishment of an Islamic regime in Iran triggered a wave of Shiite militancy in Iraq, Lebanon, and the Gulf states. Moreover, the Iranian Revolution provided the inspiration and impetus for revolutionary action by Sunni fundamentalist groups in the Arab world.

Patterns of Islamic Response

The pattern of successive waves of resurgence in response to crisis situations (Figure 2) constitutes an inbuilt sociopolitical mechanism which has enabled Islam to renew and reassert itself against internal decay and external threat. Despite the obvious similarities between the various revivalist movements, there were important differences in ideological content and modality of application. These differences stemmed from the peculiar circumstances of crisis facing the Islamic community in various epochs and geographical settings.[14] Thus, the character of each Islamic response was determined by the requirements of its crisis milieu and the personality of the revivalist leader. For example, the main catalyst of Ibn Hanbal's call to Islamic roots was the moral decline of Abbasid society. Similarly, the pristine fundamentalism of Ibn Abd al-Wahhab had been triggered by the moral degeneration of Muslim society in the Arabian Peninsula. These were movements of internal renewal in contrast to the dual imperatives of Ibn Taymiyyah's crisis milieu, which required both internal regeneration and external defense against the Tatars.

The expansion of European power and cultural influence during the nineteenth century created new conditions which were to shape the subsequent phases of Islamist response. The Sanusi began as religious missionaries but ended up fighting the Italians because of the Ottoman inability to defend North Africa. The primary catalyst of the Mahdist insurrection was the dysfunctional socioeconomic impact of Ottoman rule on the Sudan centered on a three-tiered imperialism of Egyptians, Turks, and Britons. In these cases, Islamic resurgence was a response to the internal conditions of the empire as well as to European imperialism.

A different sociopolitical situation existed in the more advanced lands of Islam—Egypt, Turkey, and India—where Europe had gained both political and cultural ascendance. These circumstances generated movements of Islamic modernism as exemplified by Abduh's Salafiyyah, which sought to use Western ideas in transforming Islamic society. The persistence of Western imperialism and the mounting socioeconomic problems of the Islamic countries precipitated a new revivalist movement of a populist type in the interwar years, centered on the Muslim Brotherhood, which challenged the Westernism of the Salafiyyah and advocated a narrow and radical fundamentalism as the basis of a new Islamic order. After a period of decline during the height of Pan-Arabism, Islamic fundamentalism reemerged as a powerful socio-spiritual force, often displaying revolutionary tendencies.

A Dialectical Perspective on Contemporary Islamic Society

The ebb and flow of Islamic fundamentalism throughout history reveals an ongoing dialectic between Islam and its social-economic-political environment. Thus, the contemporary Islamic setting, like its historical antecedents, is conditioned by the operation of multifaceted dialectical relationships, which become exacerbated in times of crisis. Nine dialectical relationships may be identified:

Secularism vs. Theocracy

The conflict between the proponents of a secular state and those advocating the establishment of an Islamic polity is a central dialectic in all Muslim societies. These diametrically opposed positions pit the Westernized secular nationalists against Islamic fundamentalists seeking to create an Islamic *ummah.*

Islamic Modernism vs. Islamic Conservatism

The clash between Islamic modernists and conservatives has been a persistent feature of contemporary Muslim society. While the modernists seek to reform Islam and adapt it to contemporary life, the conservatives cling to traditional Islamic precepts and reject Western and other influences. In this sense, the fundamentalists are ultraconservatives with a radical bent.

Establishment Islam vs. Fundamentalist Islam

This conflict pits the high-ranking clerics *(ulama)*, who are usually government appointed and supported, against the leader-ideologues of fundamentalist groups representing populist Islam. The conflict stems from their respective social-occupational positions and sharply divergent interpretations of Islam. As members of the establishment, the higher *ulama* tend to reinforce the legitimacy and actions of ruling elites through their interpretations of Islamic Law. In sharp contrast, fundamentalist ideologues reject the interpretive authority of the establishment *ulama,* and proceed to formulate doctrines of radical sociopolitical change.

Ruling Elites vs. Islamic Radicals

This is the fundamental cleavage between the rulers and their opponents seeking a change in the status quo. During the last decade, the most virulent opposition to the rulers of Arab and other Muslim countries has come from Islamic militants pressing for radical changes along fundamentalist lines. The source of their contention involves the moral basis of authority—the lack of legitimacy of ruling elites and institutions.

Economic Elites vs. Islamic Socialists

The polarization between the rich and poor pits the Islamic fundamentalists and other opposition groups against the established economic order, which is perceived as lacking social justice and moral legitimacy. The perceived linkage between economic, political, and religious elites serves as justification for the necessity of revolutionary action to restructure society along Islamist lines. Fundamentalist theorists advocate social justice through redistribution of wealth.

Ethnic Nationalism vs. Islamic Unity

These opposing tendencies have persisted since the rise of Islam. They represent the propensity of bifurcation along national, tribal, and ethnic lines in direct conflict with the quest for a united Islamic community as consecrated by the Prophet Muhammad.

Sufi Islam vs. Fundamentalist Militancy

In its stress on spiritual salvation through contemplation and mysticism, Sufi Islam is regarded by the fundamentalists as their polar opposite. The inner-directed spiritualism of the Sufis usually emphasizes a personal quest for union with God in the context of a liberal interpretation of Islamic precepts. In sharp contrast, fundamentalism insists on the strict observance of Islam coupled with political activism as a means to reshape society and gain salvation.

Traditional Islam vs. Fundamentalist Islam

The cardinal principle of fundamentalist Islam is the quest for the authentic and puritanical precepts of the faith. In various degrees, fundamentalists reject the bulk of traditions and innovations that accumulated after the early phase of Islamic history. To regenerate the Islamic ethos, the fundamentalists find it necessary to engage in a new interpretation of Islamic law *(ijtihad)* without the guidance of traditionalist juridical opinion which represents conventional Islam.

Dar al-Islam vs. Dar al-Harb

Historically, this dialectic represented the ongoing conflict between the territorial domain of Islam *(Dar al-Islam)* and the rest of the world. The latter was perceived by the Muslims as *Dar al-Harb*—a realm of inherent conflict lacking the peace of Islam and opposed to it on the world stage. This confrontation is an important part of the worldview of Islamic fundamentalists and many conventional Muslims. In the contemporary setting, the *Dar al-Harb* would include the West and the Communist Bloc.

The interplay of the foregoing nine dialectical relationships in the Islamic and world settings has progressively generated a crisis of major proportions, the specific attributes of which shall be explored in subsequent chapters.

3 The Social-Psychological Bases of Islamic Revivalism

ANY COMPREHENSIVE STUDY of contemporary Islamic fundamentalism necessitates an inquiry into its psycho-spiritual, political, social, and economic roots—the milieu which acts as the incubational environment for fundamentalist beliefs and actions. A recurrent pattern of history is the cause-and-effect relationship between social crises and the rise of religious, revolutionary, or revivalist movements which seek to transform the established order to build a new society on the basis of their particular ideological prescription. Consequently, the ideologies of these movements are both comprehensive and rigid, reflecting the responses of typically charismatic leaders to situations of crisis. It is no mere accident that fundamentalist movements in various religio-political contexts have acquired spiritual and sociopolitical potency when two interrelated conditions are met: the appearance of a leader of charismatic propensity and a society in deep turmoil. Significantly, the Islamist movements of the past have satisfied both of these conditions. The Islamist movements of the present are no exception.

Crisis Environment

A diagnostic examination of the contemporary Arab-Islamic milieu reveals the existence of a societal crisis of multi-dimensional proportions. For over two centuries the Islamic world has experienced a

25

protracted crisis encompassing the sociocultural, economic, political, and most basically, the spiritual realms. In the Ottoman context, Islam had lost much of its legitimizing force to perpetuate the ascendancy of the Turkish ruling dynasty and imperial institutions. Meanwhile, the non-Islamic minorities of the empire were pressing for political reforms and European protection from government repression. The promises of the 1908 Revolution to establish communal equality and to safeguard human rights were never implemented, as the Young Turk leadership decided to pursue policies of Turkification under its newly adopted ideology of Pan-Turanism. Beyond the threat to their collective identity, Turkification was anathema to the Arabs, since Arabic had been the sacred medium of Allah's revelation to his Arab Prophet Muhammad as written in the Quran. The consequent estrangement of the Muslim Arabs from the Young Turk government, coupled with European ideological influences, contributed to the spread of Arab nationalism. After the outbreak of World War I, the appeals of the Young Turk regime for Arab support to wage *jihad* against the Allies fell on deaf ears. The Arab nationalist leadership was suspicious of Turkish promises as it witnessed the decimation of the empire's Armenian population. The British-supported Arab Revolt of 1916 virtually sealed the fate of the Ottoman Empire.

The breakup of the Ottoman realm was followed by a fragmented Arab world under British and French hegemony. In these circumstances, Arab nationalist elites found themselves confronted with two tasks: the achievement of full independence from European control and the forging of a viable ideological synthesis to establish legitimate government. These twin objectives were only partially achieved, thereby intensifying the crisis confronting the Arabs. The removal of Anglo-French imperial influence created a vacuum soon to be filled by Soviet, American, and Israeli power. More fundamental and intractable was the Arab failure to respond to the "ideological imperative"— a persistent dilemma in Third World countries. The recent emergence of Islamist ideology can be traced in part to the abortive search for workable ideologies of nation-building and socioeconomic development.

The contemporary Arab social setting is characterized by certain specific attributes of protracted and intense crisis, which constitute the catalysts that have triggered Islamic fundamentalist responses. The identification of these catalysts requires two levels of investigation: (1) catalysts arising from crises peculiar to specific Arab states or subnational groups and (2) catalysts stemming from the larger Arab crisis milieu. The micro-catalysts found in specific national settings are analyzed in Part II. There are, however, significant cross-national similarities between crisis conditions, which permit consideration of macro-level catalysts deriving from the larger crisis environment of Arab society. These crisis attributes may be classified into six clusters; their dynamic interaction operates in a mutually reinforcing pattern, promoting social turmoil and political instability.

Identity Crisis

One consequence of Islamic decline was the crisis of individual and collective identity among the Muslims. Since Islam constituted an all encompassing life system that included religion *(din)*, state *(dawlah)* and law *(shariah)*, the task of finding a substitute framework of identity was to prove difficult if not impossible. Hence, the enormity of the identity crisis as Islam was placed on the defensive by Western military might and ideological influences.

The progressive decline of the Ottoman and Persian Islamic Empires prompted the rise of competing nationalist ideologies based on ethno-linguistic identities. The consequence was a multi-phased cen-

Figure 3
Dialectics of Ideological Transformation

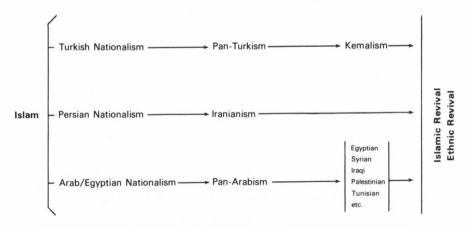

Reproduced from R. H. Dekmejian, "The Anatomy of Islamic Revival: Legitimacy Crisis, Ethnic Conflict and the Search for Islamic Alternatives," *Middle East Journal* 34, no. 1 (Winter 1980).

tury-long dialectical process, which culminated in a synthesis during the 1970s (see Figure 3).[1] In the Middle Eastern context, three indigenous nationalisms arose as substitutes for the Islamic *ummah*—Turkish, Iranian, and Arab/Egyptian.

As depicted in Figure 3, the early Turkish nationalism of Ottomanist reformers led by Ahmet Reza gave way to the Pan-Turanism of the Young Turks inspired by Ziya Gökalp, which Ataturk transformed into a secular Turkish nationalism presently under challenge by Islamic fundamentalists and ethnic nationalists (e.g., Kurds). In Iran, an indigenous Persian nationalism evolved under Reza Shah into a Pan-Iranian ideology based on pre-Islamic Aryan themes, only to be repudiated by the Islamic Revolution and emerging ethnic nationalism.

In the Arab orbit, Egyptian and Arab nationalism developed separately until the 1950s, when Nasser presided upon their convergence in the ideology of Pan-Arabism. Indeed, this was a tortuous synthesis, the process of which reflected the depth and breadth of the Arab crisis environment. In Egypt, the competing ideologies included Islamic reformism (Muhammad Abduh), Pharaonic nationalism (Taha Husayn), Western liberalism (Nahhas Pasha), Islamic fundamentalism (Hasan al-Banna), right-wing nationalism (Ahmad Husayn), and communism. In the Mashriq, Arab nationalism first developed among Christian intellectuals and rapidly gained Muslim adherents before and during World War I. Like its Egyptian counterpart, Arab nationalism experienced the competing influences of fascist, socialist, Islamic, and Western ideologies during the interwar years. However, the quest for a unified ideology in the Arab East was even more fragmented than Egypt's as a result of rivalries between Syria, Iraq, Jordan, and Saudi Arabia. The secular Arab nationalism of Syria clashed with the monarchical Arabism espoused by the Hashemites of Iraq and Jordan, and Saudi Arabia's Wahhabi fundamentalism.

In the framework of these conflictual ideologies and elite rivalries the Arab world faced its moment of truth in the Arab-Israeli War of 1947–48 with disastrous consequences. The Israeli challenge, no less than Western imperial influence and Nasser's charismatic appeal, produced a strong commitment to Pan-Arabism among the masses. As the champion of the Arab cause, Nasser appeared to have solved, in a secular context, the pervasive Arab identity crisis by overwhelming all sectarian, fundamentalist, rightist, liberal, and leftist challenges. Meanwhile, Nasserist Pan-Arabism had found a rival expression in Syrian Baathism—a movement which lacked charismatic leadership.

The Arab defeat of 1967, and Nasser's death in 1970, precipitated a sharp decline in Pan-Arabist attitudes and a new quest for an ideology of success. Indeed, by the late 1970s, the Arab ideological dialectic had come full circle: Arab thinkers and politicians had experimented eclectically with various indigenous and European ideologies and political systems for three-quarters of a century with unsalutary results. Meanwhile, the Arab masses and intellectuals had been torn between diverse value systems in their search for identity. In the brief course of a decade, Nasser's Pan-Arabism had provided in large measure a solution to the Arabs' identity crisis. The defeat of 1967 shattered the Pan-Arabist dream, and with it, the edifice of the Arabs' individual and collective personality. Thus, the old crisis of Arab psycho-spiritual identity reappeared with unprecedented intensity. The desperate search for alternatives centered on revolutionary socialism, Western liberalism, and Islamic fundamentalism. The Islamic way emerged as the dominant alternative during the 1970s.

Legitimacy Crisis

Identity crisis involves a crisis of the soul and the personality.[2] It is often characterized by acute alienation including feelings of normlessness, powerlessness, insecurity, and self-estrangement which Durkheim called "anomie."[3] In extreme cases, situations of anomie could create a growing sense of psychological distress, heightened expectations, and vulnerability to mass appeals—the propitious preconditions for a revolution led by a charismatic personality. The most immediate consequence of identity crisis and alienation is the precipitous decline in the legitimacy of ruling elites and institutions. Even prior to the debacle of 1967, Arab elites were facing acute crises of legitimacy with the singular exception of the charismatic Nasser. Ironically, it was Nasser's Pan-Arab appeal which undermined the legitimacy of his fellow Arab leaders. This legitimacy crisis had been reinforced by the failure of these leaders in the political, economic, and social domains.

Elite Misrule and Coercion

The legitimacy of political systems and elites is constantly reinforced or weakened depending on the performance of leaders. Operating from a weak legitimacy base, Arab leaders have often lacked the requisite initial "political capital" to generate effective policies that constitute the building-blocks of stable public order. Even in polities where conditions are favorable, policy making and administration have been arbitrary, discontinuous, and pursued in a milieu of large-scale official corruption. The frequent failure of elites to develop and implement socially beneficial policies has led to the erosion of their tenuous legitimacy and to a consequent increase in the use of force to maintain control. While the crises in identity and legitimacy primarily affect the psychological and political aspects of Arab society, the pervasive reliance on the instrumentalities of repression affects the everyday existence of the people. In recent decades, Arab ruling elites have often maintained themselves in power through increasing levels of coercion against opponents, who are denied institutionalized channels of free expression. Simultaneously, the coercive capabilities of these elites have substantially increased through the acquisition of administrative expertise and technological sophistication. These quantum increases of coercive and control capabilities have further contributed to the Arab crisis environment.

Class Conflict

A prime consequence of elite incompetence and misrule has been the growing maldistribution of wealth in virtually every Arab country. The availability of oil money and the impact of global market forces have greatly widened the economic gap between the social classes, in the midst of corruption and conspicuous consumption among rulers and their clients. These factors have generated class polarization and conflict in populations with high rates of growth. Despite promises made over several decades, a large number of Arab governments have failed to promote social justice.

In the mid-1970s the richest 5 percent of households in Egypt, Morocco, and the Sudan received over 20 percent of the income, while the poorest 20 percent of the households received about 5 percent of the income (see Table 1). In the same period the percent of population in absolute poverty was 9 percent in Egypt, 28 percent in Morocco, and 40 percent in the Sudan. In less than a decade the percentage of Moroccans in absolute poverty had risen from 28 to 45 percent.[4] The wide gap between rich and poor constitutes one of the most politically salient aspects of the Arab crisis milieu.

Table 1
Structure of Income Distribution[5]
1975

Countries	% of Income Received by Richest 5% of House- holds	% of Income Received by Poorest 20% of House- holds	% of Income Received by Poorest 40% of House- holds	% of Pop. in Absolute Poverty Using Official Ex- change Rates
Egypt	21.0	5.2	13.9	9
Sudan	20.9	5.1	14.5	40
Morocco	20.0	4.0	11.3	28
Iraq	35.1	2.1	—	—

Military Impotence

The fifth factor contributing to the Arab crisis situation is the persistence of military defeats. Implicit in the Arab quest for independence was the aspiration to acquire sufficient military potential to safeguard vital interests. However, this deeply felt aspiration to achieve military prowess has not been realized, despite massive sacrifices of economic and human resources by military and monarchical oligarchies. With the single exception of Algeria, no Arab state has achieved independence primarily through military means. The successive defeats by Israel culminating in the June 1967 War produced shock waves among Arabs and Muslims, engendering deep feelings of fear, insecurity, and anger. The manifest inability of Arab leaders to end Israeli occupation of Arab territory has sapped their residual legitimacy and promoted widespread disillusionment, anguish, and despair. Consequently, Arab feelings of inferiority generated under European rule have been reinforced by the continued Arab military impotence against Israel.[6]

Modernization and Culture Crisis

At the most basic level of social existence, a culture crisis permeates Arab society—a crisis exacerbated by the interaction of the preceding five catalysts: identity, legitimacy, elite misrule, class conflict, and military impotence (see Figure 1). However, the most potent catalyst of the Arab culture crisis is the disruptive impact of modernization. The motivation to modernize was originally prompted by the desire to emulate the West in achieving military strength and economic development. This dual quest for military and economic modernization, largely unsuccessful and destabilizing, has produced sharp cleavages between traditionalists and modernists since modernization involves the importation of non-indigenous behavioral norms and values. While the modernists are inclined toward the wholesale emulation of Western social theory and practice, most traditionalists advocate the selective borrowing of aspects of Western experience thought to be compatible with Islam, i.e., science and technology. The modernized sectors consist of small elite groups which often indulge in the blind mimicry of Western modes of dress and social behavior considered contrary to conservative Islamic values and practices. The superficial Westernization of political and economic elites, coupled with their non-nativist behavior and conspicuous consumption, sets them apart from their less affluent and tradition-bound subjects. This has created a politically dangerous culture gap between the rulers and the ruled, which is exacerbated by the existing ideological vacuum caused by the erosion of Pan-Arabism and the lack of a substitute ideological framework. With the exception of Nasserism and Baathism, there were no conscious attempts by political elites to achieve a synthesis of Western, socialist, and nativist theories that would suit the developmental needs and cultural ethos of Arab society. The resulting clash between the aggressive Western culture and the indigenous value system has produced a certain schizophrenia in the Arab mind and a sense of inferiority vis-à-vis the West.[7] At present, the crisis of culture pervades every Arab country, although it is probably more acute in the affluent conservative states of the Arabian Peninsula.

The Psyche of the Mutaassib

It is impossible to adequately comprehend the Islamist phenomenon without determining the personality structure of the fundamentalist individual as it is shaped by the crisis environment. On the basis of social-psychological theory, coupled with empirical observation, it is possible to construct a composite personality profile of the "true believer." In this context, the formulations of Erikson, Lasswell, Inkeles, Durkheim, Adorno, Hoffer, and Riesman are particularly useful, although not completely adequate to explain the peculiar characteristics of the radical fundamentalist *(mutaassib)*. Clearly, the Islamic cultural context possesses unique formative attributes which influence the personality development of fundamentalist individuals. Therefore, an attempt will be made to identify the "modal personality" of the Islamic fundamentalist of the radical type, on the basis of certain recurrent personality traits in the population which seem to constitute the typical pattern of psychological expression.[8] These include:

Alienation

The fundamentalist is, above all, an acutely alienated individual. His alienation, the direct consequence of the Arab-Islamic crisis environment, involves rejection of Nasserism, Baathism, liberal capitalism, socialism, and the legitimacy of Arab ruling elites. The *mutaassib's* alienation from the larger Arab milieu is often followed by a self-imposed separation from society and counterbalanced by his induction into the Islamist belief system; this will bestow upon him a new identity and even membership in a fundamentalist organization.[9]

Premature Integrity—Dogmatism

The neophyte's discovery of the new faith is typically followed by his total commitment to it as a true believer. In the case of younger converts, intense commitment produces "premature integrity" at an early age, marked by an extreme rigidity in beliefs and refusal to integrate new values into their ideological framework.[10]

Inferiority—Superiority

The feelings of inferiority among fundamentalists are a direct consequence of their alienation and inability to find a niche in society. These inferiority feelings are transformed into manifestations of aggressive superiority as soon as the neophyte becomes coopted into the Islamist faith.

Activism—Aggressiveness

Fundamentalists tend to be aggressive in their dealings with unbelievers *(kuffar)* and often with mainstream Muslims in compensation
for their deprivations in society and in their conviction that "non-
communicants" are following the "wrong path" *(dhal)*. In the quest to
impose their own beliefs and behavioral codes upon society, Islamic
fundamentalists display a high degree of activism both as ideological
propagators and potential revolutionaries. This is in sharp contrast to
introspective Sufis who usually substitute mystical contemplation for
political activism.[11]

Authoritarianism

The fundamentalists possess many of the character traits of the
"authoritarian personality."[12] This authoritarianism directly flows from
the absolutist character of their teachings and the concomitant injunc-
tion to effect a radical transformation of society—hence, the preoccupation with power and the quest for political and social domination.[13]

Intolerance

The intolerance of Islamic radicals stems from the dogmatic content of their creed and their total indentification with its strict precepts.[14] Closely related is their unforgiving attitude toward all "de-
viationists," which reflects a belief in an unforgiving God.[15]

Paranoia—Projectivity

The *mutaassib* is apt to see "evil forces" at work in a hostile
environment. He displays a deep distrust of people and governmental
institutions to which he ascribes malevolent intentions.[16] He is inclined
to divide the world into rigid categories according to clearcut stereo-
types.

Conspiratorial Outlook

The commitment of Islamic radicals to revolutionary change, combined with their negative perceptions of society, usually prompts the establishment of secret organizations to combat enemies and overthrow constituted authority. The conspiratorial tendency is also a response to state repression of Islamist groups and organizations.

Idealism—Sense of Duty

As true believers, Islamic fundamentalists display the highest sense of idealism and devotion to their cause. Convinced of the absolute truth of the Islamic message and mission, the destruction of the "sinful" state and society becomes the supreme virtue.[17]

Austereness—Hardiness

In keeping with their strict interpretation of Islam, the fundamentalists reject the easy path in their social, sexual, and political activities.[18] They manifest rigid discipline, an austere lifestyle *(ta-qashshuf)*, and readiness to struggle and sacrifice.

Obedience—Conformity

The fundamentalist pledges absolute obedience to Allah, the Prophet, and to the charismatic leader of the movement through the *bayah* (oath).[19] His behavior is conditioned by strict conformity to group norms as promulgated by the leader.

The foregoing characteristics appear to constitute the modal personality of the radical fundamentalist. It should be emphasized that this composite profile is an archetypal configuration; individual fundamentalists in real life might exhibit these character attributes in varying degrees of intensity. Indeed, some fundamentalists may display these traits in their most extreme form. Others may deviate from the norm in pursuing an attenuated fundamentalism by abstaining from explicit acts of opposition to the state. Such individuals would usually remain at the periphery of Islamist groups as sympathizers or "fellow travelers." A further category of fundamentalists includes the nebulous collectivity of extremely pious individuals *(mutadayyinin)* who share many of the *mutaassib*'s attributes, except loyalty to specific activist leaders or membership in militant societies. The politicization of this "mass constituency" is a politically salient topic to be discussed under Part III.

4 Islamist Ideology and Practice

IN ITS CONTEMPORARY EXPRESSION, the ideology of Islamic fundamentalism represents the culmination of accumulated revelation, tradition, and practice going back to the Prophet Muhammad. Thus, the content of modern fundamentalist ideology and its legitimization is consciously based on the selective interpretation of Islamic historical epochs. Indeed, present-day fundamentalist societies and movements seek to justify their very existence and mission by referring to divinely ordained duties and historical precedents, which reflect their peculiar historiography, combined with a deterministic self-view and worldview. Consequently, the burden of history lies heavily on the Islamist ideologues, as they strive to reconstruct the past in the present crisis setting, in order to shape the future.

Foundations of Fundamentalist Thought

Contemporary Islamist theoreticians base themselves on the Quran and a plethora of commentaries and compilations of traditions by both eminent and obscure writers reaching back to the second and third centuries of Islam. Significantly, these theorists trace their intellectual roots to a chain of authorities who represent a distinctly conservative, legalistic, and militant orientation in Islamic thought. There is little in

37

this corpus of theory from the contributions of "liberal" Muslim thinkers.

The chain of Islamist thought begins with the Quran and the six canonical books considered the most authoritative sources of the narrative traditions (ahadith)—Bukhari, Muslim ibn al-Hajjaj, Abu Dawud, Tirmidhi, Ibn Majah, and Nasai. In addition, the interpretations and opinions of several traditionalist imams and qadis are cited with great frequency by fundamentalist writers. One such authority is Abu Yusuf (d.798), a student of Abu Hanifa and Malik b. Anas, who became Harun al-Rashid's Grand Judge (qadi al-qudat).

Beyond these early authorities, contemporary fundamentalist thought is based on historical precedents established by revolutionary movements and events. In this sense, present-day Islamist societies emulate the pattern of early insurrectionary groups by using politicized Islam as an ideology of protest against ruling elites who are charged with deviating from the true faith. Indeed, beginning with the Kharijites and the Shiites, fundamentalism became the ideology of opposition against those in power. In the Shiite case, this revolutionary trend led to the emergence of the Fatimids and the Carmathians (Qaramitah) and their esoteric doctrines often propounded by hidden authors like Ikhwan al-Safa (Brethren of Purity). These and subsequent insurgent movements constitute important examples for today's Islamists not only for their ideological orientation but because of their revolutionary methods. A case in point is the Kharijite insurrection and its theory and practice of jihad. In sharp contrast to the Twelver Shiite belief in waging jihad under the reincarnated Mahdi, the Kharijites made jihad a fundamental article of their faith—a sixth pillar.[1] To impose their strict doctrine, the Kharijites would wage violent jihad against both Muslims and non-Muslims; hence their imprint on the militant jihadists of the present.

Apostles of Islamic Militancy: A Profile

Among the Sunni, the fundamentalist persuasion was exemplified by a succession of activist thinkers, who established important precedents in political theory and practice, which constitute the foundations of twentieth-century Islamic revivalism. The forerunners of contemporary Sunni Islamist thought include many major and minor authorities,[2] nine of whom are selected here for consideration (see Figure 2): Ibn

Hanbal (d. 855), Ibn Salamah (d. 1032), Ibn Hazm (d. 1064), Qadi Musa Iyadh (d. 1149), Nawawi (d. 1277), Ibn Taymiyyah (d. 1328), Ibn al-Qayyim (d. 1350), Ibn Kathir (d. 1373), Ibn Abd al-Wahhab (d. 1792).

As the foremost champion of strict orthodoxy, Ibn Hanbal (d. 855) is the most important precursor of present-day Sunni fundamentalism. The combination of Ibn Hanbal's legal interpretations, willingness to suffer persecution, and personal militancy made him the prototype of the fundamentalist theorist-activist, whose example has been repeatedly emulated until the present. While the Hanbali School of Law claims the smallest number of adherents among today's Muslims because of its strictness, the same characteristic has made Hanbalism an indispensable anchor for all Sunni fundamentalists. Another eminent proponent of Islamist thought was the brilliant philosopher Ibn Hazm al-Andalusi (d. 1064), who combined fundamentalist theory and practice in his calamitous political life during the most tumultuous period of Muslim Spain. Ibn Hazm's stress on doctrinal purification and simplicity, coupled with his militant advocacy of *jihad,* are considered major components of Islamist thought.[3] Two lesser figures were Imam Ibn Salamah (d. 1032) and Qadi Iyadh (d. 1149). Ibn Salamah's pugnacious conception of *jihad,* and Iyadh's strict traditionalism as an eminent jurisconsult *(faqih)* of the Maliki School of Law, have found favor in recent Islamist writings. The opposition of Iyadh to the Almohad dynasty led to his exile and death. To these militant imams, the waging of *jihad* was not simply a collective obligation *(fard kifayah)* but an individual duty *(fard ayn)* except in unusual circumstances.

The Abbasid demise and the chaotic conditions of the thirteenth and fourteenth centuries produced four major proponents of Islamic renewal, all centered in Damascus. The first was Muhyi al-Din al-Nawawi (d. 1277), a preeminent Shafii advocate of *jihad* who possessed an exceptional knowledge of the *sunnah* and a reputation as an uncompromising traditionalist. Nawawi's righteousness and willingness to challenge the government's power to exact heavy taxes prompted Sultan Baybars to expel the imam from Damascus. Nawawi was followed by a succession of militantly fundamentalist imams led by the celebrated Taqi al-Din ibn Taymiyyah (d. 1328). In the perception of contemporary Islamist ideologues, Ibn Taymiyyah is the most prominent precursor of present-day fundamentalism after Ibn Hanbal. Like his predecessor, Ibn Taymiyyah was the embodiment of the militant theoretician and activist defender of the faith. He recognized no authority except the Quran, the *sunnah* and the practices of the early

Islamic community; he violently opposed innovation *(bidah),* saint worship, and pilgrimages to shrines. Moreover, Ibn Taymiyyah preached *jihad* against the Mongols, the Ismailis, Alawis, and Druze, and advocated placing restrictions on non-Muslims. As a confirmed anthropomorphist, he attributed to God human traits and believed in the literal interpretation of Quranic references to the Diety. Despite repeated incarcerations in Damascus and Cairo, Ibn Taymiyyah persisted to the end in upholding the strict constructionism of Ibn Hanbal against a multitude of jurists belonging to the Shafii School of Islamic Law. Particularly unconventional was his self-appointed role as *mujtahid fil-madhab* (legal interpreter), thereby freeing himself from blind emulation *(taqlid)* and even consensus *(ijma)* in reaching his juridicial opinions.

As an activist *mujaddid,* Ibn Taymiyyah's overriding concern was the building of moral solidarity *(taawun)* on the basis of a reinvigorated Islamic ideology and its strict implementation in society. To him solidarity meant the spirit of brotherhood binding together all the Muslim faithful from the time of Muhammad to the time of Final Judgment.[4] Only through moral solidarity could the Muslims become God's witnesses on earth in keeping with the prophetic calling. In view of the threats facing the *ummah* during Ibn Taymiyyah's lifetime, he sought to transform the moral solidarity of the Muslims into a united commitment to *jihad* against the Tatars and the divisive forces within the Islamic community. To Ibn Taymiyyah, fighting in *jihad* constituted a higher obligation than pilgrimage, prayer or fasting.[5]

The powerful influence of Ibn Taymiyyah on contemporary Islamist theory and practice stems from his commitment to translate his teachings into action. Thus, he participated in the war against the Tatars and was repeatedly subjected to inquisition *(mihnah)* and incarceration for the valiant defense of his beliefs. Ibn Taymiyyah's resolute fundamentalism, and advocacy of militant *jihad* and free *ijtihad* have left an indelible mark upon later generations of fundamentalists. However, in certain areas of Islamic thought, Ibn Taymiyyah took a more moderate stance than some contemporary proponents of Islamic militancy. Despite his opposition to the Sufism of Ibn Arabi, he accepted a Sufism based on Islamic legalism and tradition.[6] Moreover, he showed reluctance to condone *takfir*—the excommunication of an individual from the Islamic community. In contrast to some of today's Islamist groups, Ibn Taymiyyah would prescribe excommunication only as a last resort.[7]

After Ibn Taymiyyah's death, his teachings were perpetuated by his disciples, most notably Ibn al-Qayyim al-Jawziyyah (d. 1350). As a militant preacher and writer, Ibn al-Qayyim became the foremost interpreter of Ibn Taymiyyah's teachings for which he suffered persecution and imprisonment.[8] In his efforts, Ibn al-Qayyim was joined by a Shafiite defender of Ibn Taymiyyah, Imad al-Din ibn Kathir of Damascus (d. 1373). Ibn Kathir was attracted to Ibn Taymiyyah's militant puritanism and shared the latter's distrust of speculative theology and popular Sufism. In view of the continuing threat to Islam from the Crusaders, Ibn Kathir and Ibn al-Qayyim became leading advocates of *jihad*.[9] The writings of these two imams are repeatedly quoted in the contemporary Islamist literature.

The direct spiritual descendant of Ibn Taymiyyah's Damascene group of theorist-activists was Muhammad ibn Abd al-Wahhab (d. 1792), who revived Hanbalism after a lapse of four centuries. The doctrines of Ibn Abd al-Wahhab and his Muwahhidin movement bore the clear imprints of Ibn Taymiyyah and Ibn al-Qayyim. Ibn Taymiyyah's influence resurfaced in the writings of Rashid Rida, Muhammad Abduh's Syrian disciple who founded the journal *al-Manar* in 1897. This publication was instrumental in spreading Ibn Taymiyyah's ideas in North Africa, thereby contributing to the rise of the Islamic nationalist movement led by Abd al-Hamid b. Badis (d. 1940).[10] No less significant was Ibn Taymiyyah's influence on Abu al-Ala Mawdudi of India and the radical Arab fundamentalists of the recent period—Sayyid Qutb, Shukri Mustafa, Abd al-Salam Faraj, and Juhayman al-Utaybi. In retrospect, Ibn Taymiyyah has become the preeminent *munadhdhir* (theoretician) of Sunni fundamentalism. As a token of their reverence, Ibn Taymiyyah's followers refer to him as "al-Shaykh al-Islam."

The foregoing nine exponents of Islamist thought—Ibn Hanbal, Ibn Salamah, Ibn Hazm, Iyadh, Nawawi, Ibn Taymiyyah, Ibn al-Qayyim, Ibn Kathir, and Ibn Abd al-Wahhab—represent a composite profile of intellectual and political leadership, possessing certain unique characteristics. Indeed, in terms of social background, personality, conviction, and behavior, the lives of these nine imams reflect striking similarities including:

   1. commitment to the renewal of the *ummah* by a return to Islamic roots;
   2. advocacy of militancy and *jihad* in defense of Islam;
   3. combining fundamentalist ideology with political and social activism in their personal lives; and

4. readiness to challenge religious and political authority and willingness to sacrifice for the sake of Islam.

Mujaddids and Mahdis

The epicentric role of charismatic leadership has been a persistent feature of religious and revolutionary movements. The fusion of the religious and political realms in Islam renders the charismatic leader indispensable as the fountainhead and propagator of the revivalist message.

Islamic belief and precedent permit several types of fundamentalist religio-political leadership. Among the Sunni, the primary type of leadership associated with the occurrence of revivalist movements is that of *mujaddid*. The notion of *mujaddid* is embedded in the Traditions, specifically in a *hadith* related by the Prophet's companion Abu Hurayra found in Abu Dawud.[11] As restorer of the faith, the *mujaddid* is to appear every century to defend the Traditions *(sunnah)* against innovation *(bidah)*. In his mission to regenerate the Islamic spirit, the *mujaddid* will combat worldly scepticism, impiety, and rigid conformism in legal interpretation *(taqlid)*. He will undertake *ijtihad* in pursuit of the socio-spiritual regeneration of Islam. The *mujaddid* is not a prophet sent by God; he is recognized as a *mujaddid* often posthumously as a consequence of his accomplishments.

According to Mawdudi, a *mujaddid* may pursue any one or several of nine dimensions of Islamic renewal *(tajdid)*: diagnosis of current ailments; scheme for reformation; estimation of one's limitations and resources; intellectual revolution; practical reforms; *ijtihad;* defense of Islam; revival of Islamic system; and universal revolution.[12] To Mawdudi, only an "ideal" *mujaddid* is capable of achieving all nine objectives of renewal. He maintains that the "ideal" *mujaddid* is yet to appear and that there have been only "partial" *mujaddids* in Islam beginning with Umar II. In Mawdudi's prognosis, the "ideal" *mujaddid* will appear as Al-Imam al-Mahdi as foretold in the Traditions of the Prophet.[13]

Unlike the *mujaddid,* the *mahdi* claims devine sanction for his mission. In the Sunni tradition, the concept of mahdiship is not as clearly defined as in Judaism, Christianity, and Shiite Islam. According to Ibn Khaldun, the Expected Messiah (al-Mahdi al-Muntazir) will issue from the Prophet's family *(ahl al-bayt)* to appear at the "end of time" along with Jesus (Isa), to defeat the enemies of Islam and to save his people.[14] In contrast, Mawdudi's conception of mahdiship is more circumscribed. He expects the *mahdi* to be a "modern leader" possessing special intellectual and spiritual gifts to carry out his revolutionary mission to establish "the Caliphate after the pattern of Prophethood." To Mawdudi, the *mahdi* will not perform supernatural acts, nor will he proclaim himself as *mahdi;* but the people will recognize him as such from his achievements.[15] Examples of Sunni mahdiship include Muhammad Ahmad of the Sudan (1879), and Muhammad ibn Tumart of Morocco (1130). More elaborate is the Shiite notion of mahdiship. Ismaili Shiites believe in the reappearance as *mahdi* of the seventh imam, descended from Ali, who is believed to have gone into temporary occultation *(ghaybah).* In contrast, Twelver or Imami Shiites (Jafari) await the reappearance of the twelfth imam in the line of Ali, who is believed to have gone into occultation.

The problem of leadership is a central preoccupation of present-day Islamist theorists and practitioners. Each fundamentalist group has formulated its own concept of leadership in terms of necessary attributes and modalities of selection. The Ikhwan takeover of the Great Mosque of Mecca featured a *mahdi,* while Khomeini's Islamic Republic is led by a jurisconsult *(faqih),* acting as the representative of the Hidden Imam. On the other hand, as the founder of the Muslim Brotherhood, Banna preferred the humble title *murshid* (guide), despite his powerful influence as a *mujaddid.*

The Fundamentalist Ideology

In any religious context, fundamentalist phenomena involve a return to basics—to the puritanical foundations of the faith. However, the movement back to the "pure" origins of the creed does not always imply the blind emulation of the lifeways of the Prophet's environment. Indeed, some present-day fundamentalist movements strive to incorporate, in various degrees, new practices and values to strengthen their viability in the modern context. Consequently, the ideological orientation of contemporary Islamist movements has been influenced by modern ideologies of development, such as socialism and capitalism. These alien influences, however, are not commonly acknowledged by Islamist ideologues, who ascribe to them Islamic origins.

The ideologies of contemporary Islamist movements are substantially similar in content and objectives. The salient differences between these ideologies will be discussed under Part II. The aim here is to present only the general characteristics of fundamentalist thought *(fikrah)* and ideology *(aqidah)*, which most Sunni Islamist movements of the Arab world have come to share. These characteristics are mostly drawn from the teachings of Banna, Qutb, Mawdudi, Hawwa, Faraj, and al-Utaybi.

Din wa Dawlah

Islam is regarded as a total system of existence, universally applicable to all times and places, including the hereafter. Unlike Christianity, the separation of the faith *(din)* and the state *(dawlah)* is inconceivable. Rule *(hukm)* is inherent in Islam; the Quran gives the law, and the state enforces the law.[16]

Quran and Sunnah

The foundations of Islam are the Book of God Almighty (Quran) and the Traditions *(sunnah)* of Muhammad, God's Messenger *(Rasul)*, as well as the practices of the Prophet, his companions *(sahabah)*, and the first four caliphs *(Rashidin)*. Islam is the final truth and final revelation; as the possessors of the ultimate truth, the Muslims' primary missions in life are submission to God *(ibadah)*, and propagation of Islam *(dawah)*; consequently "God stands with them."[17]

Sirat al-Mustaqim

The call to spiritual rebirth should be based on a return to the "correct path"—*sirat al-mustaqim*—which inspired the first Muslims.[18] Unless the Muslims revert to the puritanism of the *salaf*—their pious ancestors—there will be no salvation. Thus, the first community establishd by Muhammad and his companions is the supreme model for emulation.

The Sixth Pillar

The good Muslim should go beyond observing the Five Pillars (obligations) of Islam, and commit himself to a life of action in building the ideal community.[19] According to Banna and his followers, the establishment of an Islamic order *(al-nizam al-Islami)* is a religious duty which may involve *jihad.* The resort to *jihad* transcends the intellectual effort of *ijtihad,* since it connotes physical struggle, fighting *(qital),* death, and martyrdom. Consequently, the violent challenge to the status quo becomes a built-in component of militant Islamic fundamentalism. Since the obligation of *jihad* involves the possibility of martyrdom, Muslims should be ready to sacrifice themselves; for victory can only come with the mastery of "the art of death" *(fann al-mawt).*[20]

The Universal Ummah

The ultimate aim of the good Muslim should be the establishment of Allah's sovereignty over the whole of mankind. Thus, the homeland of Islam is the earth itself. In order to establish the authority of God and His Law *(Shariah),* it is necessary to dispossess worldly rulers, both Islamic and non-Islamic, of their authority through *jihad.* The resort to *jihad* should not be "defensive"—it should go beyond purifying and securing the existing Islamic world in order to conquer the obstacles placed in the way of Islam's propagation the world over. These obstacles include the state, social systems, and traditions against which the *mujahidin* (holy strugglers) will employ a "comprehensive" *jihad* including violence—*jihad bil-saif*—striving through the sword.[21] Therefore, the transformation of *jahili* society—Jews, Christians, communists, atheists, polytheists, and unrepentent Muslims—is a prerequisite for the establishment of the Islamic community, which will guarantee the freedom of man from others and from his own desires.[22] In this context, Islam alone is recognized as the savior of humanity—the religion of the future.[23]

Social Justice

Islam considers the life of man a spiritual and material unity. Thus, moral behavior determines socioeconomic justice. All property (*mal*) belongs to society and ultimately to God; man merely utilizes wealth and earns it through his labor. Islam recognizes private property but limits it in accordance with the general welfare of the community. The accumulation of wealth through dishonesty, monopoly, and usury is prohibited. The principle of *zakat* (almsgiving), coupled with state policy will prevent the division of society into classes.[24] Such practices are often labeled "Islamic socialism." The historical figure who symbolizes a vehemently "communistic" position on social justice to most Islamists, is the Prophet's companion, Abu Dharr al-Ghifari.[25]

Legitimate Rulership

Government will operate by consultation *(shura)* under the Quran; the state will be charged with the enforcement of the *shariah* (divine law). The executive authority is to be bound by the teachings of Islam and the will of the people. The ruler should satisfy the following prerequisites: Muslim, male, adult, sane, healthy, just, pious, virtuous, knowledgeable in Islamic jurisprudence, and capable of leadership. If the ruler deviates from the "correct path," he must be warned, guided, and eventually removed should he persist in his deviation. Indeed, "those who do not govern according to divine revelation are unbelievers."[26]

pg 4 - the foundations of Islamic Polity

Puritanical Society

The Islamic *ummah* should be a puritanical society based on *salafiyyah* maxims, in emulation of the Prophet's message and exemplary life. The recreation of such a virtuous society requires pious individuals, whose everyday life is patterned after the Prophet's and his companions'. The family is the cornerstone of the social structure where men are placed in a position of leadership and responsibility while women are the source of love and kindness. The mixing of the sexes should be controlled and women decently dressed *(al-ziyy al-Islami)* to maintain dignity and avoid the possibility of temptation.[27] Western values and mores are rejected as being alien to Islamic religion and culture.

Unity of Theory and Practice

In his person, the Prophet united the message of Islam and its implementation. Therefore, the Islamic way is not one of mystical contemplation *(sufism)* but one of action. Ideology should be translated into a coherent program of action *(minhaj)*.[28] This commitment to perpetual activism compels the application of *shariah* to new circumstances through open *ijtihad*, directed against the religious establishment and state authority. Thus, there would not be slavish imitation *(taqlid)* of tradition but renewal *(tajdid)* to forestall the onset of impiety and ignorance *(jahiliyyah)*.[29]

Techniques of Ideological Propagation—The Dawah

The energetic propagation of the message *(nashr al-dawah)* has been a basic feature of the Islamic faith since its inception. As a universalistic creed, Islam has sought to spread its teachings throughout the world. In this effort, the call to Islam *(dawah)* is both a collective and individual duty *(fard)*.[30]

In the fundamentalist practice, the call to Islam acquires a special meaning. While both conventional and fundamentalist Muslims share the commitment to the call, basic differences exist in the techniques, motivations, and targets of their missionary work. Conventional Muslims seek to proselytize among non-Muslims—Christians, Jews, atheists, animists and others. These groups are at best secondary targets for the fundamentalists; their primary focus of conversion and recruitment is the conventional Muslim who is invited to follow the "correct path."

Operating within the Islamic realm, the fundamentalists utilize a plethora of unique propaganda techniques, targeted at both individuals and groups. As the possessors of the "ultimate truth," the Islamists propagandize with great zeal and fervor, often covertly, depending on political circumstances. These techniques found their virtuosic use in the hands of Hasan al-Banna and his acolytes, who set the pattern that has been emulated by the new leaders of the movement. As the head of a totalitarian collectivity, the fundamentalist leader has two ongoing propagandistic concerns: (1) the reinforcement of his followers' beliefs to raise their level of consciousness, and (2) the induction of new members into his movement. The Brotherhood's Hasan al-Banna dispatched special messages *(tarif)* to educate his followers about the society's goals and activities. He also provided guidance for the spiritual, mental, and physical direction of the members' lives. Each neophyte took an oath of allegiance embodying the motto: "action, obedience, silence."[31] The action component was perpetually reinforced by the member's participation in mass gatherings marking religious holidays and political events. These rallies, which resembled Christian revivalist meetings, were conducted in highly emotional settings, with chants and slogans to generate feelings of unity, power, and collective devotion.

Mass rallies were also used to impress and recruit new members—the leader's second propaganda objective. In appealing to outsiders, charismatic speakers were especially chosen to use powerful revivalist oratory as *duat* (missionaries), as distinct from *khutaba* (preachers), who represented the appointed mosque functionaries of the Islamic establishment.[32] In the areas of fundamentalist strength, the missionary often replaced the official preacher during prayer services, as the mosque became the focus of recruitment.[33] A special section for propaganda was organized, in addition to a clearing house for publications to maintain doctrinal orthodoxy. Speakers and topics were chosen to fit the audience depending on its educational, socioeconomic, and occupational status.

The utilization of propaganda by today's Islamist groups follows a long tradition that goes back to the Prophet's time and the disputations between his successors. Indeed, there are striking similarities between the techniques employed by contemporary Islamist societies and militant groups in Islamic history such as the Carmathians and the Fatimids. The *dawah* is often conducted secretly on an individual basis, particularly when the group is conspiratorially inclined. In larger settings, modern devices are frequently used including cassettes and tape recorders.

Target Audiences of the Revivalist Call

The crisis factors that generate Islamic fundamentalism also create both distinct and amorphous constituencies of opposition to state authority. Such opposition is the consequence of widespread popular dissatisfaction with society and state. However, it should be noted that the crisis environment exercises a differential impact upon individuals and classes in society. Clearly, certain categories of individuals and social groups are more sensitive to the realities of the existing order than are others, by virtue of their socioeconomic position, psychological makeup, age, education, and occupation.

In view of the differences between Arab regime characteristics and policies, some cross-national variations exist in the target audiences of revivalist propaganda. Nonetheless, it is possible to identify certain general social strata and collectivities which have displayed special inclination toward involvement in Islamist causes. It should be noted that these target audiences and groups are often overlapping in their composition.

The Youth

The youth of the Arab countries is the most receptive social group to the Islamist call. This category includes high school, college, and university students and graduates who are apt to become the most zealous participants in Islamist societies advocating violence. A variety of crisis factors have contributed to extreme alienation among Arab youth—psychological insecurity, unemployment, lack of identity, social inequity, and loss of national dignity vis-à-vis Israel and the West. The fact that the membership of militant fundamentalist societies includes a high percentage of young people is no coincidence. Significantly, university students and graduates with specializations in science and technical fields are more prone to be attracted to fundamentalism, in contrast to those with humanistic backgrounds. The former are highly motivated, idealistic, and upwardly mobile.[34] There appear to be three reasons for the predominance of scientific and technical field preferences among fundamentalist students: (1) the desire to catch up with the West scientifically to neutralize its industrial and military superiority; (2) the quest to master fields of learning (science/technology) which are thought minimally to involve the transference of Western values to Islamic society; and (3) the attractiveness of the certainty inherent in the exact sciences as opposed to the analytical and speculative nature of the Humanities and the Social Sciences.

Newly Urbanized Elements

The unceasing tide of migration from the countryside to the cities has been a major destabilizing factor in the Middle East. The result has been the growth of massive urban agglomerations, characterized by housing shortages, unemployment, and virtual lack of social services. More significant is the culture shock that urbanization produces among the new arrivals. They experience a "culture crisis" as a consequence of being separated from the stability of their traditional middle- and lower-middle class families in the small towns and villages.[35] Thus, in urban mass society, these individuals tend to lose their psycho-social bearings as they are bombarded with the values of an alien environment. In the anomic loneliness and social atomization of the city, the new urbanites seek to find a social-spiritual niche and a "medium of salvation"—membership in fundamentalist societies. Indeed, the urban setting renders the newly urbanized elements particularly vulnerable to recruitment by charismatic leaders or their agents.

Political Malcontents

This amorphous group includes some of the most politically conscious individuals and segments of Arab society from which counter-elites are likely to emerge. Their opposition to constituted authority is usually triggered by the social, economic, and foreign policies of Arab governments. The dissidents include a plethora of Nasserist and nationalist idealists, dispossessed political, religious, and economic groups, middle- and lower-rank military officers, and the victims of state repression. Among these, the military constitutes the most potent source of Islamist insurrection.

Nativist-Traditional Elements

The traditionalist sectors of Arab society include several petty bourgeois or "middling" occupational clusters—bureaucrats, shopkeepers, professionals, teachers, clerks, artisans, and small landowners—who are opposed to the dilution of the Islamic ethos under the impact of foreign political-economic-social penetration. These are devoutly religious people whose shift to fundamentalist activism is a consequence of their perceived threat from the state and the outside world. Often the threat factor is seen as affecting both their traditional religious identity and their economic interests. A combination of state policies operating in the framework of the global economy have destabilized the socioeconomic position of the Arab middle classes during the last decade. The opportunities for middle-class individuals to acquire mobility have been significantly reduced. In fact, it has become increasingly difficult for this stratum to retain its existing socioeconomic status, producing a situation of relative deprivation.[36] The economic frustrations of middle-class elements have been compounded by their cultural alienation from the Westernized political and economic elites. This culture gap is reinforced by a widening economic gap which the middle classes are unable to bridge despite their relatively high educational level. While a college education has not brought the expected betterment in economic status, it has contributed to a historically unprecedented sharpening of social consciousness among large segments of the Arab middle class. Hence, the accute sensitivity of its members to socioeconomic injustice and the Western cultural assault on their Islamic identity.

The Lower Strata

This amorphous mass consists of three main categories—poor peasants *(fallahin)*, tribesmen *(badu)*, and the urban poor. Together, these lower classes are commonly called *mustadafin*—the oppressed or the disinherited. Two attributes render these classes proliferous sources of recruits for the fundamentalist cause. As the most traditionalist sectors of society, the *mustadafin* nurture a deep and abiding commitment to Islam. This factor, combined with their lowly socioeconomic position, makes them readily receptive to the Islamist message. Important examples of *mustadafin* include the Ikhwan warriors of Saudi Arabia and Khomeini's mass constituency. In a milieu of revolutionary fervor, the *mustadafin,* along with the youth and lower-middle class nativist elements, are likely to provide the mass support and cannon fodder in a possible seizure of power by the military and its civilian allies.

As related earlier, there are some cross-national differences in the disaffected groups which have manifested strong Islamist orientations.

This is particularly true about the "middling" sectors—the backbone of most fundamentalist societies in the Arab world. The evidence indicates that differences in the internal makeup and policies of Arab governments have produced differential impacts on the various sectors of the middle-class. For example, the policies of the Syrian Baath have had a deleterious effect on the fortunes of the Sunni urban petty bourgeoisie, which has been further alienated by the sociopolitical ascendance of the Alawite minority.[37] Thus, the Islamist protest movement in Syria is primarily based on the Sunni urban middle class.

A different situation exists in Egypt where sectarianism of the Syrian type is not an issue. Consequently, Egyptian middle-class fundamentalism is mainly the result of the government's economic, cultural, and foreign policies. Moreover, in contrast to the Syrian case, the most accutely disaffected sector of the Egyptian middle classes is probably the rural lower middle class and its urban offshoots. In Tunisia, on the other hand, the disaffected groups manifesting fundamentalist tendencies are more heterogeneous than those of Syria and Egypt. These include the traditional bourgeoisie, business and property owners who were affected by the expropriations of 1962–69, and lower middle-class elements; the average age of the Tunisian militants was between 20 to 30.[38] These questions will receive further elaboration in Part II.

The Appeal of the Islamist Alternative

It is possible to summarize the basic characteristics of the Islamist alternative which contribute to its drawing power at the mass level. As an ideology, Islamic fundamentalism:

1. bestows a new identity upon a multitude of alienated individuals who have lost their social-spiritual bearings;
2. defines the worldview of the believers in unambiguous terms by identifying the sources of "good and evil";
3. offers alternative modalities to cope with the harsh environment;
4. provides a protest ideology against the established order;
5. grants a sense of dignity and belonging and a spiritual refuge from uncertainty; and
6. promises a better life in a future Islamist utopia, possibly on earth and definitely in heaven.

The drawing power of the Islamist societies stems from their success in combining theory and practice by attempting to implement the doctrinal precepts of the fundamentalist ideology in the context of their collective existence. Specifically, Islamist societies provide:

1. a sense of brotherhood in a community of believers;
2. specific functions to be performed by individual members, thereby defining their "stations in life" and according them self-respect;
3. mutual assistance and self-help in communal settings including health care, social services, and financial help; and
4. a medium of political activism which ultimately promises to alter the "sinful" society according to Islamist precepts.

The power of Islamist ideology to attract adherents reflects its capacity to perform important social, political, and psychological functions which have gone unmet by the authorities. The consequent vacuum in socioeconomic development and socialization has been filled by Islamist ideology and its purveyors. Thus, fundamentalism offers alternative prescriptions to remedy social ills and an escape from alienation in a turbulent environment. As a mechanism for social mobilization, Islamist ideology can accommodate the political dissident as well as provide an escape from politics for those seeking spiritual salvation.

The prime targets of fundamentalist propaganda—the youth, new urbanites, political malcontents, traditionalists, and the lower strata—have already manifested considerable receptiveness to the "message." However, at the present stage of evolution, the outright resort to activism and violence has been infrequent. Yet, by all indications, the process of Islamist politicization is continuing at varying rates depending on the status of the group and the nature of the regime. The circumstances and scenarios which are likely to accelerate the transformation from passive to active fundamentalism will be outlined in Part III.

Indices of Islamic Fundamentalism

The analysis of the indices of fundamentalist behavior involves a difficult process of identification and assessment. The first task is to differentiate between conventional Muslims who practice the faith in varying degrees of regularity and fundamentalist Muslims of both the passive and radical types. The second task is to distinguish between passive and radical fundamentalism. These require the exercise of judgmental prudence on the part of the scholar, in view of the peculiar coalescence and continuity between the different modes of Islamic practice.

Passive Fundamentalism

Explicit manifestations of a return to Islamic lifeways have been an increasingly pervasive behavioral pattern in Arab society. Evidence of conspicuous Islamic collective and individual behavior may be seen in all aspects of daily life. It should be emphasized that the powerful current toward the Islamic ethos does not automatically denote mass political activism. It is rather a politically passive fundamentalism in many instances, with more or less discernible characteristics. The attributes of this amorphous socio-spiritual effervescence of Islam include:

1. regular mosque attendance, five times a day;
2. strict observance of the Five Pillars—profession of faith (*shahadah*), prayers (*salat*), fasting (*sawm*), almsgiving (*zakat*), pilgrimage (*hajj*);
3. striving for an exemplary life with a significant degree of adherence to Quranic prohibitions, such as abstaining from alcohol and pork and a conscious rejection of Western social and sexual mores;
4. regular religious meditation and reading of the Quran and other Islamic literature;
5. participation in group activities organized by religious societies within and outside the mosque. Popularly supported mosques (*ahli*) are preferred to government subsidized mosques;
6. participation in neighborhood self-help and mutual assistance societies, which provide health care, food, and social services particularly to the poor;
7. growing full beards (*lihya*) and thin moustaches as a sign of devotion and piety and often displaying short haircuts;
8. wearing of distinctive clothing; males usually wear a *gallabiyyah* which does not cover the feet; women wear loose garments

covering the body or a maxi-length skirt and sometimes a head cover (khimar).[39]

There are cross-national variations in the appearance and clothing of both men and women. For example, in the Egyptian case, conservative fundamentalist women often wear a head mask, while others use a simple head cover.

Activist Fundamentalism

The foregoing behavioral attributes apply to the general category of fundamentalist Muslims who do not routinely manifest political activism unless there is a *fitnah*—an instigation from the state or society at large. While under normal circumstances the fundamentalist masses are likely to remain politically passive, the activists among them conform to unique behavioral patterns in tightly organized groups. However, in many cases, it is difficult if not impossible to differentiate between the militant and passive fundamentalists, except in situations where the following characteristics are observable:

1. Activist fundamentalists are likely to pursue the behavioral norms of the passive fundamentalists (1 through 8 above), except with greater rigor and assiduity.

2. Activist fundamentalists tend to live together in specific neighborhoods and, in certain cases, in physical and social isolation from the Muslim population and even from the passive fundamentalists.

3. Activist fundamentalists tend to frequent specific mosques which cater to their peculiar *dawah*. Generally, they are known to attend the prayers at dawn *(fajr)* for the purposes of solitary meditation and collective worship. The sparsely attended mosque at dawn affords them the opportunity to form conventicles to organize and plan their activities. Certain activist groups attend private mosques which are funded by the faithful, in contrast to mosques supported and controlled by the authorities.

4. The activists, in contrast to passive fundamentalists, periodically engage in acts of "purifying" violence directed against places of illicit pleasure, night clubs, hotels, movie theaters, and governmental figures.

General Indices of Collective Behavior

In addition to the behavioral indices described above, it is possible to identify a residual category of collective manifestations of fundamentalism which have been increasingly observable during the last decade:

1. Mosque building—this has increased dramatically throughout the Arab world as a result of four sources of funding: government grants, endowments by affluent individuals, contributions by the faithful, and external funding from oil-rich Arab rulers.
2. Radio-television programming—there has been a marked increase in programs on Islam and interruption of scheduled radio and television broadcasts for prayer calls.
3. Observance of holidays—major and minor holidays are observed with greater fervor, as are religious ceremonies and rituals.
4. Mosque attendance—there have been growing levels of mosque attendance by both sexes.
5. The Press—there has been a greater incidence of newspaper articles and commentaries on religious subjects, including special sections devoted to Islam in the Friday newspapers.
6. Elaborate lighting has been installed to illuminate mosques during night time.
7. Religious literature—there has been an unprecedented increase in the printing of the Quran *(mushaf)* and books on Islamic history and religion.
8. Copies of the Quran are conspicuously displayed in homes, offices, government buildings, cars, and taxicabs.
9. Religious slogans—Islamic slogans are displayed on public buildings, homes, cars, trucks, public transport vehicles, newspapers, television, and streets.[40]

Verbal Indices of Collective Behavior

Another method to discern the manifestations of fundamentalism is through the identification of key words, mottos, and phraseology which Islamist speakers and writers use with great frequency. Indeed, Islamic fundamentalism has its own specialized terminology *(mustalahat)* and slogans *(shiarat),* as found in other religions and ideologies. To the faithful, these terms constitute the ideological code words which help to homogenize their beliefs and evoke emotion and action. Moreover, the language of fundamentalism shapes the worldview of the believers and, therefore, their perceptions of reality. The following is a sample of such terms:

jahiliyyah—the ignorant and sinful society consisting of non-Muslims as well as Muslims who do not follow the correct path—*sirat al-mustaqim*—as in the pre-Islamic society of the Prophet's time.

fasad—moral corruption in society, especially among the ruling elite and its allies in the economic sector.

tawhid—belief in the unity of Allah, in opposition to *shirk*—the belief in ascribing "partners" to the Godhead.

iktinaz—hoarding of goods and wealth against the interests of the Islamic community.

makruh—abhorrence by believers of impious conduct.

iftira—false accusation.

kafir—unbeliever. In the case of extreme fundamentalists, the term is applied to all non-Muslims, including Christians and Jews as well as mainstream Muslims.

ada Allah wal-insan—enemies of Allah and men.

quwwah al-sharr wal-zalam wal-jahiliyyah—forces of evil, darkness, and ignorance.

fann al mawt—"the art of death"—readiness to sacrifice one's life as martyr *(shahid)* for the cause of *jihad*.

khurafah—superstition.

bidah—innovation.

al-mumin al-qawi khayrun min al-mumin al-daif—the strong believer is better than the weak believer.

taghut—despot.

mulhid—apostate, heretic, atheist.

dhal—straying from the right path.

zindiq—atheist.

nasr min Allah, wa fathun gharib—victory is from God, and the conquest is at hand.

al-zalamah—injustice as referred to the deeds of the government and exploiting groups.

al-masakin—the wretched.

al-fuqara—the poor.

al-mufsidun fi al-ard—the corrupt on earth.

tabdhir—extravagance.

murtadd—a sinful person who rejects Islam despite being a Muslim.

yuhallilun al-haram wa yuharrimun al-halal—they legalize the illicit, and they proclaim illicit the legal, referring to the *ulama* and their verdicts in support of government policy.

Finally, it is instructive to quote the credo of the Muslim Brotherhood of Egypt:

> Allahu ghayatuna, al-rasul zaimuna,
> Al-Quran dusturuna, al-jihad sabiluna
> Al-mawt fi sabil Allah asma amanina
> Allahu akbar, Allahu akbar.
>
> God is our goal, the Prophet is our leader.
> The Quran is our constitution, struggle is our way.
> Death in the service of God is the loftiest of our wishes.
> God is great, God is great.[41]

5 Taxonomy of Islamist Societies and State Responses

$\mathcal{T}$ HE MULTIPLICATION of fundamentalist groups in the Arab countries and the larger Islamic world has been a fact of life in recent years. Despite certain basic similarities in values, beliefs, and orientation, considerable diversity exists among these groups and societies.

In view of the covert nature of many Islamist organizations, it is often difficult if not impossible to gather accurate information concerning their attributes. Only a handful of these are known to Western scholars and specialists dealing with the subject. Actually, dozens of fundamentalist organizations exist in each Arab country, operating overtly and covertly in pursuit of their political, social, and spiritual objectives. A conservative estimate of the number of active fundamentalist groups in the Arab world would be several hundred, of which ninety-one are presented in Appendix I. It should be noted that sufi orders, Islamic philanthropic societies, and mainstream Islamic associations are mostly excluded from this sample.

Aggregate Profile of Fundamentalist Societies

The ninety-one Islamist societies together provide a composite picture of the active and organized segments of the fundamentalist movement in the Arab world. It should be stressed that the data presented here are far from complete, and more research is necessary to acquire a comprehensive depiction of the Islamist reality in the Arab context. The data on the ninety-one groups have been collected from about two hundred newspapers, pamphlets, tracts, periodicals, and books in Arabic, French, English, and Farsi and from interviews with over two dozen informed individuals from the Middle East including members of Islamic societies. Underground publications were an invaluable source. Each piece of information has been cross-checked with as many sources as possible to maximize accuracy. What follows is the aggregate analysis of twelve aspects of these associations.

Names of Islamist Societies

In most cases, a group's name is chosen by its founder(s), except in those instances where an alternate name was given by the media or the authorities. For example, in Egypt, the Islamic Liberation Organization is known in the media as the "Technical Military Academy Group," and the Society of Muslims as "Denouncement and Holy Flight"—Takfir wal-Hijrah.

Often the name of a specific society reflects its sectarian or ideological orientation and objectives. Thus, the words "Fatimi," and "Zaynab" denote Shiite organizations, since they refer to the "Holy Family"—the union between the Caliph Ali and the Prophet's daughter Fatimah and their female offspring, Zaynab. It is also noteworthy that most groups associated with the Muslim Brotherhood of Egypt use the term "Ikhwan" (Brethren). Among Egyptian groups, the words "jamaah" or "jamiyyah" (society) are preferred, while the Shiites seem to have a predilection for the term "hizb" (party). Some societies operate under several names to mislead the authorities.

The names chosen by fundamentalist societies also reflect their quest to reinforce their theological legitimacy. Consequently, certain terms and phrases, used with great frequency, are meant to suggest religious and historical authenticity. These include:

> Hizb Allah—Party of God
> Al-Ikhwan—The Brotherhood
> Al-Fath—Islamic Conquest
> Al-Haq—The Truth (of Islam)
> Al-Jihad—Holy War
> Junud Allah—Soldiers of God
> Al-Tahrir al-Islami—Islamic Liberation

Mujahidin—Fighters of Holy War
Dawah—The Call
Tawhid—Oneness of God

Membership Background

By all indications, fundamentalism is observable among all segments of society, from the uppermost to the lowliest classes. However, the primary recruitment sources of Islamist organizations are the middle, lower-middle and lower classes, consisting of urban petty bourgeois elements and newly urbanized provincials and peasants. Particularly significant are students of large urban colleges and universities, many of whom have family roots in the small towns and villages of the countryside. The large proportion of students and young people in militant Islamic societies reinforces the future potency of fundamentalist groups vis-à-vis ruling elites and institutions. This phenomenon underlines the political bankruptcy of the authorities and their failure to institute effective programs of socialization to capture the loyalties of the youth. Other occupational sources of recruitment include: shopkeepers, workers, teachers, soldiers, bureaucrats, engineers, physicians, tribesmen, and lower- and middle-rank military officers.

Militancy and Ideology

A large majority (75 percent) of the ninety-one Islamist groups in the sample were judged to be "militant," in view of their revolutionary propensity or record of violence. Among the notable exceptions are the old Muslim Brotherhood of Egypt, the Damascus faction of the Syrian Muslim Brotherhood until 1980, several Sudanese parties, and some Islamic groups in the Gulf, Lebanon, and the Maghrib. For example, Lebanon's Islamic National Movement is quite "moderate," since it is led by Sunni politicians and clerics who appeal to the people's Islamic consciousness to maintain group solidarity against the dominant Maronites. Under crisis circumstances brought on by state repression, economic breakdown or defeat by Israel, the line between the middle and high levels of militancy is likely to be blurred, as passive and nonviolent fundamentalists will move toward militancy. Finally, there appears to be an inverse relationship between the size and militancy of these groups: the larger the movement, the more overt its activities and the lower its militancy. Moreover, the established movements possess an older membership who manifest lower levels of activism. The last two propositions are clearly exemplified by the Egyptian Muslim Brotherhood and several Sudanese and Maghribine Islamic associations.

In terms of ideology, some differences exist between the belief systems and practices of Islamist societies. The younger, more militant groups tend to emphasize violent *jihad* as an ongoing priority, while others will employ *jihad* tactically when the resort to violence appears beneficial to their cause. Other Islamist groups emphasize proselytization, collective social action, and economic self-help as a means to prepare themselves for a possible future confrontation with the state. Moreover, certain fundamentalist groups like Takfir wal-Hijrah advocate centralized organization and communal living thereby segregating their members from the larger society. Finally, it is necessary to differentiate between "primitivist" and "adaptationist" societies. The primitivists, like the Takfir of Egypt and the Ikhwan of Saudi Arabia strive to strictly emulate the lifeways of the Prophet's community. In contrast, the adaptationists like the Muslim Brotherhood are predisposed to the selective incorporation of modern ideas and practices into their ideology and behavior.

Sectarian Identity

As shown in Appendix I, a large majority of the Islamist societies of the Arab world are Sunni (80 percent). This finding reflects the overwhelmingly Sunni affiliation of most Arabs. Major exceptions are the Twelver groups of Iraq which claim to represent the Shiite majority and the Shiite activists of Lebanon, Saudi Arabia, and the Gulf. None of the groups of the sample represent the Ibadis, Zaydis or the *Ghulat*—Ismailis, Ali Ilahis, Alawites, and Druze.

Leadership: Charismatic vs. Bureaucratic

In view of their underground or semi-public status, the leadership of certain fundamentalist groups is unknown. Generally, the founders

Table 2
Types of Islamist Leadership

Charismatic	Bureaucratic
Ibn Abd al-Wahhab	Al Shaykh family
The Mahdi Muhammad Ahmad	Abdallahi; Al Sadiq al-Mahdi
Banna	Tilmisani
Sibai	Attar/Hawwa/Saad al-Din
Baqir al-Sadr	Baqir al-Hakim
	Muhammad al-Shirazi
	Hadi al-Mudarrisi
Musa al-Sadr	Nabih al-Barri

of Islamist societies tend to be charismatic while their successors are bureaucratic types operating within a collective leadership. The charismatic founders include such powerful personalities as Hasan al-Banna (Muslim Brotherhood); Ayatullah Baqir al-Sadr (Hizb al-Dawah of Iraq); Imam Musa al-Sadr (AMAL of Lebanon); Shukri Mustafa (Takfir wal-Hijrah); Salih Siriyyah (Islamic Liberation Organization); and Juhayman al-Utaybi (Ikhwan of Saudi Arabia). Among the bureaucratic types are: Umar Tilmisani (Muslim Brotherhood of Egypt); Shaykh Hasan Khalid (Islamic National Movement of Lebanon); Nabih al-Barri (AMAL of Lebanon); and the collective leaderships of the Syrian Muslim Brotherhood, the Sudanese parties, and Maghribine Islamic groups. It would appear that the younger the movement, the more the probability of it being led by charismatics who assume such titles as *amir* (commander), *imam, murshid* (guide), or *mahdi* (messiah). The transition from charismatic founders to bureaucratic perpetuators is shown in Table 2.

The personality profile of fundamentalist leaders indicates generally marginal backgrounds, a strong sense of alienation from society, and a powerful compulsion to compensate for personal sufferings and deprivations by seeking the destruction or the radical transformation of the ruling order. These attributes of marginality, alienation, and the quest for comprehensive change can be readily seen in such leaders as Ibn Abd al-Wahhab, the Sudanese Mahdi, Banna, Qutb, Mustafa, Siriyyah, Musa al-Sadr, Baqir al-Sadr, and Utaybi. Another significant feature of Islamist leadership is the Sufi background of several leaders which was transformed into politico-spiritual militancy under the impact of personal suffering and crisis conditions *(fitan)*. Among those who began as Sufis but turned to activism were the Sudanese Mahdi, Hasan al-Banna, and Said Hawwa of the Syrian Muslim Brotherhood.

Millenarians and Messianists

Islam, like other religions, possesses a millenarian propensity centered around a messianic promise. While the messianic notion—mahdism—has received greater theological significance among the Shiites, it is also a part of the Sunni belief system, as embedded in about fifty traditions *(ahadith)* in an unbroken chain of authority *(mutawatir).*[1] It is significant that the notion of mahdiship continues to have contemporary expression among Islamic fundamentalists. This can be seen in several of the societies in Appendix I, as well as in historical cases (see Table 3).

Size

Any judgment on the size of fundamentalist groups should remain tentative. About 40 percent of the ninety-one groups analyzed appear to possess small memberships—less than a thousand activists. Another 40 percent can be classified as medium size organizations with several thousand active and many inactive members. These include Takfir wal-Hijrah, the Jihad Organization, and the Islamic Liberation Organization. Finally, about 20 percent are large associations with active mem-

Table 3
Mahdist Leadership in Islam

Name	Movement	Locality
Muhammad Ibn Tumart (1130)	Muwahhidin	North Africa
Ibn Falah al-Mushasha (1462)	Mushashain Shiites	Khuzistan
Muhammad Ahmad (1879)	Mahdiyyah	Sudan
Shukri Mustafa (1975)	Takfir wal-Hijrah	Egypt
Muhammad ibn Abdullah al-Qahtani (1979)	Ikhwan	Saudi Arabia
Taha al-Samawi (1981)	Jamaat al-Muslimin lil-Takfir	Egypt
Al-Mahdi al-Arabi (1982)	al-Usbah al-Hashimiyyah	Egypt

berships exceeding five thousand, and followers of up to a million. The last category includes the Muslim Brotherhood of Egypt, its Syrian affiliate, the Ahl al-Dawah of Algeria, the Hizb al-Dawah of Iraq, the AMAL of Lebanon, and the Sudanese parties. However, considerations of cross-national equivalence dictate that size be assessed relative to a country's total population. In that sense, the Jordanian Hizb al-Tahrir, the Kuwaiti Society for Social Reform, and Morocco's Muslim Brotherhood may be considered large organizations. Yet, in terms of their potential for violence, smaller groups are more prone to constitute an immediate danger to established authority, although a mass uprising will require the participation of the medium and larger groups.

Current Status and Organizational Lifespan

The majority of the ninety-one Islamist societies are proscribed, and several are permitted to operate with tacit official sanction, often granted with reluctance. While most of the militant organizations have been suppressed, there is little reason to doubt their continued underground existence and threat potential. Among the suppressed groups, the Shiite organizations of Iraq have displayed a reduced level of armed activity due to the intensity of state repression. Similarly, the Syrian Islamist groups are in great disarray as a result of the government's crackdown during 1979-82. The militant societies of Egypt such as Al-Takfir, Al-Jihad, and ILO have been forced into an underground existence. Meanwhile, several large fundamentalist associations are permitted to operate in semi-public fashion. These include the Muslim Brotherhood of Egypt and its affiliates in Jordan, the Maghrib and the Gulf. Only in the Sudan have the Islamist societies come to the forefront of political affairs as a result of the accommodation reached by President Nimayri and his attorney general, Hasan al-Turabi, a leader of the Brotherhood.

Despite their proscribed status, new Islamist groups, both passive and militant, continue to mushroom throughout the Arab countries in response to local crisis conditions. As a rule these groups are founded by charismatics who gather around them a small number of disciples to propagate their peculiar version of Islam. In time, the more militant groups are likely to clash with the authorities, while some will expand in size and assume the form of political parties by toning down their ideological militancy.

Table 4
Country of Origin of Islamist Groups

Egypt	29
Iraq	12
Syria	12
Lebanon	6
Sudan	5
Saudi Arabia	5
Jordan/West Bank	4
Tunisia	4
Algeria	3
Morocco	2
Kuwait	2
Gulf	2
Yemen	1
Bahrain	1
USA	1
Israel	1
Germany	1
	91

Country of Origin and Transnational Ties

As the most populous Arab country, Egypt claims the largest number of Islamist societies in the sample (29). Iraq has twelve groups, eleven of which represent the vociferous Shiite opposition to the Baath regime. The Syrian Islamist opposition to Hafiz al-Asad is represented by twelve groups. Most of the remaining Arab countries are represented by one to six Islamist societies (see Table 4). A note of caution should be registered regarding the relationship between the number of activist groups in each country and the level of Islamist activity. While the large number reported for Egypt reflects Islamic activism, it also underlines the fractionization of the movement. Moreover, it is likely that the small number of fundamentalist groups reported in the sample for Saudi Arabia and Syria is due to the relative lack of information about these societies vis-à-vis the more open Egyptian social context. Finally, there exist many more societies in North Africa, Jordan, and the Sudan than those reported in Appendix I, because these countries were not given detailed coverage in this study.

Virtually all the larger fundamentalist organizations maintain transnational ties with counterparts in Arab and Muslim countries,

Europe, and North America. The most notable organization with transnational connections is the Muslim Brotherhood of Egypt, with affiliates and allies in Syria, Jordan, Tunisia, Algeria, Morocco, Lebanon, Libya, the Sudan, Saudi Arabia, the Gulf, Pakistan, and the West. Similarly, the once formidable Hizb al-Dawah al-Islamiyyah of Iraq has ties with Iran, Syria and the Shiites of Lebanon and the Gulf states. The Shiite AMAL of Lebanon has links to the Syrian and Iranian régimes. Jamaat al-Masjid of Saudia Arabia is active in the Gulf and even in Oman; and the Hizb Allah of Yemen has propagandized effectively in Saudi Arabia, the Gulf states, the West Bank, and Europe. The group Ansar al-Dawah is active in proselytizing among Indian and Pakistani Muslims working in the Gulf and through them in India and Pakistan. The Kuwait-based affiliate of the Muslim Brotherhood, Jamiyyah al-Islah al-Ijtimai, operates in the Gulf states in promoting Islamic culture. It is noteworthy that the Technical Military Academy Group and Takfir wal-Hijrah have maintained ties with sympathizers in several Arab countries, despite their proscribed status in Egypt. Finally, there is the unique category of several transnational Islamic organizations—Ahl al-Hadith, Harakat al-Islamiyyah and Al-Ittihad al-Islami—which operate in Europe, Canada, and the United States as extensions of larger Islamist societies based in the Arab world. On the basis of the foregoing evidence, the last decade has witnessed the emergence of an Islamic movement of truly transnational proportions. Thus, what began as a polycentric movement has been increasingly assuming a transnational character, receiving substantial reinforcement from Muslims residing in the West and throughout the world.

Islamist Groups in Evolution: A Pattern

Taken in the aggregate, a statistical analysis of the ninety-one Islamist societies indicates salient relationships between five organizational attributes: (1) lifespan of group; (2) type of leadership; (3) size; (4) level of militancy; (5) political status. *A high statistical association was discovered between small size, high militancy, clandestine status, recent nascence, and charismatic leadership. Conversely, a high statistical association was found between large size, low militancy, public existence, longevity, and bureaucratic leadership* (see Appendix III).

These relationships conform to the general patterns which seem to characterize the evolution of revivalist and revolutionary movements. At its inception, the group is small, clandestine, cultic-millenarian, militant, led by a charismatic, and composed of young radicals. In time, the group becomes a larger movement, operating openly with a reduced level of militancy, led by bureaucratic types, and consisting of an older cross-section of members.

These findings offer empirical reaffirmation to the theories of Weber and Montesquieu regarding the changing nature and role of leadership from the genesis of a movement to its institutionalization.[2] Thus, the epicentric role of the charismatic founder is eventually replaced by his bureaucratic disciples as charisma is "routinized" and the movement acquires the attributes of an organization. The transition usually entails doctrinal dilution and revisionism.

Regime Types and Responses to Fundamentalism

The emergence of Islamic fundamentalism as a major sociopolitical force has confronted the Arab regimes with an unprecedented challenge, which, in its ultimate logic, undermines the moral foundations of authority—the legitimacy of every ruling elite and institution. A taxonomic analysis of Arab state policies toward Islamist groups necessitates a multidimensional scheme of classification, which combines types of regimes with their policy attributes. The Arab states exhibit substantial diversity in regimes, ranging from traditional monarchies to leftist military autocracies, each of which has developed specific policy responses toward the fundamentalist phenomenon. The nature of state policies depends on degree of legitimacy, wealth, coercive potential, and the elite's perception of the fundamentalist challenge. Beyond these factors, the policies toward fundamentalism are strongly influenced by the specific ideologies of ruling elites and their orientation toward Islam. Arab regimes may be classified in four general categories along two dimensions: (1) Islamic fundamentalism vs. Islamic passivity; and (2) social radicalism vs. social conservatism. The Islamic dimension classifies regimes according to the extent of their reliance on Islam as an instrument of self-legitimization and as a guide to policy. The radicalism-conservatism dimension involves the extent and nature of social change being pursued by each regime which range from revolutionary to gradualist and conservative.[3] The perceived approximate position of each regime is indicated in Figure 4.

The foregoing classification may serve as the basis for a fourfold

Figure 4
Classification of Arab Regimes

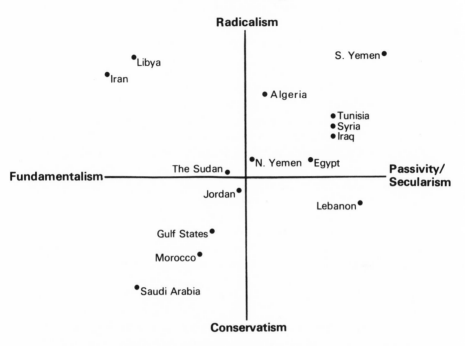

taxonomy of Arab state policies toward the fundamentalist societies and the larger Islamist movement:

Radical Islamic:	Libya (Iran)
Conservative Islamic:	Saudi Arabia, Morocco, Jordan, Oman, Kuwait, Qatar, Bahrain, United Arab Emirates, and the Sudan
Secularist Cooptative:	Tunisia, Algeria, Syria, Iraq, Egypt, North Yemen, South Yemen
Secularist Conservative:	Lebanon

Radical Islamic: Libya

By all criteria, Libya represents a unique case in the Arab context and in the world community. The *dawah* of "Brother" Muammar al-

Qadhafi is an uncommon mix of Islam, populism, socialism, and Arabism, which reflects the mercurial and restless personality of its creator. Through a combination of charismatic populism, ideological fervor, and selective repression, Qadhafi has created a Muslim *Jamahiriyyah* in his own image—an integrative populist polity which has neutralized all opposition groups including Islamist societies, army factions, and Nasserists. All insurrectionary efforts have been crushed, as the colonel continues the quest to export his brand of Islamic revolution based on his personal philosophy as stated in *The Green Book.*

Indeed, Qadhafi's approach to Islam distinguishes him from all other Muslim ideologues and governments. After attempts to revive Islamic law during the early 1970s, Qadhafi proceeded to limit its scope to religious matters and moral conduct.[4] The place of Islamic law was taken up by *The Green Book,* which Qadhafi sees as the embodiment of a new revolutionary doctrine to resolve the problems of humanity. Meanwhile, he has rejected the *sunnah* of the Prophet and the vast corpus of authoritative interpretations of the *ulama,* in favor of the Quran. In this sense, Qadhafi is a "primeval" fundamentalist whose understanding of Islam stems from his personal *ijtihad* centered solely on the Quran.

Conservative Islamic: Saudi Arabia, Morocco, Jordan, the Gulf States, and the Sudan

The monarchies pursue gradualist policies within a traditionalist Islamic framework reinforced by tribal consensus. Thus, Islam is utilized in varying degrees as the elite's official ideology, its mechanism of self-legitimation, and the religion of the state. By surrounding themselves with the halo of traditional Islamic legitimacy, these regimes seek to preempt opposition attempts to use Islam as a protest ideology. The spectrum ranges from the rigorous conservative fundamentalism of Saudi Arabia to the mild Islamic conservatism of Jordan.

In the Saudi case, the dynasty rules by virtue of Wahhabi legitimacy and has assumed the role of protector of the *Haramayn* (Holy Cities). However, this monopoly of Islam has not hindered the emergence of fundamentalist movements, both of the Sunni and Shiite varieties. Since the Shiite disturbances in al-Qatif and the Ikhwan takeover of the Grand Mosque constituted direct challenges to the monarchy, they were suppressed decisively. However, the regime was quick to expand and intensify its policies of cooptation in the wake of these insurrections by offering incentives to the Shiites and generous compensation to the families of the executed Ikhwan guerrillas (see Chapter 9).

While similar in goals, Saudi and Moroccan policies toward fundamentalism manifest important differences. Both monarchies tolerate quiescent fundamentalism so long as there is no resort to anti-regime violence. Until recently, King Hassan had managed to contain his opponents through a combination of selective repression and cooptation within an Islamic sociopolitical framework which was far more permissive than Saudi Arabia's. The situation was drastically altered by the mass rioting of early January 1984 which shook the regime and induced mass repression. While the opposition included a broad cross-section of Moroccan society, it appeared that Islamist elements had assumed a leading role in the struggle against the monarchy.[6] Meanwhile, King Hassan continues to rule by virtue of Islamic legitimacy as "Commander of the Faithful," without enforcing strict fundamentalist laws and practices.

Oman's theocratic system is less permissive than Morocco's, although it lacks Saudi Arabia's official commitment to strict Islamic lifeways. Sultan Qabus rules in the name of Islamic legitimacy of the Ibadi variety. As the non-Sunni dynast of a part-Sunni state, the Sultan has been concerned with the cooptation of his Sunni subjects— particularly Dhufaris and Wahhabi tribesmen. In recent years, the Sultan's cooptative capabilities appear to have increased as a result of domestic oil production and outside aid from the U. S. and the Gulf states (see details in Chapter 10).

The official commitment to Islam in Jordan and the Gulf States is not as total as in Saudi Arabia or Iran. There is a certain flexibility in these monarchies which translates into policies of accommodation and coexistence toward diverse ethnic and religious groups including Muslim activists. The Hashemite Dynasty of Jordan claim descent from the Prophet which serves as an important symbol of legitimacy. Innovative flexibility has been the hallmark of King Husayn's policies, particularly during the last decade. After suppressing the Palestinian threat to the Kingdom in 1970–71, the King has pursued policies of accommodation toward the Muslim Brotherhood which enjoys strong Palestinian support. The Brotherhood, led by Abd al-Rahman al-Khalifa, functions as the unofficial overseer of social morality but refrains from pressing for the adoption of strict Islamic codes. In contrast, the Islamic Liberation

Party of Shaykh Taqi al-Din al-Nabhani and the Brotherhood's radical wing represented by Dr. Abdallah Azzam have been suppressed due to their militancy and opposition to the regime, particularly on Palestinian issues. In recent years, increasing numbers of Palestinians have turned to Islamic militancy in view of the bleak prospects for a resolution of their cause.

The symbiotic relationship between the state and the Islamic societies of Jordan is also evident in the Gulf. In Kuwait, Qatar, Bahrain and the U. A. E., Sunni governments are confronted with both Sunni and Shiite Islamist movements. Of the two, Shiite fundamentalism is more militant, as a consequence of Iranian inspiration and the Sunni possession of wealth and power. The truck bombings of December 1983 of the U. S. and French embassies and other targets in Kuwait appear to have been induced by Shiite militancy within the framework of the Iran-Iraq war. The Shaykhly regimes have managed to accommodate both variants of fundamentalism with monetary inducements. These flexible policies have been extended to the Persian communities, which may be more vulnerable to Iranian Islamist propaganda than the native Arab Shiites. A somewhat special case is the Bahraini situation, where a Sunni minority rules an underprivileged Shiite majority. However, the Bahraini government has been able to contain recent manifestations of Shiite activism, while displaying some degree of accommodation in offering economic incentives.

The Sudan occupies a special position in the classification of regimes in Figure 4, because of President Jafar al-Nimayri's decision in Fall 1983 to implement *shariah* law throughout the country. This was the culmination of the Islamization process begun in 1977 when Nimayri forged a rapprochement with the Islamic parties, including the Mahdists and the Brotherhood. Thus, the Sudan first followed Pakistan's path toward Islam although in a gradualist manner because of the non-Arab tribes of the south consisting of Christians and animists. However, the recent acceleration of Islamization has precipitated an open rebellion in the southern provinces and a return to the guerrilla warfare of the 1960s. Two key personalities in the drive for Islamization are Hasan al-Turabi and Al Sadiq al-Mahdi. As attorney general, Turabi has played an important role in implementing the *shariah,* despite the criticism of his radical colleagues in the Muslim Brotherhood and opposition from the Sufi orders. Meanwhile, Al-Sadiq al-Mahdi, the great grandson of the Mahdi, has opposed the traditionalism of the Brotherhood and has advocated a modernist Islam based on reason.[7] At this juncture, the Sudanese evolution toward an Islamic system is marked by inconsistencies and excesses such as the hanging of Mahmud Muhammad Taha, the Republican Party leader, in January 1985. The attempt to establish an Islamic order appears to be a futile means to reinforce the regime's legitimacy in difficult political and economic circumstances.

Secularist Cooptative: Syria, Iraq, Egypt, Algeria, Tunisia, and the Yemens

All seven regimes have maintained varying degrees of secularism while attempting to placate the fundamentalist groups through economic, political, and symbolic incentives. However, these governments have also resorted to different modalities and degrees of suppression whenever faced with manifestations of Islamist threat. Syria and Iraq are Baathist, avowedly secularist, semi-socialist, and Pan-Arabist. Yet, the two states are led by opposing wings of the Baath Party which derive their power from different ethno-religious minorities. Consequently, the Islamic revivalist phenomenon in both countries constitutes a mortal challenge to the very survival of these regimes, since both rule over antagonistic sectarian majorities.

The Alawite-led Syrian government of Hafiz al-Asad has faced a tenacious fundamentalist challenge based on the Sunni majority, which constitutes almost 60 percent of the total population. After a decade of relatively unsuccessful cooptative policies toward the Sunnis, the Baath has responded with repression in the face of escalating Islamist opposition. However, the regime has persisted in its efforts to coopt the opposition groups (see Chapter 7).

Similar conditions exist in Iraq, where Saddam Husayn's predominantly Sunni government rules a Twelver Shiite majority (55 percent). In the face of increasing Shiite revolutionary fervor during the late 1970s, the Iraqi Baath resorted to repression. These policies have weakened the organizational network of the Shiite groups. Simultaneously, the government has attempted to win over the Shiites by including several in the governing elite (see Chapter 8).

In Egypt, the government's reaction to Islamist challenges before and after Sadat's assassination was resolute but not terroristic. The Mubarak government has gone beyond Sadat's policies by attempting to reeducate and win over the Islamist youth. While stressing its commitment to Islam, the Egyptian regime has maintained a generally secularist orientation, but has refrained from foreign and domestic policy initiatives that could provoke the Islamist elements (see Chapter 6).

In Tunisia, Bourguiba's Destourian Party has endured, although its secularist orientation has come under increasing attack especially from the bazaar sector. The regime's reactivation of Islam as the state religion and retraction of certain modernist policies[8] have proven insufficient in placating the new fundamentalist groups representing populist Islam. As in other countries, Islam has become the language of protest against official corruption, socioeconomic injustice, and Westernization. The situation culminated in the widespread riots of January 1984, triggered by the imposition of higher bread prices. The regime blamed the Islamic groups for the violence and dispatched the army to quell the rioting.[9] The price increases were cancelled by President Bourguiba in the face of unprecedented public furor. There is every indication that after Bourguiba, the growing Islamist wave will attempt to reassert itself.

In terms of ideology and policy, Algeria is better equipped than Tunisia to confront the Islamist challenge. As a state born out of a protracted revolutionary war, the ideological mix of reformist Islam and socialism was consecrated as the official creed—the basis of popular legitimacy. Under President Boumedienne, the Islamic orientation was reinforced as the government continued to monopolize Islam, while proscribing the activities of Islamist societies like al-Qiyam and Ahl al-Dawah. The revolutionary origin of the Algerian state, coupled with its cooptation of Islam provided Boumedienne with a strong ideological weapon to neutralize fundamentalist propaganda. In recent years, however, a new militant revivalism has emerged as a response to rapid modernization and Westernization. A major manifestation of Islamic militancy was the rioting by university students amid attempts to topple the regime in November 1982. These were decisively crushed by President Chadli Ben-Jadid, who initiated a campaign of Islamic "moralization" to reform the government, while refraining from the promulgation of modernizing policies that could generate controversy.[10]

The two Yemens present special problems. The northern regime is caught between conflicting pressures from its Zaydi and Shafii populations, in addition to the mutually antagonistic policies of conservative Saudi Arabia and Marxist South Yemen. The regime survives through a balancing act between the Zaydi and Shafii communities, while relying on Saudi political and economic backing to counter South Yemen. The constitution makes the *shariah* the source of all legislation. One important element in the political equation is the Islamic Front which is under the influence of the Muslim Brotherhood whose ideology is propagated by thousands of Egyptian teachers working in the country. Reportedly, the Front is pro-Saudi and four of its supporters are members of the October 1983 cabinet.[11]

As a Marxist regime, the People's Democratic Republic of Yemen (South Yemen) is unique among the Arab states. Despite its Marxist orientation, the constitution declares Islam as the state religion, and top government figures lead the faithful in prayers on religious holidays. The regime has moved cautiously in revising Islamic legislation.[12] It appears that the leadership has taken an incrementalist approach to effect social transformation, while stressing the compatibility of Islam and Marxism in official propaganda.

Secularist Conservative: Lebanon

After nine years of civil war, the Lebanese have reverted to the consociational formula of the prewar years to achieve reconciliation. Under this system, power was shared between Lebanon's seven major religious communities. Despite its sectarian base, the government operated in a substantially secularist mode that was made possible by the equilibrium between the various communities. By coopting the leaders (*zuama*) of the religious groups into the government, the Lebanese system sought to check sectarian militancy with mixed results.

Both Sunni and Shiite militancy have been evident in the Lebanese cauldron of countervailing forces. The Sunni militants of Tripoli have repeatedly clashed with pro-Syrian militias, while the Shiite AMAL and its pro-Iranian factions have fought the Lebanese army, the American and French peacekeeping forces, and the Israelis in South Lebanon.[13] The Shiite militant groups of Lebanon are to some degree the ideological and organizational projections of Shiite resurgence radiating from Iran and Iraq's Hizb al-Dawah, with extensions to Kuwait, Bahrain, and the Eastern Province of Saudi Arabia. It is too early to tell whether the new consociational formula of President Gemayel and Prime Minister Karami will succeed in stabilizing Lebanon.

Part II Islamic Resurgence in the Arab World

Case Studies

6 Egypt

Cradle of Islamic Fundamentalism

T HE SOCIETY OF MUSLIM BROTHERS, more than any other organization, has been the ideological and institutional epicenter of fundamentalism in the Arab sphere and the Islamic world. The Brotherhood has survived recurrent state suppression and internal conflicts for over fifty years. The essential dynamic of the Brotherhood's survival is rooted in the bedrock of Islamic faith and culture where the psycho-spiritual character of most Egyptians is embedded. Despite its Egyptian origins, the spiritual and political influence of the Brethren has been evident in virtually all Arab countries and beyond. Indeed, it is impossible to comprehend contemporary Sunni Islamic fundamentalism and its Arab manifestations without a firm understanding of the origins and development of the Brotherhood.

The Genesis of the Brotherhood

The Brotherhood was founded in 1928 by Hasan al-Banna in Is-mailiyya. Its establishment represented the confluence of powerful social currents and the charismatic personality of Banna.[1] Egypt during the interwar years was the focus of conflicting social, economic, political, and ideological pressures, which provided a favorable milieu for the rise of the Brotherhood. This crisis environment which preceded Banna to the second half of the nineteenth century, was characterized by European political, cultural, and economic penetration under the hegemony of the British and the non-native Muhammad Ali dynasty. Two main currents of Egyptian response developed within this crisis environment. The first was Egyptian nationalism symbolized by the revolt of Ahmad Urabi Pasha (1881) against the Khedive and his European patrons, and the struggles led by Mustafa Kamil, Muhammad Farid, and Saad Zaghlul against the British. The second was the movement of Islamic reformism (Salafiyyah) under the aegis of Shaykh Muhammad Abduh. These interrelated nationalist and Islamic responses found fertile soil during the interwar years in the midst of the triangular confrontation between the monarch, the British, and nationalist politicians led by the Wafd Party. However, in the Egyptian perception, these intellectual and sociopolitical movements had failed to liberate Egypt from the British yoke, the corrupting cultural and economic influences of the West, and the misrule of the Palace and the politicians. Nor had the Egyptian leadership been able to synthesize an ideological formula to shape the process of nation-building and socioeconomic development. Thus, Banna's reaction to the crisis milieu was to advocate a return to the basics of Islam—the call to fundamentalism. Banna's *dawah* was a direct descendant of earlier revivalist movements.

Banna: The Avatar of Fundamentalism

Hasan al-Banna, more than any other individual, can be considered the avatar of twentieth-century Sunni revivalism. He was the unique embodiment of the Sufi spiritualist, Islamic scholar, and activist leader who possessed a rare ability to evoke mass support by translating doctrinal complexities into social action. While Banna's movement lacked the philosophical depth of the Salafiyyah, it succeeded in galvanizing and organizing a mass following as no other Islamic movement had done in recent centuries. Banna was singularly unconcerned with ideological intricacies since he was committed to revival of the Islamic community without regard to its internal, sectarian, or other divisions. In promulgating the Brotherhood's ideology, Banna relied on the Quran, and the six canonical treatises of *hadith*. In addition, Banna based himself on the precedents of thought and action established by the leading exponents of fundamentalism including Ibn Hanbal, Ibn Hazm, Nawawi, and a host of other theorist-activists and heroes in Islamic history.[2]

In keeping with the universal pattern of fundamentalist leadership, the Brotherhood constituted the organizational extension of Banna's charismatic personality and the institutional reflection of his vision. Banna's emergence typifies Weber's charismatic leader who appears in times of crisis with a message of social-spiritual salvation. As a product of Egypt's conflictual milieu, Banna faced a personal crisis which he sought to resolve by projecting it to the level of society. Thus, Banna also exemplifies Erikson's inspirational leader whose quest for personal salvation is transformed into a mission to return society to "the correct path." In Banna's case, the salvational mission was directed at the Egyptian faithful seeking solutions for their psycho-spiritual, social, and economic problems. Hence, the "fit" between the charismatic's message and the society in crisis as increasing numbers of Egyptians joined the Brotherhood under the banner of militant Islamic puritanism.

The Brotherhood in a Revolutionary Setting

From its modest beginnings, the Brotherhood had become by the late 1930s one of Egypt's most powerful organizations. It attracted members from a cross-section of society—bureaucrats, professionals, students, workers, small shopkeepers, and some peasants. Banna established a powerful organizational and propaganda apparatus, and increasingly strove to play a political role in Egyptian affairs. The war years brought Banna into conflict with the British authorities and the Egyptian government. He was repeatedly arrested as the organization continued its anti-British agitation and underground activity centering on *al-Nizam al-Khassah,* the Special Organization—otherwise known as *al-Jihaz al-Sirri*—the Secret Apparatus. Meanwhile, Banna had promulgated the objectives of his organization. His classic statement underlines the anomalous relationship between Islamic fundamentalism and civil society and reflects the worldview of fundamentalist Muslims toward social reality:

> My brothers you are not a benevolent society, nor a political party, nor a local organization having limited purposes. Rather, you are a new soul in the heart of this nation to give it life by means of the Quran; you are a new light which shines to destroy the darkness of materialism through knowing God; and you are the strong voice

which rises to recall the message of the Prophet . . . You should feel
yourself the bearer of the burden which all others have refused. When
asked what it is for which you call, reply that it is Islam, the message
of Muhammad, the religion that contains within it government, and
has one of its obligations freedom. If you are told that you are political, answer that Islam admits no such distinction. If you are accused
of being revolutionaries, say "we are voices for right and for peace in
which we dearly believe and of which we are proud. If you rise against
us or stand in the path of our message, then we are permitted by God
to defend ourselves against your injustice . . ."[3]

Banna's declaration that his group was not a political party did
not prevent him and his followers from engaging in intensive lobbying,
demonstrations, and even electoral politics. At the end of World War
II, the society had reached its apogee as it struggled against the palace,
the Wafd, and the British. Meanwhile, Banna had built an organization
of a million followers with an elaborate apparatus covering all aspects
of social existence—propaganda, labor, peasants, students, professions, family life, athletics, legal services, the press, publications, and
financial and economic affairs. True to its Islamist creed, the society
had attempted to build an *ummah*—an Islamic state within the Egyptian state. By late 1948, the Brotherhood was perceived as the most
formidable threat facing the monarchy. Early in December, the government dissolved the society fearing an imminent revolution, after the
latter's involvement in street violence and the assassination of several
prominent figures. Banna's personal efforts to negotiate with Nuqrashi
Pasha's government were unsuccessful as the prime minister proceeded to unleash the full powers of the state against the Brethren. On
December 28, 1948, Nuqrashi was assassinated by a Muslim Brother—
an act that brought a reign of terror against the society, leading to
Banna's assassination on February 12, 1949, by government agents.
    The period of repression was brought to an end by the accession
of the Wafdist government in January 1950, when the Brotherhood
regained its legal status. In October 1951, Judge Hasan al-Hudaybi was
elected Supreme Guide, as the society's guerrillas began to fight the
British in the Suez Canal Zone. On January 26, 1952, massive rioting
broke out against the British presence culminating in the destruction of
Western-owned establishments in the heart of Cairo, including the
Shepheard's Hotel. The Brotherhood's complicity was suspected but
never proven. On July 26, 1952, King Faruq was overthrown by a
military junta led by General Muhammad Naguib and Lieutenant Col-

onel Gamal Abd al-Nasser, without the active participation of the Brotherhood and its leadership.

During the Revolution's first year, the Brotherhood's relations with the military regime were cordial and often friendly. However, by mid-1953, it became apparent that the Nasser-led Revolutionary Command Council (RCC) was moving toward a secular state rather than an Islamic polity.[4] Thus, in the ensuing Nasser-Naguib power struggle, the Brotherhood supported the latter by joining the outlawed parties in demonstrations calling for a civilian regime. These manifestations of opposition were crushed by the junta, as hundreds of Wafdist, leftist, and Brethren sympathizers were purged from the officer corps. By April 1954, Nasser had consolidated his power within the RCC and the Army. The RCC-Brotherhood conflict, however, did not intensify until Nasser's conclusion of an agreement with Great Britain on July 19, 1954, providing for the evacuation of the Canal Zone. The Brotherhood rejected the agreement as "treasonable" in an attempt to rally Egyptian and Arab opposition against Nasser. An uneasy coexistence marked the summer and early fall, broken by an assassination attempt (October 26, 1954) against Nasser, which was blamed on the Brotherhood. This triggered a massive repression of the society and the arrest of its leadership and over 4,000 members.[5] The proud leaders of the Brethren were tried by a People's Tribunal consisting of RCC officers Gamal Salim, Husayn al-Shafii, and Anwar al-Sadat. Six of the defendants were executed and Hudaybi was imprisoned for life; twenty-six years later an offshoot of the Brotherhood—Al-Jihad—assassinated President Anwar al-Sadat, on October 6, 1981.[6]

The cardinal hallmark of Islamic fundamentalism and its embodiment in the Brotherhood is the ability to regenerate itself after periods of remission. The military regime, which had systematically destroyed the Brotherhood's apparatus by late 1954, proceeded to capture the loyalties of the Egyptian and Arab masses in the emerging charismatic popularity of Nasser. Simultaneously, Nasser's Pan-Arabist socialist ideology had coopted a significant portion of the Brotherhood's *dawah*. For over a decade, Nasser was able to offer the Arabs much of what the Brotherhood had promised—dignity, unity, popular participation, defiance of the West, and a semblance of socio-economic justice. It was not until the early 1960s that Nasserism became encumbered with the Syrian secession, the Yemeni War, and economic problems, setting the stage for the Brotherhood's reemergence in 1964. In that year, Nasser freed the Brethren presumably to counter the Communists. But once again, the society became embroiled in a conspiracy against the regime. The plot was effectively uncovered by the security forces in mid-1965, leading to widespread arrests. Three prominent Brethren, including the society's theoretician—Sayyid Qutb—were hanged, and over one hundred members were jailed. Significantly, many of the conspirators were relatively young members of the new middle class—engineers, chemists, scientists, and students.[7] This pattern of Islamic militancy among young individuals with scientific specializations would become a salient membership characteristic of fundamentalist groups during the 1970s. The gloomy life in prison became the crucible which shaped the future course of the Islamic movement in Egypt. The intensity of repression produced a painful soul searching among the Brethren and a reassessment of their situation. There were wide-ranging debates within the prison walls, leading to fights and factionalism. Among the younger members there was deep disillusionment with the senior leaders of the Brotherhood, who engaged in petty controversies and lacked the fortitude not to break down under torture.[8]

A new opportunity for the Brotherhood's return presented itself in the aftermath of the June 1967 War. The magnitude of the debacle created a profound legitimacy crisis engulfing Arab leaders and institutions, including a perceptible diminution of Nasser's charismatic appeal. The defeat sent tremors through Arab society, triggering a wave of self-criticism and introspection unmatched in recent history. It was generally recognized that the ideological solutions of the past were inadequate in remedying the multiple ills of Arab society; hence, the call for *taghyir aqliyyah*—a change of mentality or psycho-spiritual transformation.[9] While the future direction of this moral and behavioral change could not be ascertained in the tumultuous wake of the June War, in retrospect the evidence indicates an ideological reversion to Islam among large sectors of the Egyptian/Arab population. In the face of defeat and pervasive identity crisis, the retreat of the masses from the Pan-Arab ideological model did not focus on Socialist, Western, or Marxist revolutionary alternatives but to the only available and genuinely nativistic moral-behavioral framework—Islam in its fundamentalist expression.

Paradoxically, the postwar reemergence of fundamentalism at the mass level was tolerated and even encouraged by the authorities in Egypt and other Arab states. In the face of the legitimacy crisis brought on by defeat, Arab leaders attempted to broaden their formulas of self-legitimation by coopting Islam to neutralize the Islamists and to maximize popular support. The mass media and the speeches of leaders were laced with references to Allah, the Prophet, and the Holy Quran.

A case in point was the media coverage of President Nasser's presence at mosque services commemorating the birth of the Prophet two days after the June War. Moreover, in a skillful propaganda maneuver, the regime used Islamic fatalism to escape responsibility for the defeat. Thus, the hand of God was seen in Egypt's defeat so that its people would awaken. According to this logic, "Israel had been faithful to its religion and therefore victorious; but we were defeated because our faith was not strong enough."[10] The Brotherhood agreed with the government about the need to return to God but blamed the regime for its lack of godliness. Furthermore, the Brethren saw the defeat as Allah's revenge upon the Nasser regime for its suppression of the society: "Those who fight or persecute soldiers of God (the Brethren), will be defeated, as the Pharaoh was defeated by Moses."[11] Consequently, the Brotherhood found the postwar political and ideological vacuum propitious for its revival. Meanwhile, new Islamist groups were being formed, particularly by a younger generation of angry militants.

Egypt Under Sadat: Fundamentalism Ascendant

The death of Nasser on September 28, 1970 removed a major obstacle to the full-scale emergence of Islamic fundamentalism; and the accession of Anwar al-Sadat provided the Brotherhood with a singular opportunity to reassert its presence in Egyptian life. As president, Sadat faced two immediate challenges: the consolidation of his power and confrontation with Israel in the Sinai. Internally, Sadat faced a legitimacy crisis since he lacked the charisma of his predecessor; nor did he possess a secure base in the Egyptian power structure dominated by his Nasserist rivals. To counterbalance the latter, he progressively liberated the Brothers from jail and encouraged their entrenchment in the student unions and elsewhere in society. By setting the Brethren against the Nasserists, Sadat successfully exploited their historic enmity. The process of de-Nasserization was accelerated by Sadat's purge of his opponents during May 1971 and after the October War, which began in the holy month of Ramadan under the code name "Badr"—the place of Muhammad's victory over the Meccans. The relative success of Egyptian arms in the war prompted Sadat to proclaim himself *"batal al-ubur"*—Hero of the Crossing—in an effort to maximize personal legitimacy. On the basis of this dubious claim to self-legitimation, Sadat proceeded to take three interrelated policy initiatives:

1. de-Nasserization of Egyptian society centered on the partial dismantling of the socialist public sector;

2. the institution of *al-infitah*—the opening to the West—based on expectations of foreign, particularly U.S., investments and economic assistance to create a large private sector;

3. rapprochement with the U. S. and the concomitant weakening of political, military, and economic ties to the Soviet Union.

Sadat's quest for legitimacy also involved increasing reliance on Islamic themes as a partial substitute for the ideological vacuum that he created by progressively jettisoning Nasserism. Thus, the 1971 Constitution made Islam the official religion of the Egyptian State, while the *shariah* was declared as *a* source of legislation. Despite Sadat's attempts to derive legitimacy from his pro-Islamic policies and his "heroic" wartime role, the regime was shaken in April 1974 by an attack directed at the Technical Military Academy. Also, Sadat's military and diplomatic moves during and after the war were opposed by some prominent people, including Muhammad Hasanain Heikal and Chief of Staff General Saad al-Din al-Shazli, who was dismissed and sent abroad as ambassador.[12]

The mid-seventies found Sadat pursuing a three-tiered policy in the Islamic sphere:

1. the placation of "establishment Islam" to consolidate the support of Egypt's Islamic leadership, centered in the al-Azhar University and large government-supported mosques;

2. the appeasement of the Brotherhood to neutralize the fundamentalist opposition and to utilize the society's organizational power against the Nasserists;

3. the suppression of militant fundamentalist groups whose violent activism threatened the regime.

The policy of repression that was prompted by the April 1974 attack on the Technical Military Academy continued until May 1975 when the regime moved against the Takfir wal-Hijrah group. Meanwhile, there were evident signs of cooperation between the regime and the Brethren. In 1976, Sadat allowed publication of two monthly journals—*al-Dawah* and *al-Itisam,* which represented the Brotherhood's views. Moreover, in the 1976 elections, the Brotherhood joined other political groups to marshall its followers to elect the pro-government majority in the People's Assembly. Such cooperation placed the Brethren in an awkward position during the Nasserist-led mass riots of January 1977, although some Islamist elements participated in the destruction of the proliferating night clubs, bars, and houses of prostitution. Continued support of President Sadat would have placed the Brethren in a position of compromising their ideology and losing mass support. Consequently, the year 1977 brought a parting of the ways between the two sides, soon to be reinforced by Sadat's rapprochement with Israel. The Brotherhood attacked the Egyptian-Israeli Peace Treaty, the "open door" policy, and Sadat's pro-Western cultural outlook, particularly regarding women. Moreover, it accused Sadat of supporting the Coptic Christian minority in the ongoing Muslim-Coptic confrontation. Finally, the success of the Islamic Revolution in Iran gave the Brotherhood increased confidence in pursuing its goal of establishing an Islamic order in Egypt.

The January 1977 riots set off a period of protracted crisis for Sadat, which culminated in his assassination in October 1981. Sadat's response to the growing opposition to his economic and foreign policies was to intensify his pursuit of Islamic legitimacy. The regime introduced a series of bills on Islamic penalties for usury, apostasy, theft, adultery, and drinking, most of which were withdrawn after protests by both Copts and liberal Muslims.[13] In March 1980 the *shariah* was made *the* main source of legislation through a plebiscite. The centerpiece of Sadat's quest for legitimacy was his overt practice of Islamic lifeways on the domestic front, which coincided with his emergence as a world statesman seeking Arab-Israeli peace. Despite Sadat's virtuosity as actor, his determination to play these mutually contradictory roles was to prove fatal. Indeed, Sadat's two roles and their cultural underpinnings were incompatible—the pious Muslim president versus the coopted member of the West's fraternity of leaders, displaying alien cultural traits in the midst of conspicuous opulence. Yet, despite this manifest clash of roles and identities, Sadat continued to project publicly his personal piety upon an acutely cynical and sceptical audience. In attempting to placate the Islamist constituency, Sadat was treading a dangerous path which had been followed by other Muslim leaders with mixed success. Sadat's predicament centered on his inability to convince the Islamists that he was fully committed to Islam. Consequently, Sadat's Islamic initiatives, however sincere, were found wanting because of his foreign and domestic policies as well as the inherent inflexibility of the fundamentalist creed. Indeed, there could be no middle path for the Islamic militants.

Yet the Egyptian media continued to depict Sadat as *al-Rais al-Mumin*—"The Believer President"—who extolled the traditional values of the village and the patriarchal family. Sadat claimed that Egypt constituted one big family of which he was *"kabiru al-ailah"*—head of the family—whose judgments would be obeyed by his children without objection. Such assertions were not well received given Egypt's socioeconomic conditions.[14] Presidential manifestations of piety were reinforced by the appearance of Islamic slogans in government buildings and official declarations, and in the President's speeches which typically began with *"Bismillah al-Rahman al-Rahim"* and ended with a Quranic quotation.

To those who knew him well, Sadat was a truly devout Muslim who sought to translate the noble maxims of his faith into constructive and beneficial domestic and foreign policies. The tragedy of Anwar al-Sadat was that despite his best intentions large segments of the Egyptian public harbored misgivings about the man from Munufiyya. They could neither forget Sadat's absence from his assigned post on the night of the 1952 Revolution nor overlook his ingratitude toward Nasser whose political legacy Sadat sought to erase. By the late seventies, there was a vast cultural gap between Sadat and his people. The great attention showered upon him by Western leaders and the media as statesman, peacemaker, and "best-dressed man," combined with his accommodating policies toward Israel, the Shah, and domestic corruption made Sadat the focal point of intense criticism. The regime responded by selective repression against Socialists, Nasserists, and Islamic militants, along with propaganda stressing Islamic themes such as *iman* (faith), *sulb* (toughness), *asalah* (genuineness), *sabr* (patience), *muhibbah* (love), *amal* (hope), *tawfiq* (God-given success), and *hidayah* (God-given guidance). The thrust of government propaganda was to convince the people to accept their lot and hope for a better future. This entreaty was preposterous, given the deteriorating socioeconomic condition of the great majority of Egyptians. The ideological vacuum created by de-Nasserization had now been partially filled by Islamic fundamentalism, rendering Sadat's leadership incongruous with the prevalent criteria of Islamic legitimacy. Under the circumstances, the move in the People's Assembly to declare Sadat as the fifth Rightly Guided Caliph was an act of political ineptitude bordering on sacrilege.[15] The President is known to have decried this initiative and disassociated himself from its authors.

The plain fact was that many Egyptians did not regard Sadat as their "father," and resented being called "his children," amid the frustrations engendered by the President's economic and foreign policies. Meanwhile, the Brotherhood and other Islamist groups had consolidated their position in the universities, the bureaucracy, and to some extent in the Army. On university campuses, the militants harassed Christian students and secularist faculty with impunity.[16] It appears that only in mid-1981 did Sadat realize the potential danger from the militant groups in the context of the Muslim-Christian communal clashes and rioting. In a preemptive move, the government arrested over 3,000 people in September 1981 and took direct control of all mosques. While most of the detainees were Islamists, in a balancing act the regime also imprisoned prominent Nasserists, Socialists, and Coptic leaders, including Pope Shenouda III. The suppression was accompanied by a warning from Sadat that he would arrest 5,000 additional opponents if they did not behave. Less than a month later, Sadat was assassinated by members of Al-Jihad—a militant Islamist group based in Upper Egypt. In the wake of the assassination, there was sporadic fighting, mainly in Asyut between Islamic militants and security forces. The policy of repression continued under Husni Mubarak, although the new president has pointedly refrained from Sadat's mistakes by assuming a low profile and instituting reforms. After a lengthy trial, Lieutenant Khalid al-Islambuli and four others involved in Sadat's assassination were secretly executed and over three hundred Al-Jihad members awaited trial. President Mubarak's decision to carry out the executions was condemned throughout the Islamic world and some Islamist groups called for his assassination or overthrow.[17]

In conclusion, the policy lessons of the Sadat era may be summarized as follows:

1. Not to underestimate the potency of Islamic fundamentalism in terms of its widespread influence, ideological commitment, and organizational capabilities.

2. Not to employ "the religious weapon" by coopting Islamic ideology incrementally and superficially, for the purpose of achieving political objectives not consonant with the fundamentalist ethos.

3. To pursue foreign and domestic policies which are to some degree congruent with the dominant religio-cultural value system and responsive to popular socioeconomic needs.

4. To develop a viable Islamic alternative to militant fundamen-

talism as a means of political socialization and as a guide to socially beneficial economic development and controlled modernization.

5. To implement the new ideological synthesis with a minimum of elite inefficiency and corruption, to meet the socioeconomic needs of the disadvantaged sectors of society.

Three Militant Societies

During the 1970s, Egyptian political life was shaken by the violent activities of three Islamist groups: Munazzamat al-Tahrir al-Islami (Islamic Liberation Organization), Jamaat al-Muslimin (The Society of Muslims), and Munazzamat Al-Jihad (Holy War Organization). The Islamic Liberation Organization is also known as the Technical Military Academy Group while the Society of Muslims is known as Takfir wal-Hijrah—Denouncement and Holy Flight. The ILO is also known as Shabab Muhammad (Muhammad's Youth), although there have been other fundamentalist organizations operating under this name. The group known as Al-Jihad is sometimes referred to as the "New Jihad." All three groups were born in the Egyptian crisis setting after the 1967 War. In ideological and organizational terms, these societies were the direct descendants of the Muslim Brotherhood.

Sayyid Qutb: The Crucial Link

In retrospect, Sayyid Qutb stands out as the indispensable link between the Brotherhood and the ILO, Al-Takfir and Al-Jihad. Indeed, as a militant ideologue, Qutb presided over the generational transition from the Brotherhood's atrophied fundamentalism to the youthful extremism of the 1970s. Three attributes characterized Qutb's pivotal role and influence on the new militants: (1) as a theoretician, Qutb exercised a powerful influence on the regeneration and redirection of Islamist ideology; (2) as a notable member of the old Brotherhood, Qutb provided organizational continuity between the Brethren and their recalcitrant offshoots; and (3) as an activist, Qutb's defiance of the state and his death provided the younger militants with a model of martyrdom to emulate.

Qutb had been instrumental in leading the Brotherhood's reemergence in the early 1960s. With the support of the militant wing of the Brotherhood inside and outside Egypt, Qutb's primary focus of opposition was the Nasser regime. His conspiratorial activities and advocacy of *jihad* was in sharp contrast to the more passive Islamism of Hasan al-Hudaybi, the Brotherhood's Supreme Guide who had resigned himself to preaching.[18] The government's suppression of the Brotherhood's militants in 1965–66 brought far-reaching changes in fundamentalist ideology and action. In the incubational environment of the prison, Qutb had been the dominant ideological influence, which eventually shaped the Islamist movement of the 1970s. Despite his preeminence, however, Qutb had failed to ameliorate the violent disagreements and fights among the Brotherhood's factions in jail. Yet, Qutb's more abiding influence upon the young militants both inside and outside the prison walls was to be found in his writings. Qutb perceived social reality as a perpetual dialectic between the Islamic path and *jahiliyyah*. His ideological formulations may be summarized as follows:

1. The dominant sociopolitical system of the contemporary Islamic and non-Islamic world is that of *jahiliyyah*—a condition of sinfulness, injustice, suffering, and ignorance of Islam's divine guidance.[19]

2. The duty of the faithful Muslim is to revive Islam to transform the *jahili* society through proselytization *(dawah)* and militant *jihad.*[20]

3. The transformation of *jahili* society into a genuinely Islamic polity is the task of a dedicated "vanguard" *(taliah)* of Muslims.[21]

4. The ultimate aim of committed Muslims should be the establishment of *al-Hakimiyyah*—the reign of Allah's sovereignty on earth to end all sin, suffering, and repression.[22]

As an exponent of fundamentalist thought, Qutb's ideas and style betrayed the unmistakable influence of earlier Islamist theorists. For example, in his opposition to philosophical abstractions and emphasis on the literal interpretation of Islamic precepts, Qutb followed the precedents established by Ibn Hazm and Ibn Taymiyyah and his disciples. Among twentieth-century writers, Hasan al-Banna and Abu al-Ala Mawdudi were particularly influential in shaping Qutb's theories. His concept of *al-Hakimiyyah*—Allah's authority on earth—was criticized because it lacked Quranic foundations.[23] Qutb derived the idea of *al-Hakimiyyah* from the larger notion of *uluhiyyah,* meaning divine power or sovereignty, and from the related terms *rububiyyah* and *rabbaniyyah*, both meaning divinity or Lordship.[24] In these formulations, Qutb was attempting to revive the fundamentalist theology of Ibn Taymiyyah and Ibn al-Qayyim al-Jawziyyah—the crisis theorists of the fourteenth century.[25] Thus, Qutb's ideological task was to create modalities to heighten Islamic consciousness for the purpose of establishing God's authority on earth *(al-Hakimiyyah)*. To attain this objective, it would be necessary to form a "vanguard" of dedicated Muslims prepared to undertake *jihad* against the existing sinful society. Hence the need to differentiate between the Muslims belonging to the "vanguard" and those who remain outside the organization—a problem that Qutb did not fully resolve, thereby opening the way to divergent interpretations of his teachings.

Indeed, the controversy involved nothing less than the unity of the fundamentalist movement in Egypt. The roots of the conflict went back to the Prophet's escape *(hijrah)* to Medina and the attainment of *walayah* by the Muslims who accompanied him as distinct from those who stayed behind in Mecca. Some of Mawdudi's and Qutb's writings appear to favor the legitimacy *(walayah)* of those who joined the *hijrah*.[26] This interpretation could be taken to suggest that Qutb considered the "vanguard" of activists as the possessors of greater legitimacy than the Muslims still living in *jahili* society. Yet, Qutb did not explicitly question the piety of all Muslims in the *jahili* framework who had remained outside the Islamist societies. However, he considered it imperative that the Muslims emulate the Prophet's *hijrah* by separating themselves from *jahili* society to constitute a strong "vanguard" as a prelude to final victory—the establishment of God's authority on earth.

Qutb's formulations generated conflicting interpretations among his disciples which centered on several key issues: the role of the "vanguard," the attributes of its members and leadership, the nature of separation from society, and the relations between the "vanguard" and the Muslim faithful living under the *jahili* system. Disagreement on these questions produced a split among Qutb's followers.[27] A sizeable group of young Brethren led by Shaykh Shukri Ahmad Mustafa believed in a narrow interpretation of Qutb's views and proceeded to separate itself from *jahili* society and its members against whom they leveled the charge of "unbelief" *(takfir)*.[28] This group, which called itself the Society of Muslims, later known as Takfir wal-Hijrah, was joined by some members of Jamaat al-Tabligh, while others formed similar groups based on the concept of separation from society. Among the latter were Jamaat al-Harakiyyah, Jamaat al-Uzlah al-Shuuriyyah, and Jamaat al-Takfir of Alexandria. Others involved in the controversy included members of Al-Jihad and Al-Tahrir al-Islami (ILO). Both groups rejected Mustafa's insistence on establishing a community of believers patterned after the Prophet's *ummah* which would exist in total separation from society.[29] In fact the ILO and Al-Jihad shared Qutb's recognition that the replication of the first Islamic community was impractical because of the needs of modern life.

Thus, during the early 1970s, Egypt's emerging fundamentalist movement was in a state of factionalism. The Brotherhood's old guard had been released from jail to counteract the Nasserists and the leftists. Meanwhile, the younger militants had declared *jihad* against the regime. The battle was joined prematurely with the abortive attack of the Islamic Liberation Organization on the Technical Military Academy in April 1974. This triggered a massive crackdown by the regime, leading to the arrest of several hundred ILO, Takfir, and other militants. Once again, the pattern of inter-group conflict and ideological polemics surfaced in the confines of the infamous Abu Zabal prison.[30] These quarrels crystalized the significant differences and similarities between these groups in terms of ideology, leadership, organization, and tactics.

Al-Tahrir al-Islami (ILO) and Takfir wal-Hijrah

These two militant groups, which emerged from a common sociopolitical and ideological milieu, suffered similar fates in their suppression by the authorities.[31] Because of differences in ideology and leadership, the two societies became rivals. Indeed, despite their common opposition to the state which they regarded as idolatrous and despotic *(taghut),* these groups could not form a united front against the regime. It appears that the exclusivist nature of Takfir's ideology and the uncompromising personality of Shukri Mustafa had been instrumental in aborting effective cooperation between Al-Takfir, ILO, Al-Jihad, and the lesser Islamist groups.

Ideology

As offshoots of the Brotherhood, both the Takfir and ILO shared Banna's and Qutb's fundamentalist ideals in their radical form. They advocated strict adherence to the Five Pillars of Islam as an irreducible minimum. In addition, the "good" Muslim is called upon to join others in creating a righteous community as outlined in the Quran and the *sunnah*. Consequently, the Egyptian ruling order is regarded as being corrupt and humbled by the West, Israel, and the Soviet Union.

While the ILO centered its attack mainly on the government, the Takfir condemned both the regime and the whole of society as being in the stage of *jahiliyyah*.[32] In the economic realm, both communism and capitalism were rejected as ungodly and inhuman. Both groups believed that the government's legitimacy should be based on its ability to provide social justice according to the principle of *al-adl asas al-hukm*—justice is the foundation of rule. Other criteria of rulership included election by the faithful, piety, rationality, and obedience to *shariah* law. Elected assemblies *(shura)* would check the rulers and remove them in case of failure in their duties to Allah and the Islamic community. Both groups opposed the *ulama* as being pro-regime bureaucrats, although the Takfir viewed them with greater hostility and advised its members not to pray behind them in the mosques.[33] While the Takfir advocated the strict recreation of the Prophet's community, the ILO appeared to be adaptationist in terms of borrowing modern practices to achieve its aims. Al-Takfir was far more ideological in its orientation than the ILO. In leveling the charge of *takfir*—unbelief—against everyone in society, Shukri Mustafa claimed that there was no salvation for the Muslims unless they joined his group in a conscious social-spiritual separation from the existing sinful social setting. The author of this separationist doctrine was Ali Abduh Ismail, an obscure shaykh from Al-Azhar University, who sought to pattern the Takfir's beliefs and activities after the Prophet's example during the early Meccan period.[34] Thus, at its inception, when the community was weak and vulnerable, the Prophet had refrained from *jihad* in favor of strengthening and expanding his *ummah* through spiritual and physical separation from the larger pagan setting. Similarly, at the present stage of Islamic weakness *(ahd al-istidaf)*, the Muslims are enjoined by Shaykh Ismail to practice spiritual separation *(mufasilah al-shuuriyyah)* to strengthen their allegiance *(wala)* to Islam through the Takfir organization. Meanwhile, they would desist from waging *jihad* until the group acquired sufficient strength.[35] This would necessitate joining the society with complete loyalty to its ideology and leadership since a truly Islamic life could only be achieved within the group. Indeed, Takfir members believed that all Islamic communities since the Prophet's and that of the first four caliphs consisted of unbelievers.[36]

Leadership and Organization

The ILO was led by Salih Siriyya, a Palestinian with a doctorate in science education, who had been a member of the Islamic Liberation Party, a faction of the Muslim Brotherhood of Jordan. After the 1967 War, Siriyya joined various Palestinian groups, got involved with the Libyan and Iraqi regimes, and spent some time in jail. In 1971, he settled in Egypt to work for the Arab League and began to establish underground cells *(usar)* in Cairo and Alexandria.[37]

The founder of Al-Takfir, Shukri Mustafa, was also a member of the Brotherhood. He was arrested in 1965; while in prison he became disillusioned with his older colleagues and their infighting.[38] After his release in 1971, Mustafa began to expand his movement. Like Siriyya, Mustafa had received a modern education with a baccalaureate in agriculture. Both leaders were said to possess great charisma, religious knowledge, fearlessness, and piety. While Siriyya was loved by his followers, Mustafa elicited fear with his piercing eyes. Clearly, the different leadership styles of the two men were reflected in the nature of their organizations. Siriyya presided over a twelve-member executive council which deliberated fairly democratically through concensus *(ijma)*. It is reported that Siriyya was overruled in his decision not to challenge the Sadat regime during its period of popularity following the October War; hence, the abortive attack on the Military Academy. Siriyya was executed in November 1976. Mustafa, in contrast, was an autocratic *amir al-muminin* (commander of the faithful) who made all the final judgments.[39] He was regarded as the *mahdi* whom the members obeyed through the act of *bayah* (oath of obedience).[40] Thus, in sharp contrast to the ILO, the Takfir possessed the attributes of a messianic movement.

Composition of Membership

Both groups recruited mainly from students and recent college graduates. The Takfir relied on kinship and friendship ties, while the ILO recruited young worshipers especially from the numerous popular mosques *(ahli)*. Most ILO members came from Cairo, Alexandria, and the Delta, while the Takfir recruited predominantly from Upper Egypt. A significant portion of recruits were recent arrivals to the big cities from small towns and rural communities, representing middle- and lower-middle-class backgrounds. On the average they were well educated, particularly in technical and scientific fields, and imbued with deep conviction, sense of mission, and readiness for martyrdom.[41] In several respects, the Takfir was unique. It provided a total environment of activity for its members who were kept occupied in prayer, study, athletics, propaganda, and work in the Takfir's enterprises. Thus, the membership was insulated from society and made dependent on the group for all its needs. Errant members would be excommunicated and suffer physical punishment.[42] If a member left the society he would be considered a *kafir* (infidel) since there could be no salvation outside the group.[43]

Strategies and Tactics

ILO's political strategy differed significantly from those of the Brotherhood and Takfir. The Brotherhood advocated a gradualist strategy to build an Islamic order while ILO's immediate objective was to establish an Islamic state. Thus, ILO engaged in detailed planning for a takeover of power. It infiltrated the police and the army, and, except Siriyya, its membership was psychologically oriented toward an early coup. In sharp contrast, Mustafa pursued a long-range strategy based on building a powerful nucleus of believers, patterned after the Prophet's community. The society would move against the authorities in *jihad* only when the membership of its cells had increased sufficiently to pose a credible challenge. This plan was aborted when the security forces began to arrest members of the Takfir in the aftermath of ILO's suppression. The government accused the Takfir group of kidnapping Shaykh Husayn al-Dhahabi, the former Minister of Religious Affairs, and for killing him after demanding the release of its members from prison. After fighting between the militants and the security forces, over 400 members were arrested and five Takfir leaders were executed in March 1978. Once again the state prevailed, as the media branded the Takfir organization as "the Khawarij of the twentieth century."[44] Despite the repression, both Takfir and ILO are reported to be active in the underground and encouraged by the success of the Iranian Revolution. It seems that these and other Islamist groups now regard the Iranian Revolution as a prototype to be emulated by a change in strategy to promote popular uprisings on campuses and in the streets.

The Jihad Organization

The Jihad Organization was first uncovered in 1978 as a consequence of its involvement in anti-Coptic activities. However, its full potential was not revealed until the assassination of President Sadat. The organizational strength of this group centered in Asyut, Upper Egypt, where its members engaged the security forces in several days of intense fighting soon after Sadat's assassination. During the next months, 3,000 fundamentalists were arrested, mostly belonging to Al-Jihad and Takfir wal-Hijrah groups.

In contrast to Takfir, the Jihad was prone to infiltating the military, the security services, and other governmental institutions rather than separating itself from society. In this respect, the Jihad was far more dangerous than Takfir. Moreover, the Jihad was led by a collective leadership rather than by charismatic personalities like Mustafa and Siriyya. This feature accorded the Jihad a certain flexibility in decision making and implementation. Structurally, the organization *(tanzim)* was headed by a leadership apparatus *(jihaz al-qiyadi)* and a supervisory apparatus *(jihaz al-taqyim)*. The leadership apparatus was charged with overall administration, planning, and policy making. It included a ten-member *majlis al-shura* (consultative assembly) headed by Shaykh Umar Abd al-Rahman, a blind professor at Asyut Theological College, who issued *fatwas* (legal opinions) based on Islamic law and historical precedent to legitimize the Jihad's policies and actions. Thus, the leadership apparatus would decide on specific targets of terroristic action only after seeking "clearance" from the Majlis as legal justification and sanction. The actual operation of the organization was entrusted to the supervisory apparatus which guided the activities of three separate organs. The first conducted propaganda, recruitment, research, and enforcement of religious laws. The second provided operational support in technology, engineering, arms procurement, intelligence, and other specialized tasks—printing of propaganda booklets, falsification of government seals and documents, transportation, and explosives. The third was the combat organ charged with training in martial arts, marksmanship, medical support, and weaponry (see Figure 5). Also, the combat organ sent emissaries to garner support and financial aid from members residing abroad and supervised the Jihad's domestic communication network. The members of the organization operated as parts of an indeterminate number of groups *(majmuah)* and cells *(anqud)* interspersed throughout the larger society. Each revolu-

Figure 5
General Structure of the Jihad Organization

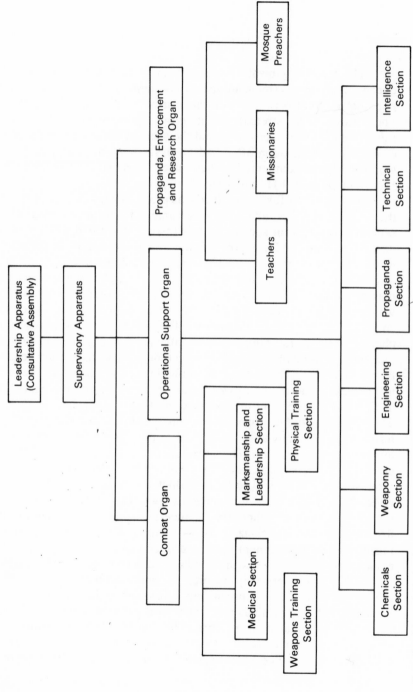

Reproduced from *Al-Jihad* (Tehran), December 31, 1982, p. 150.

tionary cell or *anqud* (literally, a bunch of grapes) was self-contained and semi-autonomous. Thus, if one was plucked from the main bunch, the other *anquds* could not be discovered readily by the security services.[45]

The foregoing *tanzim* or organizational structure of Al-Jihad was replicated in the Governorates of Minya, Asyut, Suhaj and Qina. Uniting all the regional *tanzims* was a supreme Majlis al-Shura which served as an umbrella organization. While in theory the Jihad system reflected the Leninist principle of "democratic centralism,"[46] in practice its operations were decentralized and flexible. The group which assassinated Sadat possessed a chief ideologue—Muhammad Abd al-Salam Faraj and a military chief—Lieutenant Colonel Abbud Abd al-Latif Hasan al-Zumur—who was in operational command. As ideological and military functionaries, Faraj and Zumur were in charge of implementing the decisions of the *shura* to which they belonged. While Shaykh Abd al-Rahman's *fatwa* regarding Sadat's sinfulness *(kufr)* was ambiguously formulated, the collective judgment of the *shura* to kill the President prevailed.[47] In an *anqud* meeting during January or February 1981, Faraj and Zumur initiated the process which culminated in Sadat's assassination by Lieutenant Khalid al-Islambuli and his two associates. Faraj and Zumur had considered several scenarios of assassination, which had been rejected as tactically and logistically unfeasible in view of the high probability that Sadat would escape death. It was not until Lieutenant Islambuli's appointment by his superiors to participate in the October parade that the *anqud* leaders considered it propitious to proceed with the plan. A primary source of inspiration for Lieutenant Islambuli was Juhayman al-Utaybi's book *Saba Rasail*, probably given to him by his brother Muhammad, who had witnessed the Ikhwan takeover of the Grand Mosque in Mecca. Islambuli had also read books by Ibn Taymiyyah and Ibn Kathir.[48]

The specific goals and ideological motivations of the Jihad were revealed during the trial. Lieutenant Islambuli gave three reasons for the decision to kill the President: (1) Egypt's existing laws were inconsistent with Islamic Law—a fact that brought suffering upon the Muslims; (2) Sadat's peace with Israel; (3) the arrest, persecution, and humiliation of Muslim fundamentalists in September 1981. Clearly, the assassins were reacting to the prevailing socioeconomic conditions, the Camp David accords, and state oppression.[49] These motivations were embedded in an ideological framework provided by Faraj as outlined in *Al-Jihad: The Forgotten Pillar.* It can be summarized in eleven propositions:

1. The duty of every Muslim is to strive for the Islamic *ummah*. This is a duty ordained by Allah and his *shariah*. Since the laws of the Muslim countries are the laws of unbelievers *(kuffar)*, the true Muslims must declare war *(jihad)* against their leaders who are trained in the West by Christians, Communists, and Zionists.

2. Muslim leaders or groups who reject the laws of Islam must be considered apostates *(murtadd)* despite their claims that they are Muslims. In other words, "Muslimness" has to be constantly validated since a sinful individual shall lose his status as a Muslim if he persists in his sinfulness. Apostasy is the highest level of sinfulness.

3. Cooperation with an infidel ruler who claims to be a Muslim is sin. The punishment for such a leader is death even if he is unable to defend himself. True Muslims should refrain from government work and military service.

4. Perpetual *jihad* against an infidel state is the *highest* obligation (pillar) and *only* solution for all true Muslims who desire to destroy *jahili* society and revive Islam.

5. Armed struggle is the *only* acceptable form of *jihad*.

6. *Jihad* pursued by peaceful means through rhetoric, Islamic parties, or emigration *(hijrah)* is considered cowardice and stupidity. Islam can succeed only through the force of arms as it did in the past, when a small group of earnest believers *(saff jadd)* were able to spread the message through conquest. Thus, true Muslims should engage in *jihad,* even if they are few in number.

7. First fight the internal infidel (the Egyptian state), then the external infidel (the non-Islamic world).

8. *Jihad* can be studied by every Muslim without great effort or education. Thus, the lack of knowledge is no excuse to abstain from *jihad.*

9. Leadership in Islam must be granted to the strongest among the believers, who also has more fear *(taqwa)* of Allah. He must be chosen collectively, and once chosen must be obeyed. An arrogant and haughty scholar should not be a leader.

10. Abstaining from *jihad* is the main reason for the sorry situation of the Muslims today—humiliated, degraded, disdained, and divided.

11. Allah has designated five periods in Islamic history:
a. the *ummah* under the Prophet,
b. the *ummah* under the Caliphs,
c. the *ummah* under the Kingdoms,
d. the *ummah* under dictatorships,
e. the Islam of our time when dictatorship and tyranny will be overthrown, and the *ummah* shall become controlled by a

system similar to the Prophet's community; and peace will reign.[50]

Faraj's book is clearly written and well reasoned. It is an un-abashedly militant work, which makes the resort to violence the "sixth obligation" of Islam on the basis of Quranic interpretation, historical precedent, and the writings of Ibn Hazm, Ibn Taymiyyah, Qadi Iyadh, Ibn al-Qayyim, Ibn Kathir, Nawawi, Qutb and others. In sharp contrast to Takfir, the Jihad group did not possess a single leader like Shukri Mustafa who commanded the total allegiance of his followers. Thus, Jihad's ideology was not as messianic as that of Takfir. The Jihad was not led by a *mahdi,* although it did not deny the eventual advent of a *mahdi.* Nor did the Jihad share Takfir's concept of withdrawal from society and the postponement of *jihad* until a more propitious time. Instead, it posited a new doctrine of "Muslimness," which, in its ultimate logic, could be achieved only through permanent *jihad.* The failure of the Muslims and their leaders to meet these obligations of Islam will make them infidels, undermine their legitimacy, and condemn them to destruction. As a case in point, Faraj mentions only one leader by name—Anwar al-Sadat.[51]

Egyptian Fundamentalism and State Response

An overall appraisal of Islamic fundamentalism in contemporary Egypt indicates an inexorable return to Islamic roots among a significant segment of the population. Islamist manifestations are discernible throughout Egyptian society, although militancy draws most of its support from the middle- and lower-middle classes, which are particularly vulnerable to the "call" in view of their level of education, social consciousness, and economic frustrations.

The Smaller Societies

In its organized expression, contemporary fundamentalism continues to feed on the ideological, spiritual, and organizational legacy of

Banna's Muslim Brotherhood. However, the Brotherhood's organizational influence has receded with the proliferation of Islamist groups. While groups like Takfir, Jihad, and ILO, which sprang up in the early 1970s, were the direct descendants of the Brethren, the connection between the newer Islamist groups and the Brotherhood appears tenuous. A total of twenty-nine Egyptian Islamist societies are identified in Appendix I. These range from the massive Muslim Brotherhood, which is semi-public, to medium-size groups like the Takfir, ILO, and Jihad, and a plethora of smaller societies such as Al-Faramawiyyah, Jamaat al-Ahram, Junud Allah, Jamaat al-Munazilah Shuuriyyah, Junud al-Rahman, Jamaat al-Muslimin lil-Takfir, Mukaffaratiyyah, Qif wa-Tabayyin, Jamaat al-Harakiyyah, and the Qutbiyyin. Most of the latter can be considered militant groups which operate clandestinely. However, none are thought to possess the size or the violence potential of Al-Takfir or Al-Jihad. This is not to suggest that the smaller groups are incapable of mounting limited insurrections or assassination attempts against government leaders. Many more militant and non-militant Islamist groups exist in Egypt than the twenty-nine presented here. It appears that new groups are being formed continually, as frustrations intensify especially among the youth and the unemployed. A pattern of appearance and disappearance characterizes these societies as they are unearthed by the government, then suppressed or contained, only to return to Egypt's omnipresent underground. Reportedly, the Egyptian authorities place the total number of Islamist groups at ninety-nine, while a Kuwait-based fundamentalist periodical puts their number at sixty.[52]

Two types of Islamist groups can be identified on the basis of geography. The first are those located in the small towns of Upper Egypt and the Delta, which recruit from the educated and semi-educated elements of society, including the sons of provincial bureaucrats, college students, blue collar workers, and lower-middle-class peasants. Such groups exhibit a certain primitivism in view of their remoteness from urban centers and foreign influences. Thus, they become politically dangerous only when their leadership decides to relocate in the capital city, as was the case with Shukri Mustafa. The second type of militant group is found in the large cities, particularly in the massive ghettoes of Cairo. These urban groups consist of students, unemployed graduates, blue collar workers, soldiers, and low-ranking officers. Many of these social elements lack family roots in the cities and have few prospects of finding a useful niche in society that is commensurate with their training and aspirations. Some have tried to "make it" in Egypt's freewheeling private sector without success, at a time when their friends and relatives have enriched themselves by corrupt means. Moreover, many of the provincial recruits are from underdeveloped areas like Upper Egypt, where they face competition from the large Coptic minority.

Another type of Islamist group consists of friends and acquaintances from the same neighborhood brought together in the local mosque. Such groups may begin as loose benevolent associations, or Quranic study societies which periodically meet to discuss the Holy Book as well as local and national issues. In time, these groups develop militancy in response to some *fitnah*—a crisis brought about by government provocation, injustice, oppression, or foreign policy initiative. Since the law prohibits public meetings, these groups take refuge in mosques, especially during the first *(fajr)* and the last *(asha)* prayers. After the *khutbah* (sermon) is delivered, the faithful sit in clusters on the mosque floor and begin conversing. These group discussions, often conducted in hushed tones, can involve the apportioning of functions to be performed by each person within the self-help societies active in the neighborhood—sending food to needy families, a doctor to visit the sick, or a lawyer to represent a client in court. Alternatively, the groups may discuss political matters, planning public demonstrations, and even violence, as *anquds* (cells) of a larger organization. In order to coordinate with other mosque networks, representatives from the cells would circulate throughout the day by attending successive prayer services in different mosques of the neighborhood and beyond. This modality of inter-cell communication creates vast neighborhood networks which may be mobilized effectively in relatively short periods of time. The mosque groups have already demonstrated their effectiveness as self-help societies which the government regards with caution in view of their potential organizational-ideological utility for insurrectionary activity. Yet the same government appears to lack the means or the will to perform these social services which are desperately needed by the people.[53]

Fundamentalism in the Military

Unmistakeable manifestations of religious resurgence have been evident in the Egyptian military, particularly among the higher NCOs and the lower and middle ranks of the officer corps. Religious fervor has also been evident among cadets in military academies. A case in point is the Air Force Academy where, instead of attending movies and games during recreation periods, large groups of cadets gather to pray and discuss religious literature. Commanding officers at the higher echelons are known to "bend backwards" to accommodate these manifestations of fundamentalism, despite certain breaches of military discipline. Such accommodation is prompted by the fear that any disciplinary response toward Islamist practices might trigger defiance of military discipline and even insurrection. In this connection, it is necessary to emphasize the negative feelings among both fundamentalist and Nasserist officers toward the Egyptian High Command, in particular, General Abd al-Halim Abu Ghazalah. His tenure as military attaché in Washington and assumption of the Defense Ministry in the wake of General Badawi's unexpected death have rendered Abu Ghazalah suspect to both Nasserists and Islamists.

There can be no doubt that the Islamist groups have members and sympathizers in the military and even in the state security services.[54] Purges of the military were instituted after Sadat's assassination because two of the main accomplices—Islambuli and Zumur—were army officers. It is virtually impossible to block Islamist influences from the military since it is a part of society. The Islamist groups often proselytize and recruit among relatives in the large extended families which invariably include members serving in the armed forces.

Al-Infitah: A Critical Catalyst

The increasing maldistribution of income as a consequence of President Sadat's policies of economic liberalization (al-Infitah), has been frequently cited as a primary catalyst of Islamist militancy. Indeed, the available evidence points to a growing income gap between rich and poor. This is manifest in Table 5 which represents an aggregation of comparable data from seven different sources. In 1964–65, the top 5 percent of Egyptian households received 19.2 percent of the income, while by 1979 their share had increased to 22 percent. During the same period, the income of the poorest 20 percent had increased slightly by .5 percent. The income distribution gap becomes more pronounced when the figures for 1964–65 under Nasser's socialism are compared with those of 1976 when liberalization was in full swing.

During these eleven years, the income of the lowest 60 percent of the population declined precipitously from 28.7 percent to 19.93 percent. Meanwhile, the middle 30 percent experienced an almost 50 percent income loss from 40.2 percent to 21.52 percent. An equally significant finding evidenced by the figures in Table 5 was the growing affluence of the upper classes under al-Infitah: the income of the richest 10 percent increased dramatically from 31.1 percent in 1964–65 to 58.55 percent in 1976—almost a doubling of the wealth of Egypt's economic elite.

Despite the limitations of income distribution data, it is evident that the trend is toward greater income disparity and potential class conflict. In terms of political stability, the most disconcerting development is the substantial reduction of middle class incomes as well as those of the lowest 60 percent of the population. It is no accident that these classes constitute a primary recruitment source of Islamist activists. Intense feelings of relative deprivation generate animosity toward the regime and its West-oriented allies in the private sector who profited under Sadat's policies. While lower-middle-class elements find it difficult to gain entrance into the middle-class, many members of this class have progressively lost their economic status and regressed into the lower middle class. There is no evidence that these patterns have been reversed in recent years.

Table 5
Percent Shares of Income

Households	1960	1964/65	1970	1975	1976	1979
Top 5%	17.5* (rural)	19.2[†]	—	21.0[‡]	—	22.0*
Top 10%	—	31.9[†]	—	—	58.55[§]	—
Middle 30%	—	40.2[†]	—	—	21.52[§]	—
Lowest 60%	—	28.7[†]	—	—	19.93[§]	—
Lowest 40%	—	14.1[†]	—	13.9[‡]	—	—
Lowest 20%	6.6* (rural)	4.6[†]	—	5.2[‡]	—	5.1*

* *World Tables,* Washington, D.C., The World Bank, 1980, p. 463.

[†] Shail Jain, *Size Distribution of Income* (Washington, D.C.: IBRD, 1975), Table 21.

[‡] World Bank, *World Economic and Social Indicators,* July 1978; M. S. Ahluwalia, N. G. Carter, and H. B. Chenery, *Growth and Poverty in Developing Countries,* World Bank, 1978; G. Sheehan and M. Hopkins, *Basic Needs Performance,* ILO, 1978.

[§] See R. Eckaus and A. Mohie-Eldin, *Consequences of Changes in Subsidy Policy* (Cairo: DRTPC, Cairo University, 1980). See also R. Eckaus, D. MacCarthy and A. Mohie-Eldin, *General Equilibrium Policy Models for Egypt* (Cairo: Cairo University/MIT Technology Adaptation Program, 1978).

State Responses

The Egyptian authorities and the media commonly refer to the youthful Islamic radicals as the "lost generation"—*al-jil al-dai*. Basically this is a correct description of reality since the Egyptian polity has failed to properly socialize large numbers of idealistic youth in the post-Nasser era. However, it appears that the "lost generation" included not only the youth but also the older and more settled occupational categories like workers, shopkeepers, military and police officers, engineers, professors, doctors and even landowners. This is partly revealed in the published reports on the occupational background of 303 Al-Jihad members arrested prior to Sadat's assassination. The detainees represented a cross-section of Egyptian society:[55]

College and University Students	112
Workers	41
College and University Graduates	31
Employees and Bureaucrats	26
Fugitives	21
Secondary School Students	17
Military, Police, and Intelligence Officers	11
Businessmen and Shopkeepers	10
Engineers	7
Unemployed	7
Landowners	6
Physicians	6
Professors	4
Teachers	3
Journalists	1
	303

Since the early Nasser era, Egyptian policy toward Islamic fundamentalism has combined coercive and cooptative measures to deal with this persistent challenge to state authority. Nasser's success in dealing with the Brotherhood was the consequence of his extraordinary charismatic appeal, combined with an unusually effective intelligence service. The charismatic appeal had substantially undermined the Brotherhood's ideological potency. Sadat could find no substitute for charisma; nor was he capable of developing his own ideological formulas to educate and socialize millions of Egyptian youth. Consequently, the ideological vacuum which Sadat himself created by de-

Nasserization, was partially filled by the fundamentalist *dawah* of the Brotherhood and its offshoots, to the detriment of the Egyptian state. The tragedy of Egypt was that neither Sadat nor his associates were principally concerned with the indoctrination-socialization process to educate the youth in becoming loyal citizens. Thus, Sadat's tactical move to let loose the Brotherhood against the Nasserists proved dysfunctional. All Sadat could offer the average Egyptian was the tenuous promise of joining the new private sector, with the hope of acquiring instant affluence. While some succeeded admirably, for millions of ambitious aspirants Sadat's utopian promises proved deeply disappointing. His call to Egyptian patriotism, after the moderate success of October 1973, sounded hollow in the absence of an "honorable" Arab-Israeli peace and the ever-growing gap between the conspicuous millionaires and the middle and lower classes. The periodic arrests and executions of militant leaders were not useful in promoting long-range stability, in view of the regime's lack of ideological-spiritual and material incentives to capture the loyalties of the people. Moreover, Sadat was reluctant to institute major reforms to contain the illegal practices of some relatives and associates. His purge of the Lawyer's Syndicate and promulgation of the "Law of Shame" were designed to stifle the opposition through legal means. Also, the regime mobilized the religious bureaucracy of Azharite *ulama* who unleashed propaganda campaigns through the media and the mosques against the Islamist groups. This elaborate counter-propaganda of the religious establishment was intensified in the wake of Sadat's assassination. In order to discredit the Jihad group, the Grand Mufti of Egypt, Shaykh Gad al-Haq unearthed an obscure *hadith* where the Prophet is reported to have advised the faithful to obey a Muslim government even though its members might engage in theft and adultery.[56] The Shaykh called upon the people to obey the authorities since the Mubarak government had promised to initiate reforms to correct the injustices of the past.

Indeed, Sadat's death constituted a temporary catharsis to defuse the crisis situation in Egypt, as Mubarak attempted to change the face of the regime by selective reforms. Despite his best intentions however, the new President possesses neither the ideological tools nor the dedicated cadres to address comprehensively the ills of Egyptian society. The deterioration of the economy, combined with Mubarak's determination to uphold Sadat's commitment to Israel and the U. S., have prevented the accumulation of Islamic legitimacy which he may need to govern Egypt. While the President has attempted to commence a dialogue with Egypt's youth, he has been constrained to take repressive measures against Islamist groups under the emergency laws on an intermittent basis.[57] Under Mubarak, "religious experts" are sent into the jails to convince the young militants that their interpretations of Islam are faulty. According to a report, the Azharite *ulama* have cooperated in this effort of reconversion, while the Ministry of Awqaf (religious endowments) has been reluctant to participate. During these prison discussions, some militants have feigned acceptance *(taqiyyah)* of the government's position only to resume their Islamic militancy after release.[58] Frequent resort to coercive means is alien to the nature of the President; yet his helplessness in the face of mounting socioeconomic problems, Israel's invasion of Lebanon, and absorption of the West Bank could only weaken the foundations of his government. Under these circumstances, it is difficult not to conclude that Islamic fundamentalism is likely to become a growing threat to the stabililty of the Egyptian regime.

7 Syria

Sunni Fundamentalism Against Baathi Rule

T HE SYRIAN POLITICAL SYSTEM stands in sharp contrast to the Egyptian in terms of its demographic, cultural, and economic underpinnings. Syria lacks the homogeneity and cohesion of Egyptian society and its tradition of centralized authority. Moreover, as a directly administered Ottoman province, Syria did not experience the degree of modernization achieved in Egypt's autonomous setting.

In the last days of Ottoman rule, Greater Syria had become the epicenter of Arab nationalism. The split of the Arab East into French and British spheres of influence after World War I left Syria in a state of geopolitical and ideological discontinuity. Under the mandate system, Syria's Sunni majority was cut off from its demographic extensions in Palestine, Jordan, Lebanon, Iraq, and the Hijaz. Thus, the nationalist aspirations of the Sunni Arabs went unfulfilled under Anglo-French mandatory rule. The trend toward fragmentation found encouragement from the French authorities, who divided Syria into sectarian provinces and effected its partial dismemberment—Lebanon was granted independence and the Sanjak of Alexandretta given to Turkey. Meanwhile, the French suppressed urban nationalist uprisings and the Druze Revolt (1923–24). These policies generated pro-German sympathies among the Syrians during World War II. After the defeat of the Vichy French mandatory regime by British and Gaullist French forces, Syria was promised independence, which was reluctantly granted in 1945.

The Syrian Political Process (1945–70)

The history of independent Syria has been marked by a complex interaction of ideology, geopolitics, sectarianism, one-party control, class conflict, and praetorian rule. This cauldron of counteracting forces set a pattern of coup d'état politics that sparked a rapid circulation of elites operating in an environment of persistent insecurity. The natural consequence was a legitimacy crisis surrounding Syrian elites and institutions which has persisted to this day.

The political elite which achieved independence consisted of the traditional nationalists led by President Shukri al-Quwwatli. This bourgeois democratic regime was dominated mostly by Sunni and some Christian upper- and upper-middle-class elements. Two years after independence, the new government committed the ill-trained Syrian Army to fight in Palestine with calamitous results. The Army returned from the front to blame the government for its defeat, thereby initiating a series of coups d'état beginning in March 1949 and ending in February 1954. The three colonels who succeeded each other—Zaim, Hinnawi, and Shishakli—were of Kurdish origin, reflecting the French practice of recruiting from the poorer minority groups eager to gain upward mobility. This was in contrast to the reluctance of upper-class elements and nationalist Sunnis to enter the French-led military service.[1] A partial return to civilian rule was effected in the mid-1950s, at the confluence of several powerful social and political currents. These included the rise of the Baath Party, the advent of Nasserism, and heightened communist activism. Since its founding by Michel Aflaq and Salah Bitar, the Baath had been unable to secure an electoral majority at the polls, despite its claim to represent Arab unity nationalism; hence its eagerness to recruit from the minorities—Christians, Alawites, Druze, Ismailis and the poorer Sunnis. These clusters of recruitables were social and economic marginals, many of whom populated the small towns and rural areas. Indeed, both the Baath and the military recruited from the same ethno-economic pool of marginals—a phenomenon which would determine the future course of Syrian politics.

The two major sources of challenge to the Baath during the mid-1950s were Khalid Bakdash's Syrian Communist Party and the growing movement of Nasserism. In order to reinforce its position and counter communist influence in the military, the Baath followed two strategies: (1) The aggressive recruitment of military officers, and (2) the conclusion of a Syrian-Egyptian union. Despite Nasser's initial reluctance, the Baath leaders succeeded in convincing him to establish the United Arab Republic (February 1958) which would enable them to utilize Nasserist power and charisma to rule Syria. This effort proved abortive as Baathi-Egyptian differences destroyed the union in the autumn 1961. Nasser's imposition of socialist measures upon Syria's entrepreneurial culture and heavy-handed Egyptian rule combined to overwhelm unionist sentiments.[2] In sectarian terms, however, Egyptian rule tended to moderate ideological and communal divisions in the name of Pan-Arab nationalism. Thus, the Egyptian departure rekindled sectarian conflict, as Sunni anti-Nasser officers from Damascus under Lieutenant Colonel Abd al-Karim al-Nahlawi assumed top positions.[3]

The Baath returned to power by coup d'état on March 8, 1963 in coalition with independent unionist and Nasserist officers; but the party's overtures for a new union were rejected by Nasser. The subsequent infighting between Baathi and Nasserist officers culminated in July 1963 with the victory of the Baath Military Committee over Colonel Jasim Alwan's pro-Nasser faction. While sectarianism did not play an explicit role in this conflict, the Nasserist faction was mainly Sunni, and the Baath Military Committee consisted mostly of Alawi, Druze, and Ismaili officers. The consequent purge of the Nasserist bloc by the Military Committee was accompanied by an ambitious policy of recruiting minority officers.[4] What had begun as a struggle between ideologies and personalities soon assumed a sectarian coloration partly due to the involvement of the Muslim Brotherhood. An anti-Baath revolt in the predominantly Sunni city of Hama was crushed in April 1964, as the struggle for power intensified within the Military Committee itself. In December 1964, the Alawi Major General Muhammad Umran was expelled from Syria allegedly for attempting to form a "Fatimiyyah Bloc" of heterodox Muslim officers.[5] Umran's expulsion pitted the Sunni President Amin al-Hafiz against the Alawi Chief of Staff, General Salah Jadid. Despite the belated attempts of General Hafiz to build a cohesive Sunni officers' bloc, he was overthrown in February 1966 along with party leaders Michel Aflaq and Salah Bitar. This takeover brought into power the Baath's militant left wing, which represented a symbiosis between the party and the army. Despite their growing predominance, the Alawite officers' group could not escape factionalism. After the 1967 War, the Baath politico-military apparatus was split between factions headed by Generals Salah Jadid and Hafiz al-Asad respectively. As defense minister, Asad controlled the military, while Jadid consolidated his grip on the party apparatus. In November 1970, the military moved to crush the Jadid faction, as General Asad became Syria's first non-Sunni president (February 1971). Thus, the Syrian military and the Baath party had provided the means for Syria's disadvantaged minorities, especially the Alawites, to gain upward mobility and power.

Islamic Fundamentalism as a Sectarian Movement

The peculiar character of Islamic fundamentalism in Syria is determined by the realities of power, wealth, and demography—conditions that are considerably different from those existing in Egypt. While the focus of Egyptian Islamist protest is a regime dominated by Sunnis, Syrian Islamic fundamentalism has fashioned itself into a Sunni protest movement against the Alawi-led government. In this respect, Syrian Sunni activism is similar to that of Iraq's Shiite majority, which opposes the Sunni-led Baath regime of Saddam Husayn. Both Islamist movements claim to represent two sectarian majorities which are ruled by minority regimes in the name of Baathi secularism.

The Syrian Muslim Brotherhood: Origins and Development

The origins of the Syrian Muslim Brotherhood can be traced to various Islamic *jamiyat* or social welfare societies established during the late nineteenth century. The Brotherhood was formed in 1935 in Aleppo; in 1944 it moved to Damascus, where Dr. Mustafa al-Sibai forged a merger of Syria's Islamic societies. As *Muraqib al-Am*—General Supervisor—he led the Brotherhood from 1945 to 1961 in collaboration with the Egyptian Muslim Brotherhood.[6] In structure, the Syrian Brotherhood was similar to that of Egypt. While the two societies regarded themselves as a single movement, each operated autonomously. The Syrian Brotherhood, like Egypt's, drew its support mainly from middle- and lower-middle-class elements—bazaar merchants, clerics, teachers, professionals, and bureaucrats. However, unlike Egypt, the rural lower-middle-class and its urbanized off-shoots were not an important element in Syria's urban based Brotherhood.

Sibai's ideological orientation closely followed that of Banna, although during the 1950s Sibai theorized about Islamic socialism at considerable length. Sibai's Egyptian intellectual origins went back to Al-Azhar and his friendship with Banna. Indeed, Egypt provided the crucible where Sibai began his revolutionary activities which sent him to prison in Egypt and later in French-ruled Syria. Thus, the motivational base of the Brotherhood's adherents included the French occupation and the political-economic consequences of splitting the Arab homeland into separate national units. Sibai perceived his movement as a *ruh* (spirit) and a new revolution dedicated to the establishment of a comprehensive Islamic order *(al-nizam al-Islami)*.[7] The Arab defeat of 1948 contributed to the society's expansion, which was suppressed by Colonel Adib al-Shishakli in 1952. After the latter's overthrow in 1954, the society faced serious challenges from the Baath, the Nasserists, and the Communists. Nor was the society active during the Syrian-Egyptian union, since much of its urban, middle-class Sunni support was preempted by Nasser. In fact, Sibai dissolved his group in 1958 to comply with Nasser's wishes.

The Brotherhood supported the breakup of the United Arab Republic because of its ideological opposition to Nasser. Some of its members joined the secessionist Sunni officers led by Abd al-Karim al-Nahlawi and won ten seats in Parliament. This success was short-lived as the Baath Party returned to power in March 1963 and proceeded to suppress the Brotherhood with increasing vehemence. Its new leader, Isam al-Attar, was exiled and forced to lead the society from abroad with mixed success. By the mid-sixties, the Brotherhood had emerged as an implacable opponent of the Baath, although Attar broke with other leaders by opposing armed *jihad* against the regime.[8] As one deeply committed to reformism, Attar could not condone revolutionary violence. Nevertheless, the confrontation intensified in 1964–65 due to the Hama revolt and the Brotherhood's campaign of civil disobedience led by Shaykh Habannakah. In the subsequent polarization within the Baath political-military apparatus, the Brotherhood could not play a decisive role in the context of the Asad-Jadid power struggle. From exile in West Germany, Attar supported Asad because of his ideological moderation. During the frustrating days of Arab defeat in 1967, a split developed in the Brotherhood between the moderate Damascus group supporting Attar and those of the northern cities who favored *jihad*. Among the militants was Marwan Hadid of Hama, who had been imprisoned by Nasser in 1965 with Sayyid Qutb. Hadid had begun to train with the Palestinian Al-Fatah in 1968, in preparation for the protracted challenge that the Brethren would mount against the Baath regime during the 1970s. After returning to Damascus, Hadid began a campaign to assassinate government figures. He was caught in 1976 and died in jail.

The Resort to Jihad (1976–83)

The Syrian Islamist movement passed through several stages *(marahil)* after the late sixties which were marked by increasing levels of militancy culminating in violent *jihad* in 1976. The Brotherhood's metamorphosis from a religio-political group into a fighting organiza- tion had split the movement. The division between the militant norther- ners and Attar's Damascus group was not resolved until 1980 with the formation of the Syrian Islamic Front.[9] The northern Brethren were led by Amin Yagan, Adnan Said, Shaykh Abd al-Fattah Abu Ghuddah, Said Hawwa, and Adnan Saad al-Din, who were convinced that only a well-organized armed struggle could topple the Asad regime. However, their early efforts failed to attract mass support, in view of Asad's rapprochement with Egypt, Jordan, and Saudi Arabia and his policies of reform and economic liberalization. These policies, reinforced by Arab oil wealth from the Gulf, directly contributed to the well-being of the social elements which had tended to support the Brotherhood. The situation changed in 1973 when Asad promulgated a secular constitu- tion, provoking large-scale rioting and demonstrations led by the Brethren. Sporadic strikes continued through April 1973, reflecting the increasing cooperation between the *ulama* and the Brotherhood against the government. Asad was prompted to amend the constitution to stipulate that the president would have to be a Muslim. To neutralize the criticism of his fundamentalist detractors, President Asad per- formed the small *hajj* in 1974 and has routinely attended Friday prayers in a Damascus mosque.[10]

The October 1973 War heightened Arab nationalist feelings; the regime stole the Brotherhood's thunder as most Syrians united behind their president. Yet Asad and the Syrian High Command were criticized by the Brethren for losing the Golan, joining Kissinger's "peace process," and establishing close relations with the Shah of Iran.[11] It was not until 1975–76 that a new milieu emerged to provoke a higher level of armed *jihad*. The main provocation was the Syrian role in the Lebanese Civil War; other sources of dissatisfaction were governmental corruption, the rise of parasitic entrepreneurship, and runaway inflation.[12] Asad's intervention on the Maronite side against the Palestinian-Leftist-Muslim alliance constituted a turning point. While the initial success of Syrian arms brought Asad considerable prestige, the President's inability to impose his will on the Maronites became a source of widespread criticism. Particularly offensive was the Syrian refusal to allow the Palestinian forces to relieve the Maronite siege of Tal al-Zatar, which resulted in the massacre of many Palestinians. The Brotherhood accused Asad of acting as a surrogate in Lebanon, serving Israeli, Maronite, American, and Saudi interests.[13] However, the overriding grievance of the Islamist opposition was the progressive increase of the Alawi role in the regime and the concomitant erosion of Sunni power and status. While Sunnis occupied conspicuous positions in the political apparatus (cabinet, legislature, and party), effective military power was mostly centered in the hands of President Asad and his Alawite kinsmen. The Brotherhood charged the regime as being "sectarian" and consisting of "false Muslims"—a reference to the Baath's secularism and the "questionable status" of the Alawite (Nusayri) sect in Islam. The Brethren were particularly hostile toward the President's brother, Rifat al-Asad, whose oppressive methods and unethical practices had become a source of deep resentment throughout Syria. Rifat al-Asad commanded the *Sarayah al-Difa* (Defense Squadrons) charged with defending the president and the regime.[14] This elite formation, along with Ali Haydar's *Wahadat al-Khassah* (Special Units), consisted mostly of Alawites known for their loyalty to the ruling elite.

During the mid-1970s, Adnan Saad al-Din assumed the Brotherhood's leadership as General Supervisor to prepare a new phase of struggle against the Baath. The first stage of *jihad* began in 1976 as the Brotherhood's Combat Vanguard *(al-Taliah al-Muqatilah)* employed hit and run tactics to provoke the regime into escalating its repression. The guerrillas targeted Alawi leaders, security agents, and party professionals to highlight the minority aspect of Asad's regime. Another phase of intensified *jihad* was initiatied in June 1979 with the killing of eighty-three Alawi artillery cadets in Aleppo and other spectacular forays on government buildings, police stations, and Baath Party centers.[15] In March 1980, large-scale demonstrations and boycotts took place in Hama, Homs, and Aleppo in the midst of attacks on Syrian communists and Soviet military advisors. In response, the government resorted to large-scale repression, particularly in Aleppo. An attempt to assassinate Asad prompted the regime to intensify its counter-terror, which included killings at Tadmur prison.[16] The government decreed Law 49 of July 8, 1980 making membership or association with the Brethren punishable by death.

There were indications during 1980 that the Asad regime and the Islamists were engaged in a desperate stuggle. The Brotherhood's goal of alienating the Sunnis from the regime had succeeded to a degree, although the Alawite community had rallied behind President Asad, fearing for its safety. Yet it was clear that the regime had checked the insurrection and dealt the Brethren and its allies a heavy blow.

One consequence of the Brotherhood's defeat was the establishment in October 1980, of the Syrian Islamic Front (al-Jabhah al-Islamiyyah fi Suriyya) with Shaykh Muhammad Abu al-Nasr al-Bayanuni of Aleppo as its secretary general. The Front included the Brethren, Attar's dissident faction, some ulama and smaller Islamist groups (see Table 6 and Appendix I). Its moving force was the Brotherhood's Adnan Saad as-Din of Hama, a former member of the Egyptian Brethren. He was seconded by Said Hawwa, the chief ideologue of the Syrian Islamist movement. On November 9, 1980, the Islamic Front issued a proclamation containing its program which was outlined in the charter of the movement published in January 1981. In its proclamation the Islamic Front strove in vain to split the Alawites and to rally all opposition elements behind its program, that flexibly combined Islamic concepts with liberalism and democracy. The main points of this proclamation are instructive in conceptualizing the unique features of the Syrian Islamist movement and its similarities to and differences from its Egyptian, Iraqi, Saudi, and other counterparts:

1. An appeal to the "wise men" of the Alawi community to overthrow "the regime of the Asad brothers" for the sake of preventing the tragedy of civil war.

2. An appeal for the emancipation of all citizens from "tyranny," the abolition of political prisons, freedom of thought and expression, preservation of the rights of minorities.

3. Demand for a government of separation of powers and the rule of law resting on shura (consultation), guaranteeing individual dignity, freedom, and liberty.

4. Support for the full ownership of land by farmers and the elimination of middlemen and the state from the agricultural sector.

5. Transfer of ownership of public industries from the state to the workers, who would be rewarded adequately but not excessively.

6. Opposition to the state's role as merchant, support for a free

private sector in trade and manufacturing, and encouragement of artisans.

7. Commitment to "Islamic socialism" to promote social justice under Islamic law.

8. Commitment to *jihad*—fighting in the cause of Allah—as a fixed obligation in Islam to transform the present "sectarian" regime *(taifiyyah)* into an Islamic state.

9. Strengthening of Arab nationalism and unity in the larger context of Islamic solidarity.

10. Neutrality in foreign affairs.

11. Uncompromising opposition to Israel and Zionism.[17]

The proclamation of the Islamic Front, like its charter, manifests the unmistakable ideological influence of Banna, along with Rida, Sibai, Qutb, and Hawwa. Yet, the important commonalities between the ideologies of the Egyptian and Syrian Islamists should not conceal salient differences:

1. In recognition of Syria's heterogeneity, the Front's program lacks the ideological rigidity which has characterized the ideologies of Egypt's fundamentalist societies.

2. The ideology and program of the Front reflect a greater sense of pragmatism and lack the complex doctrinal subtleties and controversies that have been a feature of the Egyptian Islamist societies.

3. The constituent groups of the Syrian Islamic Front appear to subscribe to a single ideology which represents the mainstream of Sunni fundamentalism. Messianic and cultic tendencies, as in the case of the Egyptian Takfir group, have not played a role in Syrian fundamentalism.

4. The Brotherhood and its junior partners in the Islamic Front have shown greater readiness to engage the Syrian government in comprehensive *jihad* than the Egyptian Brotherhood and its offshoots. This phenomenon may stem from the greater incentive of the Syrian Islamists to fight what they consider an illegitimate "sectarian regime" than is the case with the Egyptian fundamentalists who are ruled by a Sunni government.

The proclamation also reflects the meticulous efforts of the Islamic Front in devising its program to maximize support among the Syrian public. The document contains a most liberal interpretation of Islamic theory and political action and, as such, exhibits an accommodative attitude toward various shades of Islamic opinion, different classes and occupational groups, and even the minorities. This uncommon flexibility was prompted by the Front's enormous task—the overthrow of the Baath regime. What the Front perceived as the present "peril"—al-khatar—had brought upon the Islamic movement heavy losses.

However, the imperatives of *jihad* prompted a third phase of armed struggle which began in August 1981 and culminated in the Hama revolt of February 1982. After three weeks of fighting the insurrection was crushed and sections of Hama were destroyed.[18] Despite the intensity of the struggle and appeals from Islamic Front leaders, the Hama revolt did not precipitate a general uprising throughout Syria. The Sunni majority remained quiescent and the Army, already proccupied in Lebanon, stood by the regime.

The Islamist Movement in Syria: Social Bases and Prospects

During the 1970s, the Brotherhood and its smaller cohorts underwent a transformation from relatively small and docile associations into a large and militant revolutionary movement. Reportedly, between 1975 and 1978 the number of Islamist activists in Aleppo had grown ten-fold to an estimated 5,000 to 7,000 members.[19] A plausible estimate of the activist membership in all Syrian Islamist groups in the late 1970s would be 30,000, in addition to many sympathizers. It is also safe to assume that the numerical size of the Islamic opposition decreased after passage of Law Number 49 of July 1980 and the major losses suffered in Hama and elsewhere in the country.[20] As a result, antiregime terrorism has declind substantially, although it is unreasonable to assume that the Islamic opposition will remain dormant.

The propensity of future activism by the Brotherhood and its allies springs from three sources. The first is the theocratic imperative that only Sunni Muslims rule over a majority Muslim country. Secondly, the Brotherhood's future activism may hinge on its ability to become the leading exponent of a broadly based opposition to the Baath. Finally, the Brethren may endure if they receive continued support from the Sunni urban classes whose political and economic power has been eroded by the regime's policies. To a significant degree, the Islamist opposition has been led by social groups belonging to the *ancien régime*. Also, the Brotherhood represents the poorly paid *ulama* and the petty artisans and shopkeepers of inner city bazaars. The interests of these urban entrepreneurial groups were not well served by Baathi policies, which tended to favor the secular intelligentsia, the military, the rural elements, industrial workers, and the minorities. Nor was the "merchant bourgeoisie" pleased with the nationalization of industry and foreign trade.[21] These measures, coupled with the regime's "socialistic" policies in establishing agricultural and consumer cooperatives, were detrimental to the socioeconomic interests of traditional Sunni landed, mercantile, and manufacturing classes.[22] Clearly, the more militant Islamists came from urban middle- and lower-middle-class traditionalist families of small businessmen, professionals, and clerics. These militants possessed an additional salient characteristic—college or university education, which their fathers usually lacked. Partial data on the occupational background of 1,384 activists who were captured by the government between 1976–81 indicated a large percentage of students (27.7 percent), school teachers (7.9 percent), and professionals (13.3 percent). The latter group included 79 engineers, 57 physicians, 25 lawyers, and 10 pharmacists.[23] These patterns are also evident in the leadership of Syria's Islamist societies (see Table 6). It was no accident that in April 1980 the government outlawed the lawyers', engineers', and doctors' unions.[24]

Despite its urban social base, the Brotherhood possessed notable weaknesses which included the disunity of the Sunni community and the Brotherhood's inability to penetrate the countryside. As an urban movement, it could neither influence nor represent the peasants' interests.[25] Moreover, it appears that some of the affluent Sunni merchants of Damascus have supported both the government and the Brotherhood to hedge their bets for the future.

The Islamist Leadership of Syria: A Profile

A composite profile of the Syrian Islamist elite is presented in Table 6. In the aggregate, it reveals common patterns and characteristics which are salient in political and socioeconomic terms. Clearly discernible is the predominantly urban middle-class background of Syria's fundamentalist leadership. Equally noteworthy is the geographical background of the fifteen leaders. All the major urban centers are represented except Homs, which has remained relatively quiescent

Table 6

Leadership of the Syrian Islamist Movement

Name	Education Occupation	Family Background	Previous Affiliation	Regional Background	Present Function
Shaykh Muhammad Abu al-Nasr al-Bayanuni	Alim	Ulama family of Aleppo	Amir of Abi Dharr Society	Aleppo	Secretary General of Islamic Front; in exile
Shaykh Salim Muhammad al-Hamid	Alim	Ulama family	Brotherhood leader in Hama	Hama	Killed in fighting
Ali Sadr al-Din al-Bayanuni	Lawyer	Ulama family, brother of Muhammad al-Bayanuni	Brotherhood leader of Aleppo	Aleppo	Deputy Supervisor of MB
Adnan Saad al-Din	Educator & Writer	Lower middle class	Teacher in the UAE; leader of Northern Circle	Hama	General Supervisor of MB; one of the three leaders of the Islamic Front (Exec. Com.) in exile.
Said Hawwa	Alim; Sufi	Lower middle class; brother & father killed	Northern Circle	Hama	One of three leaders of Islamic Front (Exec. Com.); chief ideologue in exile
Marwan Hadid	Agriculture Engineer	Prosperous cotton farmer	Leader of independent Islamic group; Trained by PLO	Hama	Died in jail in 1976

Name	Profession/Education	Class Background	Role/Position	Location	Notes/Fate
Shaykh Tahir Khayrallah	Alim	Prominent religious leader	—	Aleppo	Unknown
Adnan Uqla	Civil engineer & Army officer	Middle class baker's son	Chief of military section	Darah and Aleppo	Dismissed in April 1982; Leader of dissident faction inside Syria; militant follower of Marwan Hadid
Amin Yagan	—	—	Leader of Northern Circle militants	Aleppo	Unknown
Muwaffaq Dabul	Ph. D. Mathematics, University of Damascus Professor	Middle class	Leader of Damascus Circle (pro-Attar)	Damascus	Unknown
Dandal Jabr	—	Middle class	Brotherhood organizer	Dayr al-Zur	Member of national leadership of MB
Abd al-Sattar al-Zaim	Dentist	Merchant	Brotherhood leader of Hama	Hama	Killed, 1979
Husni Abu	Teacher of French	Affluent merchant & ulama	Brotherhood organizer in Aleppo	Aleppo	Killed in fighting, 1979
Shaykh Abd al-Fattah Abu Ghuddah	Alim, Mudarris (teacher)	Family of artisans	Leader of Northern Circle militants	Aleppo	Unknown
Adnan Said	—	—	Leader of North	Latqiyyah	Unknown

during the recent disturbances. Damascus and Latqiyyah are each represented by one leader, perhaps reflecting the relative weakness of Islamist fervor in these cities. In sharp contrast, Aleppo and Hama are represented by seven and five leaders respectively, which reflects the strength of Islamist resurgence in these traditional centers of Sunni anti-regime activity. Table 6 also indicates two clusters of occupational patterns: liberal professionals and *ulama*. The latter category includes five leaders—Shaykhs Muhammad al-Bayanuni, Abu Ghuddah, Hamid, Khayrallah, and Said Hawwa—the Brotherhood's chief theorist. Six of the remaining leaders came from professional backgrounds—engineer, dentist, teacher, lawyer—many of whom were born in religious and clerical families. Adnan Uqla, who led the Brotherhood's fighters, was a civil engineer and Army officer. His predecessor, Abd al-Sattar al-Zaim, was a dentist and son of a merchant. Husni Abu who led the Aleppo branch was a teacher of French, the son of an affluent businessman, and son-in-law of a prominent imam. Dr. Dabul taught mathematics at Damascus University, Ali al-Bayanuni practiced law, and Adnan Saad al-Din was a teacher and writer.[26] These findings are revealing in terms of the social-psychological makeup of these militants. Clearly their possession of a modern and technical education was not a deterrent to their heightened Islamic idealism, as has been the case with the liberal professions in the West. Significantly, the same pattern has been observed among Egyptian fundamentalists as well as in the emerging Islamic groups of the Maghrib and Saudi Arabia. Finally, Table 6 reflects the distinctions between the moderate Damascus Circle and the militant jihadists of the Northern Circle (Hama, Aleppo, Latqiyyah), as well as between Adnan Uqla's militants and the Islamic Front. The three top leaders of the Islamic Front—Bayanuni, Saad al-Din and Hawwa—are in exile; four have been killed and the fate or location of the others is unknown. Every one of the fifteen leaders had spent time in prison, and several might still be in jail.

The available evidence suggests that the Islamic Front and the Brotherhood itself are in a period of decline due to the heavy losses suffered during 1981–82, coupled with policy disagreements among the top leaders. One major cause of dispute concerned the Front's relationship with external powers, particularly Iraq, Jordan, and Iran. The disagreement involved the Islamic "purists" under Adnan Uqla and "compromisers" led by Adnan Saad al-Din. Faced with a desperate struggle against the regime, the Saad al-Din faction joined the National Alliance for the Liberation of Syria, which is thought to have Jordanian and Iraqi support. This alliance, which is a coalition of nineteen anti-Asad groups, includes the Islamic Front, pro-Iraqi Baathists, and Nasserists. Saad al-Din's pro-Iraqi statements and reported meetings with high-ranking U. S. officials in Amman during 1982 were vehemently criticized by Uqla.[27] This manifest split in the Islamist leadership is related to the larger configuration of forces in the Middle East. Saad al-Din's rapprochment with Iraq and Jordan is consistent with the Brotherhood's necessity to marshall outside support in confronting the Asad government, which has made common cause with Shiite Iran. Indeed, the Iranian relationship with the Syrian Brotherhood has been one of irony and disappointment. While the Brethren welcomed the Iranian Revolution with enthusiasm, they were sorely disappointed by Khomeini's rapprochement with Asad and the Ayatullah's studied disregard of the Islamic movement in Syria. Despite these Iranian policies, Uqla's refusal to compromise with the Iraqi regime reflects the puritanical and principled idealism of the Brotherhood's younger activists, who regard Saddam Husayn as an anti-Islamic ruler and mutedly favor Khomeini.[28] The Uqla-Saad al-Din conflict culminated in Uqla's expulsion from the Brotherhood on April 25, 1982, which prompted him to form his own party.[29] The decline of anti-regime guerrilla activity during 1983–84 may be partly due to the split within the Islamist movement.

Regime Policies

In order to stem the tide of Islamist militancy, the Asad government has combined cooptative and repressive measures which have enabled it to survive longer than any previous regime. Indeed, despite Asad's reliance on his Alawite kinsmen, he has made a concerted effort to become the president of all Syrians. His major initiatives have included the inauguration of the policy of "rectification" *(tashih)* in 1971 and the progressive relaxation of socialist policies.[30] Moreover, Asad has made repeated overtures to Sunni elements to achieve a reconciliation. Meanwhile, the regime has countered the Islamist charge of "Alawite sectarianism" by highlighting the appointment of Sunni officials to prominent positions. These include the prime minister, the defense minister and the chief of staff. Also, the government has been sensitive to the Islamist accusation that the Nusayris (Alawites) are neither Muslim nor *dhimmi* (Christians or Jews); and therefore they are *kuffar* (unbelievers) and *mushrikin* (idolaters). The categorical stigmatization of the Alawite community has prompted the latter to reaffirm its legitimacy as a sect of Islam and seek validation of its Islamic status from Iran's Twelver Shiite clerical authorities.[31] This religio-ideological factor has reinforced the close strategic and economic ties forged between Iran and Syria during the 1980s.

However, the president has stood firm in his determination to maintain power and to preserve the secular character of the Baathi regime and its ideology. Meanwhile, Asad has pursued a militant policy toward Israel and the West in the name of Arab nationalism. The Israeli invasion of Lebanon in June 1982 proved both a blessing and a curse for the Asad regime. By confronting Israel's superior forces in Lebanon, Asad once again placed himself at the forefront of the Arab nationalist struggle. However, the defeat of the Syrian Air Force substantially detracted from Asad's credibility as a threat to Israel. By mid-1983, the president had recaptured some Syrian and Pan-Arab popular support through his lonely defiance of the American-sponsored Lebanese-Israeli agreement. The refusal to withdraw his forces from Lebanon was made credible by the Soviet willingness to resupply the Syrian army and provide a modern air defense system which included Sam-5 long-range anti-aircraft missiles. Finally, the inglorious withdrawal of U. S. forces from Lebanon and the defeat of the American-trained Lebanese Army elevated Asad to an unprecedented position of influence. Indeed, Asad's stand in Lebanon and his success in imposing his will on that country against Israeli and American objections was bound to evoke the grudging admiration of many Arab nationalists. Thus, despite the fact that Asad's Baathi secularist nationalism runs counter to the dominant Islamist current in the Arab world, the Syrian president has succeeded in retaining power and making himself a key actor in the Lebanese and Arab-Israeli contexts. Consequently, a takeover of power will elude the Islamic Front as long as the cross-sectarian coalition in the army and party leadership remains intact. The president's illness in November 1983, and the resulting confrontation between the forces of his Alawite kinsmen, did not bode well for the prospects of the regime's stability. However, in mid-1984, the president was able to reassume control by exiling the three top antagonists including his brother Rifat al-Asad. Should President Asad depart from the scene, the Syrian Baath is likely to become internally divided in a struggle for succession. Such an eventuality may prove propitious for the reemergence of the Islamic Front. Consequently, the likelihood of Islamist resurgence will depend on Asad's survival and his ability to confront Syria's economic problems and challenges in Lebanon and the larger Arab-Israeli setting. Even in the post-Asad period, the Islamists may find it difficult to assume power. Indeed, the Brethren will find it hard to convince Syria's Christian, Druse, Ismaili, Kurdish, and Alawi minorities as well as many Sunnis that an Islamic order will better serve their interests than the Baath regime.

8 Iraq

Shiite Fundamentalism Against Baathi Rule

T HE FUNDAMENTALIST MOVEMENT in Iraq represents a special genre of Islamic activism in the Arab context because of its Shiite coloration. It is the protest movement of Iraq's Twelver Shiite majority (55 percent) directed at the Baathi regime centered on the Sunni Arab minority (20 percent). In this respect, the Shiite struggle in Iraq bears strong similarity to the Sunni-based militancy in Syria against the Asad regime.

Historical Background and Conflictual Setting

The evolution of Shiite fundamentalism has been shaped by the socio-economic and political conditions of Iraq and the influences radiating from Iran and Syria. The defeat of the Ottoman Empire and the post-war settlement placed Iraq under British mandatory rule. The new order was opposed by both the Shiite and Sunni communities. In 1920 the Shiite *Mujtahid,* Muhammad Taqi al-Shirazi, led an anti-British uprising in an abortive quest for independence. Throughout the mandatory period, the British tended to favor the Sunni minority over the Shiites. The accession of King Faisal in 1921 placed the Shiites under the Sunni Hashemite dynasty of Meccan origin. However, the King pursued conciliatory policies toward the Shiite community and established a quota for Shiite representation in all cabinets. Prime Ministers

Muhammad al-Sadr, Fadhil Jamali, and Salih Jabr were Shiites. Despite such high-level representation, the Shiite role in Iraqi politics remained marginal as Sunnis like Nuri al-Said and the regent Abd al-Ilah remained politically dominant until the 1958 Revolution. Nor did the Shiites play an active role in the Iraqi military and its repeated coups against the civilian authorities.[1]

The 1958 Revolution brought Hashemite rule to a violent demise. Significantly, its leader, Brigadier General Abd al-Karim Qasim, may have disguised his Shiite origins (taqiyyah) as he assumed Iraq's presidency. To counter the demands of pro-Nasser officers to join the United Arab Republic, Qasim imprisoned his second in command, Colonel Abd al-Salam Arif, and allowed the formation of political parties. Consequently, the Hizb al-Dawah al-Islamiyyah was established as the political expression of the Shiite community. The violent overthrow of Qasim in February 1963 was followed by an unstable regime under the Nasserist Colonel Arif and pro-Egyptian Baathists. The subsequent conflict within the Baath, and between the latter and President Arif, led to the dismissal of Prime Minister General Ahmad Hasan al-Bakr and his Baathi colleagues. Arif's accidental death in April 1966 brought to the presidency his older brother, Major General Abd al-Rahman Arif, who was overthrown by the Baath in July 1968. The Arif brothers manifested a Nasserist orientation, which created foreboding among the Shiites. This attitude resulted from the fear of becoming a minority in a Sunni Pan-Arab state headed by Nasser.[2] As early as 1964, manifestations of Shiite protest were suppressed as the government established a special security branch to counter their activism. The same year saw the arrival of Ruhalla Khomeini, an exiled Iranian cleric who attracted a large following as a religious teacher.

The Baath takeover of 1968 made the Shiite position more precarious. The new regime was dominated by Iraqi Baathists and fugitives from the Syrian Baath's "right wing" led by Aflaq, who had lost power in February 1966. A combination of four behavioral attributes and policies characterized the new order:

1. A secular Arab nationalist orientation.

2. A heightened sense of paranoia and the concomitant determination not to be overthrown.

3. A predilection to recruit key officials from Takrit, the hometown of President Hasan al-Bakr and Vice President Saddam Husayn, particularly centering on the latter's kinsmen from Takrit's al-Awja district.

4. Economic and demographic policies which promoted maldistribution of income and hardship among the poorer classes, particularly the Shiites.

Every one of the foregoing Baathi policies had an alienating effect on the Shiite religious leadership and people. The regime's secular and Arabist orientation constituted a double threat: as a secular state, the regime was regarded as "infidel," and Baathi schemes for Arab unity were considered a danger to the majority status of the Shiites. Moreover, the Baath's deep-seated fear of counter-revolution and its secular ideological commitment created a dual compulsion to sponsor massive programs of indoctrination, combined with liquidation of its perceived enemies. In this sense, the Shiites were a natural target, particularly in view of the regime's narrow sectarian base in the Sunni community. While Shiites were recruited into the party and the military, supreme power was effectively concentrated in the hands of a Sunni Takriti oligarchy centering around Saddam Husayn. Finally, the Baath's socioeconomic policies tended to reinforce the economic inferiority of the Shiite community.[3] Despite Iraq's growing affluence from oil, the Shiite multitudes of the South and Baghdad remained in a state of relative deprivation. These crisis factors were responsible for the emergence of Shiite fundamentalism during the 1970s.

The Anatomy of Shiite Fundamentalism

The existence of large Shiite communities in Iran and Iraq created a symbiotic relationship between the clerical establishments of the two countries. For centuries, the Iranian faithful and clergy had been attracted to the three holy cities of Shiism located in Iraq—al-Najaf, Karbala and al-Kazimayn. In return, Iraqi Shiites looked to Iran's Shiite majority for political support as a counterweight to their Sunni rulers in Baghdad. These relationships made the Iraqi Shiites a ready target for Iranian subversion under both the Shah and Khomeini. Thus, Iranian influence was an important factor in the ideological and organizational development of Iraqi Shiite militancy.

A plethora of groups arose to represent the Shiite resistance to Baathi authority, many of which had Iranian connections (Appendix I). For example, the Hizb al-Fatimi under al-Khurasani brought together

Shiite intellectuals and officers of Arab and Iranian origin to subvert the Baathi regime during the early 1970s. However, the foremost revolutionary group was the Hizb al-Dawah al-Islamiyyah, which constituted the core of Shiite resistance. There is some dispute regarding the origins of the Hizb al-Dawah. It appears that the Hizb was founded by Ayatullah Muhammad Baqir al-Sadr in 1958–59.[4] This was a mass party led by young educated clergymen who had been inspired by Iraq's foremost charismatic *mujtahid,* Baqir al-Sadr. Its membership was mostly middle and lower class, centered in Baghdad, the holy cities, and the South. The Party's propaganda was conducted through the mosques and religious schools under the guidance of the Hawza— the theological faculty of Al-Najaf. Its activist members were tightly organized in *halaqat* (chains), consisting of *usar* (cells), which operated according to the principle of *tanzim khayti* (thread organization), whereby the individual member's knowledge of fellow conspirators was circumscribed.

It was not until the rise of the Baath in 1968 that the Hizb was progressively propelled into violent activism, since it considered the government's secularist policies as being against Islam. These included selling pork, bringing Islamic schools under state control, suspension of religious publications, obstructing mosque repairs, and persecution of Shiite clergy. Such policies constituted a provocation of the first magnitude for Iraq's Shiites, who rallied behind the Hizb in a series of violent confrontations with the regime. In 1974, the *husayni* processions commemorating the killing of Imam Husayn turned into angry political protests. The government responded with selective and collective arrests and repression. The agitation of the Hizb reached a climax during the Shiite observance of Muharram early in 1977, when the security forces attempted to interfere with the mourning procession *(masirah* or *mawkib)* halfway between Najaf and Karbalah. The Shiite crowds responded with fury, attacking a police station and chanting anti-regime slogans.[5] This was followed by widespread arrests of young and old Shiites, trials, executions, and incarceration in the infamous Jail Number One.

During the late 1970s, the Hizb and the Shiite community were radicalized by the Islamic Revolution of Iran. In 1978, after years of exile in Najaf, the Iranian Ayatullah Ruhalla Khomeini was expelled from Iraq as a consequence of the 1975 Iraq-Iran rapprochement. While it is said that Khomeini spurned the Hizb due to its Iranian connections, there was no doubt about the kinship ties and close collaboration between the Ayatullah and top Iraqi Shiite clerics. The victory of the Islamic Revolution in 1979 generated a new wave of Shiite unrest. The 1979 Muharram demonstrators demanded social reforms and the establishment of an Islamic state. In view of Khomeini's explicit encouragement of Shiite militancy from Iran, the Iraqi government perceived the Hizb as a "fifth column," aiming at a merger between Iraq and Iran. In response, the government arrested Baqir al-Sadr in June 1979, triggering massive demonstrations in Baghdad's Shiite al-Thawrah ghetto, which were crushed by the regime. The magnitude of repression caused a split within the Revolutionary Command Council, which may have prompted the execution of twenty-two top Baathi officials soon after Saddam Husayn's assumption of the presidency in July 1979. Ayatullah Sadr's declaration of absolute support for Iran's Islamic Revolution and encouragement of armed opposition to the Baath compelled the regime to charge him with treason for planning to establish a Shiite state in Iraq. Baqir al-Sadr and his activist sister Bint al-Huda were taken to Baghdad and executed in April 1980.[6] The death of one of Shiism's most distinguished *maraji* (religious authority) added a new and symbolically potent martyr to the firmament of Twelver saints.[7]

Baqir al-Sadr and the Iranian Connection

Uncertainty surrounds the precise roles of Baqir al-Sadr and Khomeini in the Shiite insurrection and its ties to Iran's Islamic Revolution. While one author asserts Sadr's and Khomeini's non-involvement in the Hizb,[8] Shiite sources ascribe to them central roles in the movement. Both clerics symbolized uncompromising Shiite opposition to the Baath. As a committed religious idealist, Baqir al-Sadr persisted in rejecting Saddam Husayn's entreaties, since he considered cooperation with the regime as *haram* (unlawful) under Islamic law because of its secular and oppressive nature.

The paramount role of Baqir al-Sadr as the chief ideologue and inspirational leader of Iraq's Shiites is beyond question. His lucid writings, combined with his reputed courage and uprightness made him the vital fountainhead of Iraqi Shiite activism.[9] Equally important was Baqir al-Sadr's relatively unknown role as one of the intellectual godfathers of Iran's Islamic Constitution. Indeed, the evidence indicates that this Arab Ayatullah contributed notably to the ideological framework of the Islamic order in Iran. Reportedly, Baqir al-Sadr and Khomeini were in frequent contact both before and after the revolution in Iran. Soon after Khomeini's victorious return to Tehran on February 1, 1979, Baqir al-Sadr sent his colleague six studies entitled "Islam Guides Life," which contained an explication of Islamic theory on the structure of the *ummah,* the leading role of the religious authorities *(marjiiyyah),* the distribution of executive and legislative powers, and an outline of Islamic economic theory. The first of these studies appeared as a prescriptive commentary on the juristical foundations and makeup of the Islamic Constitution that was being framed in Iran during 1979. Baqir al-Sadr had sent a similar document to a group of Lebanese Shiite *ulama* in response to their inquiry on the formation of the nascent Islamic polity in Iran. His political thought may be summarized as follows:

> 1. God is the source of all sovereignty, authority, and wealth. This principle frees man from the servitude and exploitation of other men.
> 2. The *ummah* is the representative of God on earth; it is responsible before God to perpetuate His trust.
> 3. Islamic law is the source of legislation and the constitution itself.
> 4. The rightly guided *marjiiyyah* (supreme religious authority) is the legal expression of Islam, and the highest *marji* is the deputy general or representative of the Imam (hidden). As such, the *marji* is entrusted with all-important functions:
> a. He is the highest representative of the state and supreme commander of the armed forces.
> b. He determines the legality of constitutional questions in terms of Islamic law and decides on the constitutionality of laws enacted by the legislative assembly *(ahl al-hall wal-aqd)* which is popularly elected.
> c. He approves the nomination of candidates seeking election as head of the executive authority.
> d. He appoints a high court to guard against deviationism, a council of grievances to redress acts of injustice, and a council of one hundred clerical scholars, preachers, and religious intellectuals to conduct the work of the *marjiiyyah.*[10]

The paramount position assigned to the *maraji* in Baqir al-Sadr's conception of the Islamic polity necessitates the selection of an exemplary personage. To Baqir al-Sadr, the qualities of a prospective *marji* must include righteousness, sincerity, and the ability to lead and to exercise independent judgment. Since the *marjiiyyah* is a divine covenant *(ahd)* to perpetuate the Prophet's and the Imams' testimony *(shahadah)* and succession *(khilafah)*, it embodies their absolute righteousness and infallibility *(ismah)*. While not infallible, the *maraji* should strive for righteousness.[11] His writings should reflect a clear ideological commitment to the Islamic state and its preservation. He must also enjoy wide support among the clergy, theological students, preachers, and religious thinkers. Finally, any candidate to the *marjiiyyah* must be nominated by the Marjiiyyah Council; in case several qualified individuals are nominated to the *marjiiyyah*, a plebiscite will determine the choice of a supreme *marji*.

Baqir al-Sadr's theoretical and political formulations were to provide powerful reinforcement to Khomeini's position on the dominant role of the jurisconsult in the Islamic state. Indeed, through his writings Baqir al-Sadr was seeking to intervene in the political struggle that was being waged in Iran throughout 1979 between Khomeini's supporters and those opposed to his insistence on a constitution stipulating the supremacy of the jurisconsult. In theoretical and practical terms, Baqir al-Sadr's rule of the *marji* and Khomeini's *wilayat al-faqih* are synonymous. They represent the culmination of a significant evolution in Shiite political thought and practice which had begun as late as the mid-nineteenth century.

Clearly, Baqir al-Sadr had propounded a comprehensive theory of social and political revolution for the establishment of an Islamic polity, which found its realization under Khomeini's rule. Ayatullah Sadr is regarded by the Shiites as an authority equal to the stature of Sayyid al-Murtada (d. 1043), Shaykh Abu Jafar al-Tusi (d. 1068), and Allama Ibn Mutahhar al-Hilli (d. 1325). It was no coincidence that Iranian broadcasts in Arabic referred to Sadr as "the Khomeini of Iraq;" his execution plunged Iran into national mourning.[12]

Regime Policies and the Shiite Future

The failure of the Shiite revolution in Iraq, in contrast to its success in Iran, was due to several factors. The Baath was relatively cohesive and had the support of the Sunni Arab minority, which feared the prospect of Shiite rule. In addition, the Hizb lacked the clerical apparatus of the Iranian Revolution, partly due to the comparatively small size of the

Iraqi Shiite clergy.[13] Finally, the Shiite failure was the consequence of Saddam Husayn's policies which combined comprehensive repression with incentives to the Shiite leadership and rank-and-file. In its propaganda, the Baath appealed to the Arab feelings of the Shiite population, while reiterating its belief in the "spirit of Islam," rather than its ritualistic aspects.[14] Meanwhile, Saddam Husayn proclaimed the birthday of Ali ibn Abi Talib a national holiday, visited Najaf, and announced his personal descent from the Prophet. By spending great sums on mosques and Shiite religious centers (husayniyyah), the regime succeeded in coopting some Shiite clerics, although many top clergy refused explicit cooperation with the Baath.[15] The chief marji, Ayatullah al-Uzmah Abu al-Qasim al-Khui, has not assumed Baqir al-Sadr's activist role. Reportedly under house arrest, the chief marji is in his eighties and unable or reluctant to express explicit support or opposition to the Baath.

The combined effect of the state's cooptative and repressive policies had substantially weakened the Shiite opposition as Iraq attacked Iran in September 1981. The regime's propaganda and the war itself deepend Persian-Arab ethnic cleavages. Some Shiites have opposed identifying their cause with the Iranian Revolution amid strains between Arab and Persian Shiite clerics.[16] Meanwhile, Saddam Husayn's policy of granting material rewards has won over several prominent Shiites, including Kelidar Sayyid Husayn, the warden of Ali's mausoleum in Najaf, Imam Ali Kashif al-Ghita of Karbala, and Shaykh Ali al-Saghir of Najaf. In addition, the well-known Shiite poet al-Atayshi has been honored by the regime. President Husayn's attempts to capture Shiite allegiance are also reflected in the composition of the political elite. A comparative analysis of ministerial backgrounds in the cabinets of 1979 and 1982 reveals some increase in the Shiite presence. Furthermore, the Shiite membership of the Baath Regional Command (Qiyadah al-Qutriyyah) stands at four—an all time high. Included are a number of prominent Shiites who have been closely associated with Saddam Husayn: Naim Haddad, Speaker of the National Assembly; Sadun Hammadi, Foreign Minister; and Rahi Farun, a top Baath functionary.

The political significance of the increased Shiite presence should not be exaggerated. The Shiite ministers of the present cabinet constitute a minority which almost matches the Kurdish presence. Moreover, the Shiites are given mostly non-sensitive portfolios such as housing, health, and trade. Somewhat larger is the percentage of Shiites in the Baath leadership. In both the party and government, the Sunni Arabs are dominant, which is also true of the security services and the military leadership.

The Shiites' situation has not improved economically, and security agents are reported to keep them under close surveillance, particularly in the mosques.[17] The revolutionary movement has been fragmented, with no single leader available to fill the shoes of Baqir al-Sadr. Several new organizations have emerged to challenge the Baath (see Appendix I). During 1979, a small group called *Mujahidin* revealed itself through armed action. While professing to be inspired by Baqir al-Sadr, the *Mujahidin* are reportedly opposed to clerical leadership patterned after Iran,[18] although some regard this group as the militant wing of the Dawah Party. Another faction of the party that split in 1980 is Munazzamah al-Amal al-Islami (Islamic Action Organization) led by Shaykhs Muhammad al-Shirazi and Hadi al-Mudarrisi. This group is inclined to oppose short-range adventures, and favors long-range activism.[19] A third group is Jamaat al-Ulama under the exiled Ayatullah Muhammad Baqir al-Hakim; this clerical society serves as an umbrella organization for various Shiite militant groups.

Nevertheless, the Hizb al-Dawah has remained the most potent of the Shiite movements. It continues to attract members from the army's lower ranks, students, professionals, and tribal people. A Shiite source reported in late 1982 that the defection rate from the Iraqi Army was exceeding 35 percent, most of whom were presumably Shiite soldiers.[20] The military arm of the Hizb—the Revolutionary Army for the Liberation of Iraq—has continued to operate against the regime, reportedly with Iranian and Syrian help. It is supported by the United Islamic Front against Saddam Husayn, which represents a coalition of the Hizb, the Syrian regime, the AMAL movement of Lebanon, and the Islamic Republic of Iran. Also, the Shiite underground has belatedly established ties with Kurdish groups and the Iraqi Communist Party, both of which oppose the regime. In the meantime, the Higher Council of the Islamic Revolution centered in Iran continues to act as the supreme body directing the Shiite struggle in Iraq. This Council under Ayatullah al-Hakim consists of Iraqi *ulama* and laymen who escaped to Iran early in 1980.[21] Through its publications and broadcasts, the Higher Council has attempted to reinvigorate the revolutionary zeal of Iraq's Shiites.[22] It appears that the Hizb is the most important element in the Higher Council, which has developed ties with sympathetic Sunni groups in the Arab world and Shiite student groups in Europe and the United States. The propaganda themes of the Higher Council reflect those of the Iranian Revolution: anti-

Americanism, and fierce opposition to the Saudi dynasty and the Egyptian government. A major theme in the Higher Council's propaganda reveals its special concern with the Egyptian presence in Iraq. This preoccupation springs from the Baath's policy of importing over a million Egyptian farmers and army veterans for a dual purpose: to equalize Iraq's Shiite-Sunni demographic disparity and to provide fighters for the Iranian front.[23] This "silent partnership" between Saddam Husayn and the Sadat-Mubarak regime runs counter to Iranian and Iraqi Shiite interests. Consequently, the Shiite clergy has appealed to Umar al-Tilmisani, the leader of the Egyptian Brotherhood, asking his support for the Islamic revolution in Iraq and Iran.[24] Meanwhile, the Sunni fundamentalists of Iraq, led by the Muslim Brotherhood, have refrained from opposing the Baathi regime.

The Impact of the Iran-Iraq War

The Shiite movement in Iraq continued to exhibit militancy during 1982 and 1983. However, a Shiite overthrow of the Baath appears unlikely in view of the regime's technological and organizational capabilities of control. Only a major Iranian breakthrough on the war front could assure the success of Iraq's Shiite movement. Indeed, the military-ideological goals of the Iranian regime and the revolutionary objectives of Iraq's Shiite insurgents have converged in the single imperative of overthrowing President Saddam Husayn. The quantum escalation of Iran's military commitment to the war has been accompanied with persistent calls to both Iraqi Shiites and Sunnis to rise against the Baath. In the war itself, Shiite fundamentalist mass fervor is pitted against Iraq's technologically superior military machine. The enormity of human losses in Iran's massed attacks are consistent with Shiite eschatological beliefs in the readiness to face martyrdom.

9 Saudi Arabia

Sunni and Shiite Militancy Against an Islamic State

IN SHARP CONTRAST to the majority of Arab regimes that profess varying degrees of secularism, the Saudi Kingdom claims to be an Islamic state. Yet despite this claim, the monarchy has not been immune to the fundamentalist challenge from within and from the Islamic Revolution in Iran. In recent years, the Islamist challenge assumed significant proportions, culminating in the takeover of the Grand Mosque in Mecca and the Shiite riots in the Kingdom's oil-producing Eastern Province. These Sunni and Shiite insurrections reflect the ideological and social cleavages in a society increasingly suffering from the culture shock of haphazard and rapid modernization. Equally significant is the fact that these anti-regime eruptions had their origins in the conflictual beginnings of the Saudi state.

A Retrospective View: The Saudi-Wahhabi Nexus

The peculiar symbiosis between militant religion and imperial power found its classic expression in the Saudi state at Dariyyah in the mid-eighteenth century which was based on an alliance between Muhammad ibn Saud and Shaykh Muhammad ibn Abd al-Wahhab. Ibn Saud took the title of *imam* as political-military chieftain, while Ibn Abd al-Wahhab provided a puritanical religious ideology as Al Shaykh. His doctrinal teachings were based on the strict constructionism of Ibn

Hanbal and Ibn Taymiyyah. The Shaykh accepted only the Quran and the *sunnah* and rejected as heretical all subsequent theological interpretations, mysticism, and superstitions *(khurafa)*. Furthermore, he repudiated the legitimacy of the Ottoman Sultans and preached strict adherence to the Prophet's maxims and practices. He forbade the use of the rosary, tobacco, wine and luxuries, and the visitation of shrines. In view of Al Shaykh's total emphasis on the absolute oneness of God *(tawhid)*, his followers were called *Muwahhidin,* commonly known outside Saudi Arabia as the Wahhabis.[1]

The Saudi state expanded rapidly in the early 1800s with the capture of Mecca and Medina, only to be crushed by Muhammad Ali's son Ibrahim Pasha in 1818. The mid-nineteenth century saw the reemergence of Saudi power in Najd, soon to be defeated by the Ibn Rashid dynasty in 1891. A decade later Abd al-Aziz ibn Abd al-Rahman Al Saud returned from Kuwait to organize the Ikhwan warriors recruited from the tribes of Mutayr, Utayba, Harb, and Ajman.[2] The Ikhwan (sing. *akh*) or the "Brethren" were tribal settlements of militants *(hujar)* who had emulated the Prophet's example in *hijrah*—in escaping from corruption to Islamic puritanism. As such the Brethren became the prime instrumentality in the hands of Abd al-Aziz to conquer and unite most of the Arabian Peninsula between 1912 and 1925. His successive victories over the Ottomans, Rashidis, Hashemites, Yemenis, and the Shiites of the Gulf culminated in the establishment of a unified Saudi Kingdom in 1932. The combined motivational power of Wahhabi fundamentalism and the lure of booty was Ibn Saud's formula of success. However, this formula contained its internal contradictions which raised difficulties for Ibn Saud and his successors. These included the tribal basis of the Ikhwan and the zealousness inherent to the fundamentalist ethos. Despite his great power and prestige, Ibn Saud could not always exercise total control over the militant tribes and their leaders. Nor could he prevent the latter from using the two-edged sword of Islamic fundamentalism to challenge his centralized rule.

By the mid-1920s, the dissident Ikhwan were openly disobeying Ibn Saud and attacking the British mandatory areas in the North. In the Battle of Sabala (1929), Abd al-Aziz finally defeated the Ikhwan led by Faisal al-Dawish and Ibn Humayd Sultan ibn Bijad, the leaders of the Mutayr and Utayba tribes respectively. It was no coincidence that these tribes were well represented among the rebels who occupied the Grand Mosque in November 1979.[3] The salient connection between the Battle of Sabala and the mosque takeover was the persisting challenge to the legitimacy of the Saudi monarchy among certain elements of the population. The twin foundations of Saudi legitimacy—Wahhabi fundamentalism and tribal consensus—have been partially eroded as a consequence of the political, socioeconomic, and foreign policies of Ibn Saud's successors. Thus, the legitimacy system which the king established may prove detrimental to his heirs. Earlier in the century, Ibn Saud's governor of al-Ahsa, Abdallah ibn Jalawi, warned his master about the dangers of the Ikhwan movement: "It is like a fire that consumes everything."[4] There can be no doubt about the present-day relevance of this admonition.

The Saudi State in a Modernizing Milieu (1953–79)

At the death of King Ibn Saud in 1953, the monarchy was already experiencing the modernizing pressures of the world milieu. The kingdom's ever-increasing oil wealth, combined with its security concerns, were progressively involving the Saudis in Arab and world affairs. Hence, the gradual erosion of the kingdom's self-imposed isolation, which pitted its fundamentalist culture against a rapidly-changing world environment. The accession of King Saud ushered in a period of profligacy and misrule. The King's shortcomings in character and performance prompted his deposition in 1964, through the combined consensus of the senior members of the royal family and the *ulama*.[5] The investiture of King Faisal marked the continuation of reformist initiatives begun during his premiership. These included the establishment of provincial governments and a judiciary, in addition to social welfare measures, price controls, and the abolition of slavery. Furthermore, Faisal created a corpus of laws regulating labor, insurance, mining, and foreign investments.[6] In promulgating these measures, the King followed his father's precedent in legitimizing the new initiatives through *shariah* law. Faisal's greatest external challenge was Nasser's Pan-Arabism which brought an Egyptian-Saudi military confrontation in the Yemen civil war (1962–68). His response was to fall back on Islamic legitimacy at home and the encouragement of Pan-Islamic movements abroad.[7] Meanwhile, Faisal placed restrictions on his Nasserist and ultra-fundamentalist critics, who strongly opposed the King's foreign and domestic policies.

King Faisal's assassination in 1975 and succession by King

Khalid opened the way for considerable relaxation of the regime's socioeconomic and foreign policies. In view of Khalid's precarious health, Crown Prince Fahd assumed operational responsibility for the affairs of the kingdom. Under Fahd, Faisal's conservative and gradualist policies were replaced by ambitious developmental schemes, which necessitated the massive importation of foreigners. The kingdom's growing wealth increased its sense of insecurity, which prompted the forging of extensive security relationships with the U. S. The combination of Saudi developmental efforts and security concerns brought a large increase in the American presence.[8] The consequences of these developments included corruption and conspicuous consumption among certain members and associates of the royal family, and an increase in the relative deprivation of the tribes and urban middle and lower classes. The combined impact of affluence and Western influences on Saudi puritanism produced a cultural crisis of major proportions threatening the very foundations of monarchical rule. In this milieu a new wave of Islamic resurgence appeared during the 1970s.

The Return of the Ikhwan

The opposition to the monarchy during the 1960s was centered on a coalition of Nasserists, Baathis, leftists, and Islamic fundamentalists. The latter's role, however, was muted, since the center stage of opposition was occupied by Nasserist Arab nationalists under Prince Talal. Despite Faisal's attempts to win over opposition elements, there were arrests of some nationalist officers in 1969 who were suspected of plotting a coup. However, the nationalist movement entered a period of decline during the seventies; its place was taken up by Islamic fundamentalism which constituted a more authentically nativist ideology of resistance.

The beginnings of the new Ikhwan movement may be traced to the early 1960s. Reportedly, it was headed by Prince Khalid ibn Musaid ibn Abd al-Aziz and some of his friends. It appears that by 1965, this small movement had become a potential threat to King Faisal in opposing his policies of incremental modernization, especially the introduction of television. In August 1965, Prince Khalid was killed along with Saad ibn Hulail and other followers.[9] Ten years later, Faisal ibn Musaid assassinated King Faisal to avenge the death of Prince Khalid, his older brother.[10] These episodes do not seem to indicate an oganizational linkage between the new Ikhwan and the remnants of the old Ikhwan under

King Abd al-Aziz. Equally tenuous seems to be the linkage between Prince Musaid's group and the Ikhwan militants responsible for the Grand Mosque takeover. What is clear however, was the existence of numerous Islamist societies which had been proliferating during the 1970s in many sectors of Saudi life. Paradoxically, these groups were now using fundamentalism to challenge the legitimacy of an avowedly fundamentalist regime. To a significant extent, history was repeating itself. As in the days of King Abd al-Aziz, the grass-roots fundamentalism of the Ikhwan was challenging the institutionalized Islamism of the state, except that the *fitnah* (provocation) of British imperialism was now replaced by the American presence and the improbity of certain members of the ruling elite.

While the new Ikhwan lacked organizational links with the earlier groups, the ideological continuity is clearly evident, despite the generational gap. In point of fact, the ideological commitment of the new groups may be deeper than that of their tribal grandparents under Abd al-Aziz, who were partly motivated by booty. Also, unlike their illiterate predecessors, the new Ikhwan are mostly young, educated, and to some degree, urbanized; consequently, they have been exposed to Westernizing influences. However, the one salient characteristic of the new Ikhwan is its pristine fundamentalism—its *dawah* preaches an uncompromising return to the Holy Book and the *sunnah*. Thus, the Ikhwan's opposition to the monarchy includes the Saudi's Wahhabi creed, although the group reveres Ibn Abd al-Wahhab and his teachings.[11]

Juhayman's Dawah

The ideological leader and moving force behind the takeover of the Grand Mosque was Juhayman ibn Saif al-Utaybi. Juhayman's background contained all the attributes of marginality vis-à-vis the Saudi ruling order. His class background, combined with his life experiences and personality, set him on a collision course with the regime, culminating in the Mosque episode. As an Utayba tribesman, Juhayman's tribal roots and family history predisposed him to oppose Saudi centralized authority. His grandfather had been killed at the Battle of Sabalah—an episode that constitutes a link between the old and new Ikhwan ideologically and in the imperatives of tribal vengeance. Juhayman served for eighteen years in the tribally recruited Saudi National Guard from which he resigned around 1974. He is known to have studied under Shaykh Abd al-Aziz ibn Baz at the Islamic University in Medina, which he left to pursue Quranic learning independently of the *ulama*. After the mid-1970s, Juhayman spent his time spreading his message and organizing his followers to confront the regime. The combination of his lower-class tribal background, family history, religious devotion, and experience in the military created in Juhayman a fundamentalist rebel of the first magnitude bent on destroying the monarchy. In his leadership style, Juhayman conformed to the charismatic prototype seen in other fundamentalist movements. Reportedly, he possessed a magnetic *(jazzabah)* personality, piercing eyes and great courage, all of which brought him tribal respect and obedience from his young followers.[12] He was also a popular poet and writer on Islamic themes. Juhayman's *dawah* is synthesized in *Saba Rasail*[13]—*Seven Letters*—which were illegally published and circulated. Its main themes, announced over the loudspeaker during the Grand Mosque takeover, included:

> 1. The imperative to emulate the Prophet's example—revelation, propagation, and military takeover.
> 2. The necessity for the Muslims to overthrow their present corrupt rulers who are forced upon them and lack Islamic attributes since the Quran recognizes no king or dynasty.
> 3. The requirements for legitimate rulership are devotion to Islam and its practice, rulership by the Holy Book and not by repression, Qurashi tribal roots, and election by the Muslim believers.
> 4. The duty to base the Islamic faith on the Quran and the *sunnah* and not on the equivocal interpretations *(taqlid)* of the *ulama* and on their "incorrect" teachings in the schools and universities.
> 5. The necessity to isolate oneself from the sociopolitical system by refusing to accept any official positions.
> 6. The advent of the *mahdi* from the lineage of the Prophet through Husayn ibn Ali to remove the existing injustices and bring equity and peace to the faithful.
> 7. The duty to reject all worshipers of the partners of God *(shirk)*, including worshipers of Ali, Fatimah and Muhammad, the Khawarij, and even music and technology.
> 8. The duty to establish a puritanical Islamic community which protects Islam from unbelievers and does not court foreigners.[14]

Juhayman implemented his *dawah* with meticulous planning and precise execution, culminating on November 20, 1979 in the Grand Mosque seizure. After closing the forty-eight gates of the sanctuary,

Juhayman's brother-in-law, Muhammad ibn Abdallah al-Qahtani, claimed mahdiship in front of an astonished multitude of pilgrims. This act conformed to the belief that a *mahdi* would appear at the turn of the Islamic century—Muharram 1400 A. H. or November 20, 1979. The militants numbered over 300 men and their families,[15] who fought for two weeks before being killed or captured. King Khalid convened a council of *ulama* to seek a *fatwa* (legal opinion) permitting the assault to recapture the privileged sanctuary. The *mahdi* died during the fighting and Juhayman was captured with sixty-two companions and executed.

According to well-placed sources, the chain of events began with a dispute involving real estate. An undetermined number of lower-class families were evicted by an influential notable. The dispossessed families then appealed to the Amir of Mecca who failed to provide them with alternate living accommodations, which prompted them to move their belongings into the Grand Mosque. This act of seeking shelter in the House of Allah may have been intended as a protest against injustice. However, the situation was politicized when Juhayman and his followers made common cause with the displaced families by joining them in the Mosque to defy Saudi authority.

The Grand Mosque episode raised serious questions about the Saudi political system. Most basically it underscored the monarchy's deficiencies in maintaining internal security. Juhayman and his group had been arrested several times, and in mid-1978 three hundred Ikhwan had been jailed, only to be released upon the intercession of the respected Shaykh Abd al-Aziz ibn Baz.[16] Moreover, the conspiracy had been hatched under the very nose of the regime, including the procurement of arms and military training. Equally serious was the government's indecisiveness in confronting the insurrection.[17] At a more fundamental level, the mosque episode underlined the monarchy's uncertain legitimacy base. A social background analysis of the insurgents indicates substantial tribal affiliation centered on the Utayba and to a lesser extent on the Qahtan, Harb, Anaza, and Mutayr tribes. In geographical distribution, a large number of the insurgents came from Najd with a few from Shammar and Asir. Among the captured, there were twenty-two non-Saudis, mostly Egyptians and Yemenis along with a few Kuwaitis, a Sudanese, and an Iraqi.[18] The large Najdi presence indicated opposition to the monarchy centered in its ancestral power base. Moreover, the significant number of theological students from the Islamic universities of Mecca, Medina, and Riyadh reflected the failure of Saudi socialization policies. According to observers, the rebels had sympathizers among the urban petty bourgeoisie, students, lower-ranking clerics, technocrats, and tribal leaders opposing centralization and sedentarization.

In retrospect, it is difficult to judge the scope of Juhayman's influence and ties to other opposition groups. While some sources have reported the creation of a coalition of secular and fundamentalist opposition groups, the mosque seizure was apparently a unilateral move by Juhayman's Ikhwan. It would seem that in organizational and ideological terms, Juhayman's group represented a relatively narrow faction among the monarchy's fundamentalist opponents. This was dictated by the messianic character of Ikhwan's ideology and the primeval strictness of its beliefs and lifeways. Indeed, for many potential sympathizers of the Ikhwan's political objectives, its takeover of the Holy Sanctuary may have constituted a doctrinally illegitimate act and a tactically foolhardy move. Nor could the claim to mahdiship by Juhayman's brother-in-law be helpful in attracting broad support from the mainstream of popular fundamentalism. Clearly, the old Ikhwan and its Hanbalite Wahhabism lacked a mahdist orientation. In the contemporary Sunni mass consciousness, a claim to mahdiship could find social validation only in periods of mass expectancy when an extraordinary personage reveals himself "at the end of time"—*akhir al-zaman*. Thus, the new Ikhwan's messianic millenarianism, social separationist tendencies, and total objection to modernization tended to reinforce its cultic nature, much like the Egyptian Takfir wal-Hijrah. Significantly, both groups were charged by the authorities as being *khawarij*—a derogatory term referring to the terroristic religio-political "seceders" of early Islam.

Shiite Fundamentalism

Shiite unrest in the kingdom's Eastern Province coincided with the Ikhwan's seizure of the Grand Mosque. The Saudi opposition press has attempted to link the two episodes in its propaganda.[19] While there is no evidence of coordination between the two events, they symbolized the breadth of opposition to the monarchy. In contrast to the Sunni Ikhwan, the Shiite fundamentalist inspiration in late 1979 came directly from the Iranian Revolution. However, in both cases similar indigenous factors prompted anti-regime militancy.

The Eastern Province contains Twelver Shiite concentrations

which are demographic extensions of the Shiite majorities in Iran and Iraq. Since the occupation of the East by King Abd al-Aziz in 1913, there has been periodic opposition to Saudi rule from indigenous Shiites. In 1925, a popular assembly was created under Muhammad al-Habshi to articulate local demands, only to be outlawed by the government. With the discovery of oil, the Eastern region assumed new importance as many of the indigenous Shiites were employed in the oil industry. During and after World War II, these Shiite workers were proletarianized and showed increasing resentment toward the government and the affluent American community. In 1948 the Shiite unrest culminated in the outbreak of large-scale demonstrations and disorder in the al-Qatif area led by Muhammad ibn Husayn al-Harraj.[20] The insurgents, calling for secession from the Kingdom, were easily crushed. During 1949, the government discovered the existence of a revolutionary society in al-Qatif operating under the guise of an educational association. The society was dissolved and one of its leaders, the leftist Abd al-Rauf al-Khanizi died in prison.[21] This movement, which has spread to Jubayl, was finally crushed in 1950. Meanwhile, there were major labor strikes during 1944, 1949, and 1953 to protest working conditions; also there were boycotts during the 1956 and 1967 Arab-Israeli wars to cut off oil supplies to the West. In 1970, the National Guard was dispatched to al-Qatif to seal off the city to contain unrest. Another outbreak in 1978 brought large-scale arrests and casualties.[22]

The mass rioting in al-Qatif and Sayhat late in 1979 coincided with the period of Shiite religious mourning *(Ashura)*, the taking of American hostages in Tehran, and the Grand Mosque seizure in Mecca. The concurrence of these episodes in the wake of the Iranian Revolution seemed ominous to the Saudis. Indeed, to the 250,000 Shiites of the Eastern Province, the call of Ayatullah Khomeini constituted an invitation to rebellion. On November 19, the National Guard returned to crush Shiite resistance, as unrest continued well into December 1979.

Saudi Policies Toward Dissident Groups

In recent years the kingdom has increasingly pursued policies of reform and cooptation toward its internal and expatriate opponents. Two categories of opposition groups may be identified. The first consists of leftist and nationalist organizations that have a secularist orientation:

1. Arabian Peninsula People's Union—Nasserist
2. National Front for the Liberation of Arabia—Communist
3. Baath Party—Arabist socialist
4. Popular Democratic Union—Marxist pro-Palestinian.
5. Democratic Popular Front for the Liberation of the Peninsula—Radical socialist
6. Arab Liberation Front—Arab nationalist
7. Arab Socialist Labor Party—Socialist nationalist

The second category consists of Islamist organizations including:

1. Islamic Revolutionary Organization of the Arabian Peninsula—Shiite
2. Liberation Party of the Peninsula—Shiite
3. Society of Propagation—Sunni
4. Ikhwan—Sunni

Despite their proliferation, the secular nationalist and leftist groups have become mostly ineffective during the last decade. The monarchy's extensive policy of offering financial rewards to its expatriate opponents has succeeded to a large extent. More complex, however, is the problem of winning over the growing Islamist opposition. In the Shiite case, the Saudi policy of cooptation appears to be half-hearted. The magnitude of internal and external Shiite opposition to the regime will depend on the institution of reformist policies and the ultimate outcome of the Iranian-Saudi confrontation. The domestic excesses of Khomeini's regime and its inability to defeat Iraq decisively have considerably reduced the influence of the Iranian Revolution on Saudi Shiites. Yet the recent reforms instituted in the East may not be enough to dampen significantly the Shiite opposition since Wahhabism and Shiism seem to be ultimately irreconcilable. On the Shiite side there has been a fear of assimilation into the Sunni majority, and a reluctance to take advantage of governmental loans, subsidies, and educational programs.

In sharp contrast are the kingdom's more sustained attempts to coopt Sunni opponents living in Saudi Arabia and abroad. It is virtually impossible to assess the effectiveness of this policy. The Sunni Islamist groups, within and outside the kingdom, maintain close ties with fundamentalist societies in the Arab world, particularly the Muslim Brotherhood of Egypt and its Kuwaiti, Maghrebine, and Gulf affiliates. Indeed, King Fahd is faced with powerful pressures from Sunni Islamist groups. Since the Grand Mosque seizure, widespread manifestations of religious resurgence have appeared, particularly among university students and faculty. These new fundamentalists have organized themselves into *Jamaat al-Dawah* (Societies of Propagation) which, despite their puritanical fervor, have not displayed as yet revolutionary tendencies. It is relatively easy to identify these individuals and groups by their appearance:

1. Full beard with thin or no mustache.
2. Very short haircut—three millimeters.
3. A short white robe *(thawb* or *gallabiyya),* over underwear, covering from the navel to knees. The *thawb* does not cover the feet since long dress denotes affluence or false pride.
4. A *taqiyyah* (cap) and cloth over the head *(ghutrah)* instead of the usual Arabian *iqal* which is considered *bidah* (innovation).
5. A watch and chain and no *tasbih* (rosary) in hand.

Manifestations of puritanical garb and demeanor are particularly evident in the scientific faculties of the University of Mineral and Petroleum Resources, King Faisal University Faculty of Medicine, and King Saud University in Riyadh. Nor is campus fundamentalism limited to external appearances. The new wave of Islamist thinking may be summarized as follows: "We cannot strengthen ourselves under these weak regimes by simply reading the Quran and history, but by studying science, to use Western technology against the West."[23]

This explains the new interest among the youth to master science and technology. Concomitantly, fundamentalist students have shown increasing opposition to studying in American and European universities since they believe that this policy is prompted by the government's desire to dilute their Islamic spirit. Islamic revivalism is also rampant among Saudi students in the United States, who are under strong peer pressure to excel.

The striking feature of Juhayman's *dawah* was its total rejection of Saudi dynastic rule, along with the Wahhabi ideology and its bureaucratic purveyors. Two centuries after Ibn Abd al-Wahhab, his descendants of the Al Shaykh family have become the monarchy's official apologists, which the Ikhwan and other fundamentalists oppose with vehemence. In view of the radicalism of Ikhwan's challenge, the monarchy was constrained to prove that it was more fundamentalist than its detractors. Thus, the government's new quest for fundamentalism, coupled with its restrictive policies, have intensified social constraints placed over average citizens. On the positive side, the kingdom has instituted reformist policies designed to placate its internal opponents. A month after the Grand Mosque seizure, Prince Fahd promised to issue a "basic law" which would include a consultative assembly *(majlis al-shura)* and modalities *(asalib)* of governance. However, the constitutional committee created in March 1980 under Prince Nayif has yet to produce the promised document.[24] Simultaneously, the kingdom has redoubled its efforts to win over domestic and expatriate opponents with generous promises of jobs and financial rewards.[25] However, these policies are bound to have limited success since they fail to address the root causes of alienation and unrest. Unless the monarchy adopts a program of comprehensive reform, its attempts to promote domestic tranquility are likely to prove abortive.

The growth of indigenous grass-roots Islamism has rendered King Fahd's tasks formidable. His difficulties are multiplied by declining oil income, along with a possible lessening of Saudi prestige and influence. In assuming the mantle after Khalid's death in the inauspicious circumstances created by the Lebanese War, Fahd has come under criticism for his perceived pro-Western orientation. The King has adopted a low profile in foreign policy, while attempting to safeguard his reputation as a good Muslim by imposing strict observance of Islamic laws. In a dramatic move on June 15, 1983, the King called upon Islamic scholars to hold an international conference to modernize Islamic law through rigorous *ijtihad*.[26] It is too early to evaluate the response of the Saudi public to the King's initiative. However, despite its problems, the Saudi polity has shown uncommon flexibility in adapting to new conditions in its quest for internal stability.

10 Islamic Fundamentalism in the Gulf

A UNIQUE SOCIOPOLITICAL ENVIRONMENT surrounds Islamic fundamentalism in the Arab Gulf states. Several characteristics define this milieu:

1. Dynastic rule by Sunni families, except in Oman, over a population which includes significant Shiite concentrations.
2. Political and economic dominance of native Arabs over nonindigenous populations.
3. Substantial Western economic and cultural penetration of the region in the context of rapid modernization.
4. Conspicuous opulence in the midst of class cleavages.
5. Great power rivalries and pressures from powerful neighboring states—Iran, Iraq, Saudi Arabia, Pakistan, Syria, Israel, and Jordan.

The foregoing factors, peculiar to the Gulf, have produced a relatively nonmilitant fundamentalism in contrast to the revolutionary nature of Islamist manifestations in Iran and Saudi Arabia. A number of similarities are discernible in the Islamic ethos of the Gulf states. All five dynasties rule on the basis of Islamic legitimacy and tribal consensus. Yet, none has been able or willing to impose strict Islamic constraints on their relatively open and polyglot societies. Nonetheless, conspicuous riches and profligacy have contributed to the rise of fundamentalism both in its Sunni and Shiite forms. Sunni fundamentalism can be found among middle, upper-middle, and tribal Arabs who resent

149

dynastic power and wealth. A more pronounced resurgence is detectable among non-indigenous Arab and non-Arab Sunni Muslims— Palestinians, Egyptians, Pakistanis, Yemenis, Syrians, Iraqis, and others, most of whom occupy middle- and lower-middle-class positions. Similarly, Shiite fundamentalism is a middle-, lower-middle class phenomenon observable among Arabs and Arabized Persians and Iranian citizens working in the Gulf states.

Despite its affluence, there has been considerable tension in the Gulf generated by the confluence of internal and external pressures. Great disparities of wealth combined with demographic imbalance and haphazard modernization have created potentially destabilizing conditions in the region. Equally threatening are the pressures from revolutionary Iran, the Iraq-Iran war, the Arab-Israeli conflict, and the ongoing superpower rivalry in the Gulf. In this milieu of complexity and potential crisis, resurgent Islam has emerged as an authentic, enduring, and pervasive force. In essence, it is a populist fundamentalism which poses a challenge to establishment Islam. As in other Arab states, the popular Islam of the Gulf is articulated through several types of fundamentalist societies representing Sufism, Shiism, shades of reformism, and strict puritanism.[1] The Gulf rulers have responded with socioeconomic reforms coupled with strengthening the Islamic establishment.

Kuwait: Islam in a Liberal State

Kuwait is the most liberal, modern, and affluent of the Gulf states. In March 1981, 50,000 Kuwaiti male citizens elected a consultative parliament to function under the ruling Al Sabah family which has been in power for over two centuries. But in reality, the decision-making process is mostly limited to the ruling dynasty and two dozen affluent merchant families. However, this decision-making elite does not constitute a closed group since it remains sensitive to public opinion expressed through the parliament and the press.

Despite the country's rapid modernization, Islam continues to be the main basis of individual and collective identity. Since the decline of Pan-Arabism in the seventies, Kuwait has experienced a significant resurgence of Islam particularly among students. By all indications, the growth of Islamic consciousness of a non-political type has been encouraged by the government. There has been an increase in the use of Islamic themes in the rhetoric of the authorities, and among political, economic, technocratic, and intellectual elites.[2] As elsewhere in the Arab world, there are those who use Islamic terminology because it is fashionable and useful to placate the religious masses.

Yet Kuwait's Islamic role transcends its boundaries. As a relatively liberal state, Kuwait is host to the political expatriates of the Arab world, who are permitted considerable freedom to write and publish. These expatriates range from Arab leftists to liberals and fundamentalists who publish several high-quality journals. Among these are influential Islamist publications which analyze critical issues and engage in *dawah*.[3] The foremost fundamentalist journal is *Al-Mujtama,* the organ of Jamiyyat al-Islah al-Ijtimai—the Society for Social Reform. The ideology and activities of this important association are patterned after the Egyptian Muslim Brotherhood, with which it has close ties. In Kuwaiti terms, the society can be considered sizeable. While it refrains from displaying excessive political activism in the Kuwaiti context, the society pursues an aggressive line toward secular Arab regimes, particularly the Egyptian and Syrian governments. A case in point is the assassination threat made in the pages of *Al-Mujtama* against President Mubarak in the wake of Lieutenant Islambuli's execution.[4] The Journal is also critical of other Arab governments which pursue oppressive policies toward Islamist groups, e.g., Libya, Tunisia, Algeria, and Morocco. In contrast, the journal usually refrains from criticizing Iraq, Jordan, Saudi Arabia, and the Gulf states except Oman, which it considers an American client. The society's membership consists of upper- and upper-middle-class bureaucrats, intellectuals, professionals, and students recruited from indigenous Kuwaitis and non-native residents. The composition of its leadership reflects the truly transnational character of this organization; it includes Moroccans, Egyptians, Palestinians, Syrians, Sudanese, and Jordanians—all of whom are accorded a relatively safe haven for their Islamist activities within certain prescribed limits. There is no question that the society enjoys the sympathy and protection of several prominent figures in the regime and the ruling family. Nonetheless, its activities are watched by the authorities, lest they compromise Kuwait's carefully tuned balance in foreign policy. Indeed, the government has chosen to confiscate certain issues of *Al-Mujtama* which were considered injurious to Kuwait's relations with certain Arab states. Within Kuwait, the society actively promotes Islamic culture and education through lectures and sponsorship of Quranic classes held in dozens of locations.⁵ Also, the society presides over a network of branches throughout the Gulf states.

In contrast to its Sunni counterpart, Shiite fundamentalism is the protest movement of Kuwait's large but less privileged Twelver minority (24 percent). While its membership includes both Arabs and Persians, the latter are more apt to participate in demonstrations and display enthusiasm toward Iranian propaganda. The most important organizational and intellectual expression of Kuwaiti Shiites is the Dar al-Tawhid. This group has been active in publishing and propaganda which are somewhat favorable to the Iranian Islamic regime. At the present time, Kuwait is caught between conflicting pressures from Iraq and Iran. While supporting Iraq as an Arab state, Kuwait has tried, with limited success, not to alienate the Iranians. In view of Kuwait's financial aid to Iraq, Iran has assumed an increasingly threatening posture. The truck bombings of the American and French embassies and other targets on December 12, 1983 may have been manifestations of Iranian displeasure carried out with the help of Shiite militants residing in Kuwait. Iran has disclaimed any responsibility for the attacks, although Hizb al-Dawah members have been arrested.⁶

Since the bombings of December 1983, Kuwaiti society has begun to experience significant strains in political life. New measures have been instituted to maintain internal security against potential terrorists. Beyond possible threats from the Shiites and Iran, the government has shown increasing concern about the growth of Sunni Islamist activism and the polarization between the latter and secular nationalist elements. In all likelihood, the regime will strive to support the secular nationalist groups as a counterweight to the Islamist activists.

Bahrain: Shiite Majority in Ferment

Bahrain has been a focal point of the Shiite resurgence in the Gulf states both before and after the Iranian Revolution, as a direct consequence of the Shiite demographic and socioeconomic status on the island. The Shiites constitute a majority with respect to the politically dominant Sunnis. Both the ruling family of Shaykh Isa Al Khalifah and most of the political elite belong to the Sunni persuasion. The alienation of the Shiite community is further reinforced by the Persian origin of some of its members. Thus, there has always been a marked pro-Iranian sentiment among Bahraini Shiites. In addition, Iran's long-standing claims to the island have intensified the Sunni-Shiite cleavage. Against this background, Shiite fundamentalism emerged as a strong protest movement in the wake of the Iranian Revolution.

In contrast to the Shah's efforts to annex Bahrain, the Khomeini regime has attempted to revolutionize the Shiite majority to undermine the Al Khalifah family. The main vehicle of Shiite militancy was the Jabhat al-Islamiyyah lil-Tahrir al-Bahrain—the Islamic Front for the Liberation of Bahrain (see Appendix I). One of its leaders was Hujjat al-Islam Hadi al-Mudarrisi who had been exiled in 1979 for claiming to be Khomeini's representative *(wakil)* in Bahrain. This Iranian cleric was also associated with the Munazzamat al-Amal al-Islami which opposes the Iraqi Baath. Since his exile from Bahrain, Mudarrisi has been actively engaged in radicalizing the Shiites with his "incendiary broadcasts" from Iran. According to the Bahraini government Mudarrisi was also the organizer of the abortive coup of December 1981.[7]

On December 16, 1981, Bahrain and Saudi Arabia announced the arrest of sixty-five Shiite conspirators who reportedly were trained by Mudarrisi in Iran. The conspiracy caused serious concern in Saudi Arabia and Bahrain, prompting the conclusion of a joint security pact on December 20, 1981. The depth of Saudi apprehension was indicated by Interior Minister Prince Nayif's accusation that "The Iranians have become the terrorists of the Gulf."[8] The Prince offered Saudi security assistance to all Arab Gulf states against Iran's "aggressive intentions."[9]

It was significant that none of the accused were executed, although the three ringleaders received life sentences. The relative leniency of the government reflected its commitment to a policy of accommodation toward the Shiite community. In recent years, the authorities have attempted to give the Shiites a larger role in government and business. In contrast to the Shiites, the Islamist fervor of the Sunnis lacks militancy. The entrepreneurial milieu of banking and business has militated against the emergence of an activist Sunni Islamist movement.

Qatar, Oman, and the United Arab Emirates

Militant Islamic movements do not play a major role in the politics of the Lower Gulf. This is not to suggest that Islam is unimportant to the region's politics and society. However, possibly due to the extensive non-indigenous presence and entrepreneurial imperatives, Islam has assumed a generally non-militant posture.

The Qatari state is ruled by the Al Thani family which officially adheres to Wahhabism. In practice, Qatari Wahhabism lacks the rigor of its counterpart in Saudi Arabia. It has been diluted by the affluent "oil culture" and the commercial predisposition of the population. In recent years, however, anti-establishment fundamentalist trends have appeared among both the tribal and educated Qataris. These trends have been reinforced by expatriate members of the Egyptian Muslim Brotherhood who occupy important advisory and educational positions. Yet there is no evidence that fundamentalism constitutes an organized opposition to the dynasty. More pronounced is the Islamist fervor of the Shiite minority which constitutes about 16 percent of the total population. The Persian origin of most Qatari Shiites has heightened their vulnerability to Iranian Islamic propaganda. However, in contrast to Bahrain, there has been little evidence of Shiite militancy.

As the home of Ibadi Islam, Oman stands alone in the Islamic world. Ibadism evolved from the Kharijites who killed the fourth Caliph Ali and contested the right of the Prophet's Qurashi descendants to lead the Islamic community. Instead, the Khawarij reaffirmed the original tribal practice of selecting the caliph by Muslim notables, subject to the expression of obedience by the people.[10] Since the mid-1700s, the Ibadis have been ruled by the Al Bu Said dynasty. During the mid-1800s, Oman came under increasing British imperial influence which has continued, in diluted form, to this day. Under Said ibn Taymur (1932–70), Oman was isolated from the outside world, as the xenophobic sultan ruled through British, Indian, and Baluchi agents and mercenaries to the exclusion of Ibadi Arabs.[11] The sultan's heavy-handed rule led to several uprisings, the most serious being the Dhufar rebellion in the mid-1960s. In response, the British replaced Sultan Said by his son Qabus, who proceeded to crush the rebellion with Iranian and Jordanian troops.

The ruling Ibadis constitute the majority element in Oman. The large Sunni minority is concentrated in the poorer Dhufar region and in the Wahhabi tribes of the interior. The sultan's reformist policies seem to have reduced Dhufari antagonism, although any Soviet-sponsored initiative from South Yemen could well trigger another Sunni rebellion. The small Shiite community does not pose a challenge. However, the sultan faces opposition from his own Ibadi sect, mostly centered in the tribes of the Jabal al-Akhdar mountainous region. This opposition goes back to the revolt of the 1950s under Imam Ghalib who was the leader of the Jabal al-Akhar tribes, based in the traditional center of the Ibadi sect at Nazwa. Since his defeat Imam Ghalib has lived in Saubi Arabia.

Should these opposition elements converge with external Sunni, Shiite, and Marxist dissidents, they could pose a threat to Qabus. The sultan's absolutism, tenuous support for the Palestine cause, closeness to Britain, and growing ties to the United States have made him the focus of intense criticism by Arab nationalists and fundamentalists. The resulting isolation of Oman from the Arab orbit has prompted the sultan to seek an ongoing accommodation with his neighbors in the newly-established Gulf Cooperation Council.

The United Arab Emirates is a mosaic of seven shaykhdoms that came together in a federation in 1971. This ingathering of large and small emirates under British auspices was an attempt to resolve diverse dynastic, tribal, and economic conflicts which had been intractable for centuries. The federal experiment has had mixed success due to the reluctance of the various rulers to sacrifice their individual prerogatives for the common good. These dynastic rivalries are further exacerbated by disparities in wealth, boundary and tribal disputes, and pressures from outside powers, especially Iran, Iraq, Saudi Arabia, and Oman.[12] Moreover, persistent antagonism has existed between the two largest units of the Federation—Abu Dhabi and Dubai—which have pursued often conflicting foreign policies. Within the foregoing political parameters, U. A. E.'s demographic makeup constitutes a salient issue from the fundamentalist point of view. All seven emirates have been affected by the immigration of substantial non-indigenous communities—Arabs, Westerners, Indians, Pakistanis, Iranians, and other South-Asian peoples. The attraction of oil wealth, combined with the compulsion for economic development, has created a major population imbalance—a factor which has contributed to the rise of Islamist opposition.[13] All seven ruling families of the U. A. E. are Sunni, as is most of the native Arab population. In view of the minority status of indigenous Arabs in the Federation, and their monopoly of power and economic resources, considerable tension has developed between the latter and the non-indigenous majority. However, the diversity of the nonnative groups and their need for jobs have rendered these frictions manageable. Within this context, three main sources of fundamentalism can be identified, none of which pose an immediate threat to the Federation and its ruling families. The most important locus of fundamentalism is the Persian Shiite community representing about 30 percent of the population, two-thirds of which are U. A. E. citizens. Most Shiites are concentrated in Dubai where some are prominent in business, banking, and politics. Originally invited by Shaykh Maktum to serve his business interests, these Shiites have sometimes exhibited pro-Iranian sympathies both under the monarchy and the Islamic Republic. While usually quiescent, the Shiites are regarded as a potential Iranian "fifth column" by the federal authorities. Significantly, Shaykh Maktum of Dubai has been careful to cultivate friendly relations with both the Pahlavi and Khomeini regimes to appease local Shiites, and as a counterweight to the other emirates led by Abu Dhabi. Another source of Islamism is the expatriate community of Pakistani and Indian Sunnis and Shiites, who do not constitute a major political threat. Somewhat more important is the resurgence among native students and tribal elements of the smaller and poorer emirates like Ajman and Ras al-Khaymah. This constituency is likely to generate some opposition to the rulers, in alliance with the non-indigenous Arab fundamentalists. However, the financial rewards of working within the system usually outweight the resort to Islamist activism. In order to placate these elements, the U. A. E. ruling elite is careful to adhere to Islamic practices, although with substantial flexibility and accommodation.

The Iranian Revolution has had an important and diverse influence on the U.A.E. While the ruling shaykhs have been concerned with the military and ideological threat of revolutionary Iran, they have also managed to distance themselves from the Iran-Iraq war. Shaykh Zayid has made several attempts to end the war through mediation efforts. Moreover, the Emirates have maintained substantial commercial ties with the Islamic Republic despite the Western embargo during the hostage crisis. In June 1982, the U. A. E. declared its neutrality in the Iran-Iraq war which was welcomed by Ayatullah Khomeini.[14]

On the internal front, middle-class nationalist and fundamentalist natives have been encouraged by the success of the Iranian Revolution to press for a more centralized federal union, limits on foreign immigration, genuine political participation, and a fairer distribution of wealth.[15] The continued rivalry between the ruling shaykhs has precluded any serious attempt to implement the far-reaching reforms necessary to build a more viable and united federal state.

Prospects for Fundamentalism in the Gulf

Despite its generally non-militant nature, the resurgence of popular Islam may well become a major source of instability in the Gulf. The various manifestations of this resurgence reflect the dissatisfaction of different social, economic, and ethno-sectarian groups with the existing political and economic order. Thus, the Islamism of indigenous middle class and tribal Sunnis represents their quest for political participation and a more equitable sharing of wealth held by the rulers and the upper classes. Moreover, nativist fundamentalism provides a medium of protest against the rulers' policies of large-scale importation of foreigners, which is regarded as a threat to the socio-cultural integrity of Gulf societies. In contrast, the fundamentalism of the expatriate workers is a protest movement against both the rulers and their native Sunni subjects. Finally, Shiite resurgence reflects the politically underprivileged status of the Twelver minority.

Consequently, the Islamist movement of the Gulf does not represent a homogeneous phenomenon. It is internally divided and its various segments vie for power and influence. Some of the extremist Sunni groups have ostracized the Shiites for their religious beliefs and uncertain loyalties. For their part, the Shiites have reaffirmed their allegiance to the authorities while continuing to cling tenaciously to their sectarian ideology. It is to the credit of the Gulf rulers that the Shiite communities have been spared extensive persecution. Such a policy would force the Gulf Shiites into desperation and even rebellion, possibly with Iranian support.

Part III Islamic Fundamentalism

Consequences and Prospects

11 Prognostic Factors in Crisis Environments

$\overline{A}$NY ATTEMPT TO PROGNOSTICATE in the Arab context can be foolhardy, in view of the plethora of variables and the high probability of accidents and unforeseen events. The most relevant parameter of prognosis is that of profound and pervasive social crisis—one that is at once a crisis of identity, legitimacy, rulership, culture, economic development, and military credibility. External challenges from the West, Israel, and the U. S. S. R., no less than internal ferment caused by maldistribution of wealth, social injustice, misrule and improbity, have combined to set the stage for an era of intense political instability. Within this crisis milieu the potential role of political Islam and Islamist groups needs to be analyzed. Figure 6 outlines the perceived causal relationships and the framework of the prognostic environment within which the Arab world is likely to evolve.

The six components of the Arab crisis environment, as identified at the outset of this study, can be expected to persist in the foreseeable future. Indeed, one might state with some certainty that these crisis catalysts which seem to have triggered fundamentalist responses are not likely soon to disappear from the scene. Under these inauspicious circumstances, three determinants are considered salient in shaping the ongoing confrontation between Islamic militancy and constituted authority: (1) elite behavior, (2) external stimuli, and (3) Islamist initiatives.

It should be noted that the causal effect of the foregoing determinants will be conditioned by their mutual interaction in the crisis environment. In other words, the performance of elites will be affected by

Figure 6
Prognostic Environment

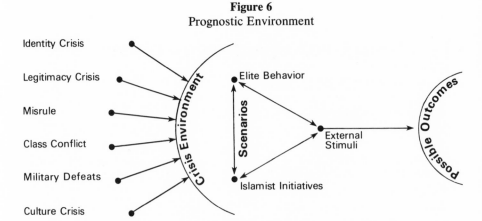

their crisis milieu, as well as the types of external stimuli and internal opposition that they are likely to face. Thus, the quality of political leadership becomes central to the identification of possible outcomes in regime stability or instability.

Elite Policies

The potential effectiveness of the policies of Arab ruling elites toward fundamentalist groups and movements can be seriously questioned. While there exists some variation between regimes, the overall effectiveness of state policies cannot be considered high in long-range terms. In point of fact, this unsalutary leadership role transcends the fundamentalist groups to cover the whole range of elite performance. To stem the fundamentalist tide and reduce the level of social tension, Arab elites need to pursue three interrelated policies—comprehensive reform, systematic socialization, and moderation in the use of state power against opponents. The history of the region suggests that the prospects for major reform are only moderately encouraging, since this requires elite self-discipline and dedication combined with energy and vision. Effective cooptation of Islamic militants requires that ruling elites set an example of fairness and incorruptibility, while pursuing effective socialization through an alternative ideology. The tragedy of the Arabs is that even with the best of intentions among leaders, there has not been a viable ideology since the demise of Nasserist Pan-Arabism. Many Arab leaders are not sufficiently conscious or concerned with the existing ideological vacuum and the imperatives of political socialization. Only Libya's Qadhafi has achieved a modicum of success in this endeavor. While Saudi, Syrian, and Iraqi leaders have recognized the ideological imperative, they are faced with serious incongruities between their respective ideologies, policies, and sociodemographic settings. President Mubarak's efforts to reindoctrinate Islamic militants in prison appear to have had limited success, in view of his non-ideological posture, failure to institute far-reaching reforms, and general inability to distance himself from Sadat's legacy.[1] Nor does the government possess the means to reverse Egypt's economic decline in the face of a growing population. It would appear that a possible course of action for President Mubarak is to effect a careful Islamic-Nasserist synthesis to revive the nationalist sentiment as a counter to fundamentalism. This type of policy may be the only alternative to the prospect of a rising Islamist threat. Simultaneously, Mubarak will need to extract major concessions from a future Israeli government regarding a Palestinian entity. The Egyptian dilemma is uniquely acute; yet its general contours are detectable in most Arab countries. A summary of the Arab states' reformist, ideological, and cooptative policies toward fundamentalism is presented below.

The summary assessment in Table 7 covers four interrelated dimensions of regime performance and capability. These are defined as follows:

1. *Reformist Zeal:* The degree of the leadership's commitment to effect genuine and comprehensive reforms in the political, social, and economic spheres.

2. *Ideological Potential:* The extent to which political elites are able to develop a viable and internally consistent ideological framework which can be utilized in the process of socialization to strengthen the legitimacy of elites and institutions.

3. *Cooptative Capacity:* The aggregate capabilities of elites and the larger political system to increase citizen participation and support through systematic socialization, commitment to reform, and economic incentives.

4. *Islamist Potential:* The current status of fundamentalist organizational militancy in each Arab country and level of its threat potential to the constituted authorities.

Table 7
Regime Performance and Capability

	Reformist Zeal	Ideological Potential	Cooptative Capacity	Islamist Potential
Egypt	medium	low	low	medium/high
Syria	medium	medium	low/medium	medium/high
Iraq	medium	low/medium	low/medium	medium/high
Jordan	medium	medium	medium	low/medium
Saudi Arabia	medium	medium	medium	medium/high
Kuwait	medium/high	medium	medium/high	medium
Libya	medium/high	high	high	low
Algeria	medium/high	medium	medium	low/medium
Tunisia	low/medium	low/medium	low/medium	medium
Morocco	low/medium	low	low/medium	medium
Sudan	low	low	low	medium/high

It would seem that regimes with low and medium/low levels of reformist commitment and ideological potential are likely to register modest levels of cooptative capability. In these situations, Islamic activism is expected to be high, thereby evoking coercive responses from the authorities. At the point when the latter become incapable of marshalling sufficient coercive means to contain the fundamentalist threat, a regime overthrow may be the likely outcome. Intervening variables, such as wealth, may change the outcomes in such countries as Saudi Arabia and the Gulf states. Furthermore, a government may increase its coercive capabilities by basing itself on mobilized sectarian minorities and/or large-scale foreign support. Such a strategy could safeguard the regime in the short-range, despite its low levels of reformist, ideological, and cooptative capabilities.

External Stimuli

To a significant degree, the evolution of Islamic fundamentalism is shaped by external factors. A perceptible increase in Islamic militancy in Egypt can be expected to have major repercussions throughout the Arab world. More serious would be an Islamist takeover in one of the larger Arab states. Indeed, the "Khomeini factor" may have been virtually irrepressible had the revolution been led by a Sunni charismatic

in a major Arab country. Except for its continuing potency in Iraq and
the Gulf area, the Iranian Revolution seems to have lost some of its
original appeal among Sunni Arab fundamentalists. Yet, the Ayatullah
continues to evoke admiration from Muslims in Egypt, Algeria, Syria,
Jordan, Tunisia, Lebanon, and Libya. The Iranian revolutionary experience is seen as a successful model to emulate. Also, close ties exist
between the Iranians and some Arab fundamentalist groups.
Nonetheless, it would seem that Iran's influence in the Arab sphere
will remain limited so long as the Iraq-Iran war is in stalemate and
Iran's domestic front remains chaotic. Moreover, Khomeini's appeal
has been limited by his support of the Syrian Baathi regime and his
inability to dilute sufficiently the Shiite character of the Islamic Revolution.

Another powerful external stimulus is the Arab-Israeli conflict.
Arab military impotence toward Israel has been a powerful weapon in
the Islamists' propaganda arsenal to attack virtually *all* Arab leaders.
On this issue, the depth and breath of vehement Islamist criticism is
shared by nearly all segments of Arab society. In this context, the
American "connection" to Israel and key Arab states has had a de-
bilitating impact on the eroding legitimacy and credibility of Arab
elites. The U.S. military relationship with Egypt, Jordan, and Saudi
Arabia is seen by the Islamists as the imposition of permanent military
inferiority on the Arabs against Israel, coupled with unwelcome U. S.
economic and cultural influences. The progressive deterioration of the
Arab position with respect to Israel, combined with the American failure to achieve a mutually acceptable Arab-Israeli settlement, are likely
to contain the future seeds of Islamist and nationalist rebellion against
pro-American Arab elites.[2] Other possible external stimuli include a
general Arab-Israeli war or a Soviet-instigated revolt.

Modes of Fundamentalist Initiative

The evolution of the Islamic fundamentalist movement will also depend on the quality of its political and intellectual leadership. At this
juncture, the movement is seriously lacking in ideological, political,
and tactical guidance. The leading activists of the various militant Islamist groups have been killed, including Siriyya, Mustafa, Juhayman,

Musa Sadr, Faraj, Baqir al-Sadr, and Marwan Hadid among others, and some are in jail. It may be several years before new leaders emerge, although there may well be any number of charismatic aspirants in the newly formed underground societies. The leadership of the Brotherhood in Egypt and other Arab states is old and tired after years of imprisonment and persecution. But its cadres are intact and their political experience unparalleled among the Islamist organizations. A younger activist successor to Umar Tilmisani could revitalize this large organization and transform it into a credible threat to the regime. For the present, the Brotherhood remains in an anomalous situation of desiring to participate legally in politics as an opposition group, while maintaining its Islamist outlook. On the whole, however, the Brethren have been cautious not to be drawn into a premature confrontation with any Arab state. In fact, it appears that the Brotherhood and its large affiliates in the Arab world are determined to prepare for the future, instead of making ill-timed attempts to seek power and risk repression as in Syria. There has been a clear tendency among the larger fundamentalist societies to Islamize the political order through policies of peaceful gradualism, a method of Islamist action that can be seen in the efforts of Turabi in the Sudan and Tilmisani in Egypt. Yet it is highly possible that any violent action by the smaller militant groups would trigger large-scale repression which may include gradualist Islamists like the Brotherhood, thereby aborting the opportunities for peaceful Islamization. Also, the pattern in Egypt and Saudi Arabia may repeat itself, whereby violent but limited anti-regime acts by young militants may preempt the onset of a wider fundamentalist revolt. The ultimate challenges facing the Brotherhood and other Islamist groups center on three tasks:

1. *To develop a broad and flexible Islamic ideological program which possesses the widest possible appeal to major segments of the population.*

Such a program would be a prelude to organizing a "national front" with non-fundamentalist groups which oppose the government. This approach bears some resemblance to the Iranian clerical role in the broad coalition which overthrew the Shah. The Syrian Brotherhood and the Iraqi Hizb al-Dawah have already moved in this direction. Similar moves are discernible in Egypt, although the smaller Islamist groups and the Brotherhood's own militants may not be prone to compromise their ideological purity. Moreover, it is doubtful whether the Islamist movements themselves can agree on a single profession of faith, except those under the Brotherhood's direct influence.

2. *To develop strong transnational links between Islamist groups,*
both within and outside the Arab world.

There is every reason to believe that the level of Islamic transnational cooperation has greatly increased in the last decade. Once again,
the Egyptian Brethren are a key factor. As the oldest fundamentalist
organization in the Arab and Islamic spheres, the Brethren have had a
half-century to propagate their ideology in every Arab country and
beyond. Exiled Brethren living in various countries have become missionaries around whom natives and exiles gather to pursue Islamist
objectives. This process of proselytization, which began after the
Brotherhood's suppression by Nasser, has produced significant results.
As shown in Appendix I, many of the Islamist groups in the Gulf,
Jordan, Saudi Arabia, Syria, the West Bank, Lebanon, the Sudan, and
the Maghrib, share the Brotherhood's mainline fundamentalism and its
sociopolitical objectives. Some of these groups are the extensions of
the Brotherhood, although the latter is not known to maintain a "supreme command" in Cairo. However, the various Brotherhoods maintain close ties with each other, which are at once spiritual, political, and
financial in nature. The Brethren also maintain relations with Islamist
groups throughout the world, including some Shiite organizations and
the Iranian clergy. The Brotherhood's networks have already played
important political roles in inter-Arab affairs, including the isolation of
the Egyptian and Syrian regimes, the reduction of some Gulf economic
aid to Syria, and support for Arafat against Asad. More than any other
factor or organization, the Brotherhood and its affiliates have contributed to Islamic reawakening at the mass level throughout the Arab world.
Through patient propaganda over the last thirty years in the midst of
deepening crisis, the Brotherhood has created a massive constituency
of politically conscious Muslims.

3. *To develop capable leadership cadres.*

It appears that the Brotherhood lacks, even in its Egyptian epicenter, a closely knit revolutionary "vanguard" that can emulate the
Leninist or the Khomeinist models of revolutionary organization. It
also lacks charismatic leadership. Nonetheless, the Brotherhood does
possess an organization and an unambiguous ideology—a combination
that some governments cannot match. In certain types of crisis environments, these capabilities may prove sufficient to assume power in
one or more Arab countries, or at least to create enough instability to
topple pro-Western regimes. Assuming that the catalysts of crisis are
already present, the question remains one of identifying the possible
"triggers" that could set the revolutionary dynamic into motion.

Scenarios of Conflict

The emergence of future fundamentalist militancy will depend on a variety of internal and external developments and events, only some of which may be identified on a tentative basis. Among scenarios of possible developments which are likely to trigger immediate or long-range fundamentalist responses, four are considered important in terms of their regional and international repercussions:

The Iraq-Iran War

The ultimate outcome of the war between Iraq and Iran can be expected to have a substantial impact on the evolution of militant Islam in the Arab world. A decisive Iranian victory could bring changes in the Baathi order in Baghdad which may be transformed into a pro-Iranian regime of Shiite coloration. Such an outcome would significantly increase the pressure for revolutionary change in Saudi Arabia and the Gulf states. Nor will the Baath regime of Syria become immune to Iranian Islamist pressures, despite its record of friendly relations with Iran. Moreover, an Iranian victory is bound to radicalize the Shiite communities of Lebanon and the Gulf states. Finally, the ascendance of Iranian fundamentalism is likely to serve as a spur to both militant and gradualist Sunni Islamists to emulate the Iranian revolutionary example. Indeed, an Iranian victory would cast the halo of divine provenance upon the Islamic Revolution and immeasurably strengthen its chilliastic élan of transnational militancy in the Arab world.

Arab Defeat by Israel

A period of protracted Arab-Israeli armed confrontation is likely to shift the focus of Islamic militancy from the Arab governments to Israel. Both militant and passive fundamentalist individuals and movements are irrevocably opposed to Israel and the ideology that sustains its existence. In view of this uncompromising stance, the Islamist groups would welcome any opportunity to fight Israel, although they are convinced that the Arab regimes, including Syria's, are unwilling to challenge the Jewish state. Thus, they consider most Arab elites as "foreign agents" who have imposed upon their people a status of permanent military inferiority with respect to Israel. Against this perceptual background, any Israeli victory over one or more Arab regimes is bound to trigger widespread opposition to the U.S. and pro-American Arab governments. In view of the prevailing configuration of forces in Arab society, opposition elements are likely to unite under the Islamist banner in a broad coalition against those in power.

U. S. Military and Political Initiatives

Arab feelings of anti-Americanism have increased significantly in recent years. During the last decade, the Arab popular mind has come to associate the U.S. with every evil that has befallen the area, from military defeats to economic misfortune. Against this perceptual backdrop, U. S. military intervention will be unwelcome, with the singular exception of countering an outright Soviet attack—an unlikely possibility from the Arab perspective. The more likely scenario is U. S. military action possibly to save a faltering regime. Such an initiative may well generate a ripple effect evoking mass fundamentalist militancy. Even if successful, the American effort is likely to destroy the ruling elite's tenuous bases of legitimacy. Another likely catalyst to trigger militant Islamist reactions may be a major U. S. policy initiative in favor of Israel, the most obvious example being a decision to transfer the U. S. Embassy to Jerusalem.

Instability in Egypt

Several objective criteria make Egypt the *key* state in the Arab world and the Middle East. There can be no strategic substitute for Egypt in terms of its geopolitical location, homogeneous popular base, cultural centrality, and military potential. Also, Egypt is the home of the largest Islamist movement in the world—the Muslim Brotherhood and its militant offshoots. Any projection of scenarios of conflict in the Egyptian setting will have to consider at least six variable factors:

1. Magnitude of socioeconomic crisis
2. Elite capabilities

3. The opposition: Islamists and Nasserists
4. Efficacy of coercive and cooptative means
5. The trigger mechanism
6. The public mood

Crisis Milieu and Elite Capabilities (1, 2)

There can be no doubt about the enormity of Egypt's socioeconomic burdens. The quantum growth of its population within a circumscribed habitable area with scarce resources is sufficient to confound the best efforts of any leader, however capable and innovative. On this account, the Egyptian elite's performance has been undistinguished despite President Mubarak's generally salutary but incremental initiatives and personal reputation as an upright individual. Contrary to Western misconceptions, Sadat's policies of economic liberalization *(infitah)* significantly increased the maldistribution of wealth. Meanwhile, heightened popular expectations of economic gain from Sadat's switch to the "American peace option" were dashed. In the face of these challenges, the leadership capabilities of the Egyptian elite may be found wanting. The cooptative capacity of the political system is limited, since it can offer neither strong ideological inspiration nor sufficient economic incentives.

The Islamist-Nasserist Nexus (3)

Two types of Islamic phenomena became manifest during the 1970s as a response to social crisis: (1) the proliferation of both militant and quietist Islamic societies and, (2) the spread of Islamic behavioral practices among large segments of the population. In ideological terms, the Islamist ethos first seemed to displace Nasserism; during the late-1970s, however, Nasserism and Islamism began to converge, producing a peculiar ideological blend centering on anti-regime protest. The first indications of this convergence were seen at the mass level during the dangerous rioting of January 1977. The possible confluence and symbiosis of these two mass constituencies could well represent a potential danger to the ruling elite.

Trigger Mechanism, State Responses, and Public Mood (4, 5, 6)

Despite the presence of crisis factors in Egyptian society, it is impossible to predict when and how these dissatisfactions will lead to open challenges to the regime. Insurrectionary timing depends on accidental or planned triggers, as well as the peculiarities of the public mood. The last factor is difficult to assess because of the natural quietude of the Egyptian national character. In sharp contrast to other Arabs, the Egyptians possess great patience and disinclination toward mass activism. Only in rare instances have they risen en masse—the burning of Cairo (1952), Nasser's resignation (1967), Nasser's funeral (1970), and the food price riots against Sadat (1977). Will they rise up against President Mubarak or will the "pharaonic imperative" of Egyptian history continue to insure the dominance of the state? The possibility of popularly based insurrectionary activity depends on several interrelated factors:

1. The degree to which the Nasserist constituency is alienated from the regime. It is not clear if the Nasserists have given up on Mubarak, considering his reformist policies and partial revival of Nasser's historical legacy.

2. The degree to which Mubarak's relations with the Brotherhood and its Islamist constituency have deteriorated, as a result of pressures against the fundamentalist groups.

3. The extent to which Mubarak and the ruling National Democratic Party will permit institutionalized channels of free expression, particularly in the electoral process.

4. The emergence of a catalyst that could trigger the insurrectionary process. This could come as a provocation committed by the government or by an external agent which flies in the face of the dominant culture and public sensitivities. A list of potentially explosive provocations include:

- Widespread arrests, repression, and torture.
- Major economic policy decisions that negatively affect the lives of many people.
- Large-scale Arab-Israeli fighting, culminating in Arab humiliation.
- Major U. S. military or policy moves in the Arab world including armed intervention.
- Escalation of local fights between the people and police as a consequence of sewer flooding, water shortages, student demonstrations, or official harrassment of religious groups.

Any one of the foregoing could generate public unrest in one or several urban areas, which may well spread throughout Cairo and the country. The Mubarak government seems to be aware of the danger and seeks to avert it by three methods:

1. The maintenance of a low profile by the president and state officials, and reluctance to undertake grand policy initiatives on the domestic and foreign fronts;

2. The resort to extensive security precautions directed at the Islamist societies, while using "soft" rhetoric to placate the masses;

3. The localization of conflict particularly in Cairo, by quickly sealing off areas of unrest, blocking the main bridges, and imposing a communication blackout to prevent coordinated action in different parts of the city.

The aim of the Egyptian security forces is to abort the replication of the explosive conditions of January 1977. The prospect of large-scale and around-the-clock rioting constitutes the essential element of any unfolding revolutionary scenario. The 1977 riots demonstrated the insufficiency of the state security forces to contain massive, twenty-four-hour popular demonstrations and lawlessness; hence, the call to the military to save the regime. The dangers inherent in the use of the professional military to quell domestic unrest have been well documented in the scholarly literature. Such action demonstrates the bankruptcy of civilian authority and reinforces the military's self-view as the supreme embodiment of national virtue and arbiter of last resort. In the Egyptian case, the problem would be complicated by the persistence of Nasserist and Islamist ideological orientations in the officer corps, some members of which oppose the regime and are likely to be sympathetic to their kinsmen rioting in the streets. The Egyptian officer corps, officially depoliticized under Sadat, has lost its ideological bearings. In less than five years it was told to change its ideological polarity from Pan-Arabism to an ill-defined role in the Western security system in the Middle East. The impact of this abrupt reorientation has not been salutary. These ideological ambiguities, coupled with strong Islamist and Nasserist orientations among officers and NCOs, makes the Egyptian military an unreliable instrumentality of internal control. This conclusion is reinforced by the army's well-known reluctance to engage the civilian population, with which it shares close social and kinship ties. In a future contingency, the longer the military's deployment as a police force, the greater the probability of a military coup against the government. In emulation of the Nasserist model of revolution, a prospective coup d'état may bring together nationalist and Islamist middle-ranking officers, who could receive support from the Nasserist left and the Islamist groups led by the Brotherhood. Other variants of coup-making scenarios could include an army takeover to prevent chaos or a military coup organized mainly by Islamist officers. The establishment of a fundamentalist revolutionary regime in Egypt would constitute an achievement of the first magnitude for the Islamist transnational confraternity. Once the proud "nucleus state" of Nasser's Pan-Arab movement, Egypt would become the epicenter of Arab Pan-Islamic fundamentalism, with incalculable consequences for the Middle East, the West, and the Soviet Union.

Islamic Fundamentalism and U. S. Interests

The emergence of Islamic fundamentalism as a pervasive transnational phenomenon has confronted the U. S. and its Western allies with serious challenges. American responses to fundamentalism, particularly in the Arab sphere, have not been informed by a clear understanding of the Islamic ethos as a prerequisite to the judicious formulation and application of policy. The price of ineptitude can be disastrous to American strategic and economic interests, as in Iran and Lebanon.

In the fundamentalist view, there have been certain constants in American foreign policy which place the U. S. on a collision course with the Islamist movement. These policy constants have included:

1. Support for secularly oriented Arab regimes because of their pro-American orientation.
2. Virtually unconditional support for Israel, thereby perpetuating Arab military inferiority which is reinforced by the American military presence in several Arab countries.
3. Pursuance of economic policies which promote maldistribution of income in Arab countries.
4. The spread of American-Western values and cultural lifeways considered alien to Islam.

There is no likelihood that the foregoing Islamist convictions will undergo significant modification in the foreseeable future. Thus, the logic of the situation would suggest the persistence of protracted conflict between U. S. interests and Islamist objectives. Indeed, theoretically there can be no ground for mutual accommodation. However, in the realm of practical politics, it might be possible to discern specific areas of coexistence and even limited cooperation, depending on regional developments and modifications in U. S. policy. Indeed, some restructuring of American policy is likely to reduce the Islamist fervor and prepare the groundwork for possible cooperation with "moderate" fundamentalist or nationalist elements. At present the U. S. is perceived as a major source of external and internal stimuli which have provoked fundamentalist responses. Consequently, two lines of policy need to be pursued as viable responses to fundamentalism to safeguard vital U.S. interests in the Arab-Islamic orbit:

> 1. Peaceful settlement of the Arab-Israeli conflict, which would provide for a Palestinian entity along with an unambiguous Islamic presence at the holy sanctuaries in Jerusalem.
> 2. Explicit American encouragement and support of sociopolitical reforms, particularly in pro-American Arab states, to promote greater socioeconomic justice and to safeguard basic human rights.

Significant progress in these two policy dimensions would immeasurably strengthen the legitimacy of pro-American elites by removing two major provocations that have evoked fundamentalist responses. The consequent amelioration of the crisis milieu is likely to neutralize the more extremist exponents of fundamentalism and provide a propitious environment for reformist elites to emerge.

U. S. Relations with Pro-American Regimes

In view of the great diversity of Arab regimes, it is unfeasible to formulate uniformly applicable guidelines for U. S. policy. However, it is possible to suggest flexible modalities of dealing with pro-American governments which could produce future salutary results. These can be summarized as follows:

1. The U. S. should avoid pressing friendly Arab governments (such as Jordan, Saudi Arabia, Egypt) to participate in politically tenuous and risky peace processes with Israel. Given the Islamist reality, any peace process which does not culminate in the establishment of a Palestinian entity and an Islamic presence in Jerusalem is bound to prove politically dangerous to all Arab ruling elites, particularly those friendly to the U. S.

2. The U. S. does not possess the resources and capabilities to

defend every pro-American Arab regime from Islamist or nationalist opponents in the midst of incipient revolutionary situations. It is practically impossible to reverse a revolutionary process once its inexorable march has begun. Thus, any American preemptive effort would have to be applied well in advance of the revolutionary outburst. In addition to providing intelligence, arms, and organizational know-how to these regimes, there is no substitute for American persuasion to institute political and economic reforms. Ultimately, American assistance can do little for regimes which are unwilling to promote comprehensive social justice. Generous U. S. economic aid to countries like Egypt should not be used to exacerbate class conflicts by increasing the existing maldistribution of wealth.

3. On the basis of past experience, excessive economic, cultural, and military penetration has proven detrimental to long-range U. S. interests. Such policies are particularly dysfunctional in Islamic societies which are acutely sensitive to foreign influences. Highly visible and large diplomatic, technical, and military contingents usually become the targets of popular resentment.

The Islamist Alternative: A Critique

In its ultimate logic Islamic fundamentalism rejects the very concept of the contemporary nation-state and its transplants in the Arab-Islamic setting. The Islamist challenge transcends the Arab states to include the modern nation-state system in its entirety, since fundamentalist Islam does not recognize national boundaries. In the context of the present socio-political crisis, the Islamist alternative has once again become credible with its moral fervor and political militancy. In the short period of five months from October 1983 to February 1984, Islamic fundamentalism had manifested itself in Lebanon, Kuwait, Tunisia, and Morocco in various modalities of political action. In every one of these cases, the Islamist challenge to the state was unambiguous. The question remains—is the Islamist alternative viable?

At least four functional modalities have characterized the emergence of contemporary Islamic resurgence: (1) A spiritual medium of escape from alienation; (2) An ideology of protest against socio-political injustice; (3) An ideology of revolutionary mobilization and;

(4) The ideological foundation of a political community—an Islamic order. In these functional areas, the Islamist alternative appears to possess varying degrees of viability. Clearly, fundamentalism has succeeded in providing a deep sense of spiritual belonging and brotherhood to millions of alienated and disinherited Muslims. Indeed, the spiritual message of Islam has retained its vigor and socioethical relevance to modern life. No less significant has been the role of Islamic fundamentalism as an ideology of protest against arbitrary rule and socioeconomic injustice. In the absence of other institutional and ideological channels of opposition, fundamentalism has provided a religiously sanctioned means for the articulation of popular dissatisfaction.

However, all too frequently, social protest has brought state repression and the escalation of political conflict in many Arab and Islamic countries. At this juncture, protest turns into revolution as mass discontent seeks a medium of revolutionary expression against constituted authority; hence the utility of Islamic fundamentalism as an ideology to mobilize the masses. But does militant Islam constitute an effective medium of revolution in the modern context? The answer would be in the affirmative given the ascendance of Islamic power in Iran. However, the predominantly Sunni context of most Arab states and their individual socio-political peculiarities could militate against the replication of the Iranian Revolution. One salient factor is the absence of a large politicized and radicalized clerical vanguard which possesses substantial religio-political and moral authority. Indeed, the Sunni *ulama* have generally lacked the moral and political influence of their Shiite counterparts; nor do they command the juridical authority to perform *ijtihad*. More notably, the Sunni *ulama* do not possess the corporate cohesion of the Shiite clerics in the context of hierarchical organizational networks. Yet there are indications that the Sunni *ulama* are not immune to radicalization and organization. This has been observed in Syria and to a lesser extent in Egypt, Jordan, and the North African countries. Syrian *ulama* have played a prominent role in the leadership of the Islamist movement. In Egypt, many well-known preachers have been identified with the fundamentalist cause, such as Shaykhs Mahallawi, Hafiz Salamah, Yusuf Badri, Abd al-Hamid Kishk, Adam Salih, and Abdallah al-Samawi.[3] Furthermore, the recent re-traditionalization of society brought about by the revival of Islamic lifeways, combined with increasing unemployment, is bound to produce a growing influx of students pursuing religious studies. The consequent emergence of a large and socially pervasive clerical class like

Iran's is expected to intensify the long-term Islamist challenge to political authority.

Nevertheless, the fundamentalist movement of today is in a fractionalized state in most Arab countries. Differences in ideology and tactics, no less than conflicts between leaders, have often promoted disunity among the Islamist groups. Ideological conflicts have resulted from diverse interpretations of Islam's original message as well as from differences in the social bases of various Islamist groups and leaders.[4] Thus, the fundamentalism of the urban middle class would tend to reflect its predominant interest in shoring up its eroding socioeconomic status; hence, the inclination of the urban middle class to support the mainstream fundamentalism of the Brotherhood and its affiliates. In contrast, the Islamism of the rural lower-middle class and its newly urbanized offshoots is likely to display provincial primitivism, heterodoxy, millenarian mahdism, and revolutionary extremism. The greater revolutionary propensity of this class, relative to the urban middle class, could be the result of its deeper feelings of relative deprivation and more intense social-psychological disorientation experienced in the urbanization process.

These factors of diversity and disunity in the Islamist movement coupled with police harassment have worked against the creation of a revolutionary "vanguard of earnest believers" that Sayyid Qutb had advocated. In the absence of a vanguard organization, the inevitable struggle between the fundamentalist societies and the state is likely to favor the latter, at least in the immediate future. Despite declining levels of legitimacy, most Arab and Islamic states seem capable of marshalling sufficient levels of coercive power and support to prevail against the fundamentalist threat. The state apparatus, reinforced by modern technology, remains ascendent and continues to command the tacit and often the reluctant support of secularists, minorities, and entrepreneurial classes who fear anarchy and the prospects of an Islamist victory.

The foregoing circumstances may abort the staging of an Iranian-style grass-roots Islamist revolution in the Arab sphere. However, the state apparatus may not be invincible, in view of mounting social and economic problems confronting the Arab and Islamic countries brought about by declining oil incomes, drought conditions in North Africa, and unchecked population growth. Given the long-term propensity of crisis conditions, the present resurgence of political Islam is not likely to constitute a temporary phenomenon—a revolutionary catharsis that would be overwhelmed by the state apparatus.[5] Indeed,

Islamic militancy shall persist as long as crisis conditions persist and groups of "earnest believers" are prepared to sacrifice their lives "in the path of God" to establish God's sovereignty on earth. Thus, the Western and Marxist practice of approaching the fundamentalist phenomenon from a socioeconomic perspective can provide at best partial answers. The total faith and absolute commitment of men like Banna, Qutb, Baqir al-Sadr, and Khomeini to the fundamentalist Islamic ideal cannot be explained simply by their class origins. The moral challenge of the Islamists to authority does not spring primarily from the material interests of particular classes or that of humanity itself, but from the absolute certainty that they are the instruments of God's will. Herein resides the moral superiority and politico-spiritual potency of the fundamentalists' claim to power.

No state in the Arab/Islamic orbit, except Iran, can advance a divinely ordained claim to legitimacy. In view of the popular appeal of the Islamists' claim in the present crisis milieu, the state apparatus may not constitute an effective block to fundamentalism. In the face of protracted disorder, a faction of the military could well assume power and proceed to establish an Islamic order with support from fundamentalist organizations. Alternatively, faltering ruling elites may resort to an evolutionary adoption of fundamentalism under pressure from powerful Islamist groups.

Yet an Islamist takeover in an Arab country does not guarantee success in establishing a viable political community. The Iranian case illustrates the multi-faceted problems that need to be solved to transform a revolution into a stable polity. In the Sunni fundamentalist context, doctrinal and policy controversies are likely to present major difficulties in the task of converting political theory into practical politics. The task of bridging the gap between Islamic doctrine and the requirements of contemporary society will require vigorous *ijtihad* by creative jurists and intellectuals. It is not at all certain that future Islamist leaders and theorists will be able to cope with complex economic and developmental problems and secure basic human rights for Muslims and non-Muslims alike. Indeed, like other religious and political ideologies, the Islamic tradition contains the prescriptions for both democracy and totalitarian autocracy. The ultimate shaper of the future Islamic community on earth will be the pious Muslim and his capacity to practice the noblest maxims of his faith in tolerance and humility.

Appendix I Islamist Societies in the Arab World

Name of Organization	Beliefs and Membership	Militancy	Sect	Leadership	Size	Current Status	Outside Ties	Country and Region
1. Faramawiyyah (The Faramawites)	Abstain from medicine and education, only Quran	High/Medium	Sunni	Charismatic?	Small	(New)	Malaysia	Egypt (Upper)
2. Hizb Allah (Party of God)	—	High	Sunni	Yahya Hashim (District Attorney)	Small	Active, underground (New)	Yemen (N.)	Egypt
3. Hizb al-Tahrir (Liberation Party)	—	High	Sunni	Charismatic	Small	Suppressed under Mubarak (New)	Arab countries	Egypt
4. Ikhwan al-Muslimin (Muslim Brotherhood—M. B.)	Middle, Lower-Middle, and Lower	Medium	Sunni	Hasan al-Banna; Tilmisani	Large	Active, public (Old)	Gulf States Syria Jordan Maghrib Europe S. A.	Egypt
5. Jamaat al-Ahram (Pyramid Society)	—	High	Sunni	Charismatic	Small	Underground (New)	—	Egypt
6. Jamaat al-Fath (Society of Conquest)	—	High	Sunni	Charistmatic	Small	Underground, suppressed by Mubarak (New)	—	Egypt
7. Jamaat al-Haq (Society of Truth)	—	High	Sunni	Charismatic	Small	Underground, suppressed by Mubarak (New)	—	Egypt
8. Jamaat al-Harakiyyah (Society of Action)	Opposed to "sinful leaders," not society	High	Sunni	—	Small	Very secretive (New)	Libya	Egypt

Appendix I (*continued*)

Name of Organization	Beliefs and Membership	Militancy	Sect	Leadership	Size	Current Status	Outside Ties	Country and Region
9. Jamaat al-Islamiyyah (The Islamic Society)	Middle, Lower-Middle	Medium	Sunni	Collective	Large	Active (New)	—	Egypt (Cairo)
10. Jamaat al-Islamiyyah (The Islamic Society)	Students	High	Sunni	Collective	Medium	Active, partly suppressed (New)	Saudi (?)	Egypt (Minyah)
11. Jamaat al-Khalifah (Caliph's Group)	—	High	Sunni	Charismatic	Small	Underground (New)	—	Egypt
12. Jamaat al-Munazilah Shuuriyyah (Society of Spiritual Separation)	—	Medium	Sunni	Abd al-Munim al-Sabruti (founder)	Medium	(New)	—	Egypt
13. Jamaat al-Muslimin lil-Takfir (Taha al-Samawi Group) (Society of Muslims for Accusation of Disbelief)	—	High	Sunni	Charismatic Small *Amir*, estab.: Taha al-Samawi	Small	Active, suppressed; ties to Al-Jihad (New)	—	Egypt (Bani Suaif)
14. Jamaat al-Muslimin (The Muslim Group)	—	High	Sunni	Taha al-Sawi	Small	Unknown (New)	—	Egypt
15. Jamiyyah al-Shariyyah (Society of Islamic Law)	Grassroots (tied to M.B.)	Medium	Sunni	Collective (Journal: *al-Itisam*)	Medium	Semi-public (New)	Gulf States	Egypt
16. Jamaat al-Tabligh (Society of Transmission)	Passive Muslims turned activists (1975)	High/Medium	Sunni	Charismatic	Medium	Jailed by Sadat (1975) (New)	Gulf States	Egypt

180

Name	Social Base		Sect	Leadership	Size	Status		Location
17. Jamaat al-Takfir (Society of Denouncement)	—	High	Sunni	Charismatic	Small	Jailed by Sadat (1975) (New)	—	Egypt (Alexandria)
18. Al-Jihad (Holy War)	—	High	Sunni	Charismatic, Ali al-Maghrabi (founder)	Small	Related to old Shabab Muhammad (New)	—	Egypt (Alexandria)
19. Junud Allah (Soldiers of God)	Middle, Lower-middle; Attack Churches, police, clubs	High	Sunni	Charismatic	Small	Underground, suppressed in 1977 (New)	—	Egypt (Alexandria)
20. Junud al-Rahman (Soldiers of the Compassionate)	—	High	Sunni	Charismatic	Small	— (New)	—	Egypt
21. Mukaffaratiyyah (Denouncers of Infidels)	—	High	Sunni	—	Small	Suppressed (New)	—	Egypt
22. Munazzamat al-Jihad (Jihad Organization)	Middle, Lower-Middle; Killers of Sadat	High	Sunni	Collective, Sh. Abd al-Rahman, A. Zumur, M. Faraj	Medium	Underground, suppressed in 1977, 1981 (New)	—	Egypt
23. Munazzamat al-Tahrir al-Islami (Islamic Liberation Organizational/Technical Military Academy Group)	Middle, Kinship, Students	High	Sunni	S. Siriyya, Charismatic, Palestinian, pro-Libya	Medium	Underground (New)	Syria Jordan Sudan W. Bank	Egypt (Cairo, Alexandria, Delta)
24. Qif wa Tabayyin (Halt and Prove)	—	High	Sunni	Charismatic, Muhammad Abd al-Salam and Dr. Umar	Small	Suppressed (part of group that killed Sadat) (New)	—	Egypt

181

Appendix I (*continued*)

Name of Organization	Beliefs and Membership	Militancy	Sect	Leadership	Size	Current Status	Outside Ties	Country and Region
25. Qutbiyyin (Followers of Qutb)	—	High	Sunni	Charismatic	Small	Sayyid Qutb's followers (New) suppressed	—	Egypt
26. Samawiyyah (The Heavenly)	—	High	Sunni	Charismatic	Small	Underground (New)	—	Egypt
27. Shabab Muhammad (Youth of Muhammad)	Youth, Students	High	Sunni	Collective?	Medium	— (Old)	—	Egypt
28. Takfir wal-Hijrah (Denouncement and Holy Flight or Society of Muslims)	Rural/Small Town, Middle, Lower, Kinship ties	High	Sunni	Shukri Mustafa, Charismatic, Muh. Abd al-Fattah, Muassab Abu Zayd, Mahdist	Medium	Suppressed, underground, active (New)	Kuwait Turkey Gulf States Jordan Libya Saudi Arabia Pakistan Syria	Egypt (Minya)
29. Usbah al-Hashimiyya (The Hashemite League)	Lower-middle, Lower Esoteric	Medium	Sunni	Charismatic messianic (Al-Mahdi al-Arabi)	Small	Jailed, freed (1983) (New)	—	Egypt (Upper)
30. Ansari (The Supporters)	Youth, Students	High	Sunni	Charismatic	Small	Suppressed, underground, active (New)	—	Syria (Aleppo)

182

Group	Social base	Religiosity	Sect	Leadership	Size	Status	Countries	Location
31. Ikhwan al-Muslimin (Muslim Brotherhood—M. B.)	Middle, Lower-middle	High	Sunni	Said Hawwa Adnan Saad al-Din Collective	Large	Suppressed, underground (dominant group of the Islamic Front) (Old)	Egypt Europe Austria Canada Iraq Jordan Gulf States U.S.	Syria
32. Ikhwan al-Muslimin (Muslim Brotherhood/Political Solution—M. B.)	Middle (Workers, Shopkeepers, Students, Soldiers)	Medium/High	Sunni	Isam al-Attar (Sibai founder)	Medium	Suppressed (Old)	Egypt Gulf States Iraq Europe	Syria
33. Jamaat Abi Dharr (Society of Abi Dharr)	Youth, Ulama	High	Sunni	Charismatic, Shaykh Muhammad al-Bayanuni	Small	In 1981 joined Syrian Islamic Front (New)	—	Syria (Aleppo)
34. Al-Jihad (Holy War)	—	High	Sunni	Charismatic	Small	Suppressed (New)	—	Syria
35. Junud Allah (Soldiers of God)	Appears and disappears	High	Sunni	Charismatic?	Small	Support Muslim Brothers (New)	—	Syria
36. Kataib al-Haq (Phalanges of Truth)	—	High	Sunni	Charismatic	Small	Suppressed (New)	—	Syria
37. Kataib Muhammad (Muslim Brotherhood of the Interior/Phalanges of Muhammad)	Middle, Lower-Middle, Merchants, Ulama	High	Sunni	Charismatic, Marwan Hadid (founder); Adnan Uqla	Medium	Suppressed in 1965 (New)	Egypt Europe	Syria (Aleppo and Hama)
38. Khulasah (The Puritans)	Youth, Students	High	Sunni	—	Small	Suppressed, active (New)	—	Syria (Aleppo)
39. Salafiyyah (The Puritans)	Cooperates with Syrian M. B.	High	Sunni	Charismatic	Small	Underground (New)	Egypt	Syria

Appendix I (*continued*)

Name of Organization	Beliefs and Membership	Militancy	Sect	Leadership	Size	Current Status	Outside Ties	Country and Region
40. Tahrir al-Islami (Islamic Liberation Party)	—	High	Sunni	Founded 1963 in Aleppo	Small	Supports M. B. and Islamic Front (Old)	Jordan	Syria
41. Talia al-Muqatila lil-Mujahidin (Combat Vanguard of Fighters—M. B.)	M. B. faction	High	Sunni	Charismatic; Marwan Hadid (died in prison/1976), Salim Muhammad al-Hamid, and Adnan Uqla	Medium	Suppressed, underground (New)	Iraq Egypt Europe	Syria
42. Hizb al-Dawah al-Islamiyyah (Islamic Propagation Party)	Middle, Lower-middle	High	Shiite	Charismatic, Ayatullah Baqir al-Sadr	Large	Suppressed, underground (Old)	Iran, Gulf States U. S. England Kuwait Dubai Bahrain Lebanon	Iraq (S.)
43. Hizb al-Fatimi (The Fatimi Party)	Mostly Iranian origin	Medium	Shiite	Collective	Small	Suppressed (pro-Shah?) (Old)	Iran	Iraq (S.)
44. Hizb al-Thawri al-Islami (Islamic Revolution Party)	—	High	Shiite	Charismatic	Small	Suppressed (New)	Iran	Iraq (S.)

45. Ikhwan Muslimin (The Muslim Brotherhood—M. B.)	Middle class	Low	Sunni	Collective	Medium	Inactive, coopted by Saddam Husayn (Old)	Egypt Syria Jordan Saudi Arabia	Iraq (N./Central)
46. Ittihad al-Islami li-Talabat al-Iraqi (Islamic Union of Iraqi Students)	Students	High	Shiite	—	Large	Suppressed, underground	Iran Gulf States Europe U. S.	Iraq (S.)
47. Jamaat al-Ulama (Society of the Ulama)	Umbrella organization	High	Shiite	Ayatullah Muh. Baqir al-Hakim	Medium	Underground (New)	Iran	(Iraq (S.))
48. Majlis al-Thawra al-Islamiyyah (Islamic Revolutionary Council)	—	High	Shiite	Charismatic?	Small	Suppressed (New)	Iran	Iraq (S.)
49. Mujahidin (Fighters)	Intellectuals stress on economic development	High	Shiite	Charismatic, Inspired by Baqir al-Sadr	Medium	Underground (faction of Hizb?) (New)	Iran	Iraq
50. Munazzamat al-Amal al-Islami (Islamic Action Organization)	*Ulama*, Cross-section	High	Shiite	Collective, Shaykhs Muh. al-Shirazi, Hadi al-Mudarrisi	Medium	Underground (New)	Iran (Mudarrisi implicated in Bahrain Coup, 1981)	Iraq
51. Rabitat al-Islamiyyah (Islamic Association)	—	High	Shiite	Charismatic	Small	Suppressed (New)	Iran	Iraq

Appendix I (*continued*)

Name of Organization	Beliefs and Membership	Militancy	Sect	Leadership	Size	Current Status	Outside Ties	Country and Region
52. Rabitat al-Mara al-Muslimah (Association of Muslim Women)	Women	High	Shiite	—	Medium	Suppressed (New)	Iran Gulf States	Iraq (S.)
53. Zaynab (Women's Association)	Women (University students)	High	Shiite	Charismatic	Medium	Suppressed (New)	Iran	Iraq (S.)
54. AMAL (Hope) (Afwaj al-Muqawamah al-Lubnaniyyah) (Lebanese Resistance Detachments)	Middle, Lower	High	Shiite	Imam Musa Sadr (founder), Nabih al-Barri Muhammad Shams al-Din, A. Qabalan	Large	Active, pro-Iran, pro-Syria, split (New)	Iran Syria Iraq	Lebanon
55. Al-Harakah al-Wataniyyah al-Islamiyyah (Tajammu al-Islami) (Islamic National Movement)	Politicians, Bureaucrats, Clerics	Low	Sunni	Hassan Khalid (Shaykh)	Medium/ Large	Active, public (Old)	Arab States	Lebanon
56. Al-Jamaah al-Islamiyyah (Islamic Society—M. B.)	Middle, Middle-Lower	Medium	Sunni	Collective Shaykh Shaaban	Medium	Active, public (M. B. of Lebanon) (Old)	Syria Jordan Egypt	Lebanon
57. Jihad al-Islami (Islamic Holy War)	—	High	Shiite	Charismatic?	Small	Underground, Anti-Israel and U. S. (New)	Syria? Iran?	Lebanon (S.)
58. Junud al-Rahman (Soldiers of the Compassionate)	—	Low	Sunni	Ahmad Dauq	Small	Semi-active, spiritual (Old)	—	Lebanon

Organization								
59. Islamic AMAL/Hizb Allah (Party of God)	AMAL faction	High	Shiite	Charismatic, Husayn Musawi	Small	Active, terrorist (New)		Lebanon S./E.
60. Al-Hizb al-Jumhuri (Republican Party)	—	Low	Sunni	Mahmud Muhammad Taha	Medium	Active (Old)	—	Sudan
61. Hizb al-Shaab al-Dimuqrati/Khatimiyyah (People's Democratic party)	Middle-Lower	Medium/Low	Sunni	Shaykh Ali Abd al-Rahman, Sharif al-Hindi	Large	Active, public (Old)	—	Sudan
62. Hizb al-Ummah (Islamic Ummah Party) (Ansar)	Middle, Lower	Medium	Sunni (Mahdist)	Sadiq al-Mahdi	Large	Semi-public (Old)	—	Sudan
63. Ikhwan al-Muslimin (Muslim Brethren)	Middle, Lower-Middle	Medium	Sunni	Collective	Medium	Active, public (Old)	Egypt	Sudan
64. Jabhat al-Mithaq (The Charter Front—M. B.)	Middle, Lower	Medium	Sunni	Charismatic, Dr. Hasan al-Turabi	Large (60,000)	Active (Old)	Egypt Saudi Arabia Jordan	Sudan
65. Hizb al-Tahrir al-Jazirah (Liberation Party of Jazirah)	Middle	High	Shiite	—	Medium	Suppressed 1979–80	Iran Gulf States Iraq Bahrain	Saudi Arabia (Eastern Province)
66. Al-Ikhwan (The Brothers)	Lower-middle, Tribal	High	Sunni	Charismatic, Juhayman al-Utaybi (killed 1979), Mahdist	Small/Medium	Suppressed after mosque takeover (New)	Egypt Pakistan Gulf States Yemen	Saudi Arabia
67. Jamaat al-Masjid (Mosque Society)	Middle	High	Sunni	Collective	Medium	Active (secret), specialize in preaching (New)	Gulf States Oman	Saudi Arabia

187

Appendix I (*continued*)

Name of Organization	Beliefs and Membership	Militancy	Sect	Leadership	Size	Current Status	Outside Ties	Country and Region
68. Munazzamat al-Thawrah al-Islamiyah Shubuh fi al-Jazirah al-Arabiyyah (Islamic Revolutionary Organization in the Arabian Peninsula)	Middle	High	Shiite	Charismatic, Said Saffar (now in Iran)	Medium	Suppressed (Now)	Iran	Saudi Arabia (Eastern Province)
69. Jamaat al-Dawah (Society of Propagation)	Students, Cross-section	Medium	Sunni	Decentralized	Large	Public (New)	Egypt (M. B.) Kuwait	Saudi Arabia
70. Ansar Harakat Asna al-Quran (Supporters of the Sons of the Quran)	Cross-section (Palestinian)	High	Sunni	—	Small	Active, underground, opposed to Iraq/Jordan (New)	Jordan W. Bank Israel	Jordan W. Bank
71. Harakat al-Tawhid (Movement of Unicity)	Anti-Arafat Palestinian	High	Sunni	Charismatic, Publishers of Al-Tawhid	Small	Underground, anti-Jordan, anti-Iraq, Pro-Iran (New)	Israel W. Bank U. S.	Jordan
72. Hizb al-Tahrir al-Islami (Islamic Liberation Party)	Palestinians (split from M. B.)	High/Medium	Sunni	Founded in 1952, Shaykh Taqi al-Din al-Nabhani	Medium	Suppressed in Libya (1980), semi-public in Jordan (Old)	Beirut and other Arab countries Libya Turkey	Jordan W. Bank
73. Ikhwan al-Muslimin (The Muslim Brotherhood—M. B.)	Palestinian Jordanian	Medium	Sunni	Muh. Khalifa (1948 Commando Leader) opposed by Dr. Azzam	Medium	Public (Old)	W. Bank (good relations with Jordan)	Jordan W. Bank

Organization	Constituency	Level	Sect	Leadership	Size	Status	Presence	Country
74. Amal al-Islami/Khawanjia (Islamic Action—M. B.)	Intellectuals, Students, Middle, Against smoking and dancing	High	Sunni	Charismatic	Medium	Active, suppressed (New)	Egypt	Tunisia
75. Ittijah al-Islami (The Islamic Orientation)	Youth, Intellectuals, Bourgeoisie, Sons of Landowners and Businessmen	High	Sunni	Charismatic (jailed in Sept 1981, Qanushi and Muru) estab.: early 70s	Large	Semi-active, suppressed (New)	—	Tunisia
76. Hizb al-Islami (Islamic Party—M. B.)	—	High	Sunni	Collective (in jail)	Large	Active, suppressed (Old)	Egypt (M. B.)	Tunisia
77. Jamiyyat Hifz al-Quran (Quran Preservation Societies)	Quranic study groups, Recruits in mosques	Medium	Sunni	Shaykh Naifar (Propaganda through preaching: early 70s)	Many small groups	Active, suppressed?	—	Tunisia
78. Ahl al-Dawah/Al-Qiyam (The People of the Call—M. B.)	Bureaucrats, Businessmen, Students	Medium	Sunni	Collective Malik Ben Nabi	Large	Active (outlawed in 1970, Spring 1981 widespread unrest, underground (Old)	Egypt (M. B.) Tunisia Morocco	Algeria
79. Harakat al-Islamiyyah (The Islamic Movement)	Muslims in dispersion	Medium/ Low	Sunni	Ben Bella	Small	Active (New)	France Europe Switzerland Iran	Algeria
80. Jamaat al-Islamiyyah (Islamic Society—M. B.)	—	High	Sunni	Sahnun (in jail)	Medium	Active, repressed (Old)	Egypt (Maghrib) (M. B.)	Algeria

189

Appendix I (*continued*)

Name of Organization	Beliefs and Membership	Militancy	Sect	Leadership	Size	Current Status	Outside Ties	Country and Region
81. Ikhwan al-Muslimin/Shabibah al-Islamiyyah (Muslim Brothers—M. B.)	Middle, Lower, Students, Engineers, Merchants	High	Sunni	Al-Zaytuni	Medium	Semi-suppressed (New)	France Egypt	Morocco
82. Shubban Islamiyyah (Islamic Youth)	Students, Intellectuals	High	Sunni	Collective, Feb. 1981: First Official Declaration	Medium	Underground, anti-King, anti-U. S.	Journal: *al-Mujahid* publ. in Belgium and France	Morocco
83. Dar al-Tawhid (Unicity Publishers)	Intellectuals	Medium	Shiite	Collective	Medium	Active (Old)	Iran Iraq	Kuwait
84. Jamiyyah al-Islah al-Ijtimai (Society for Social Reform—M. B.)	Upper-Middle, Bureaucrats, Businessmen, Students	Medium	Sunni	Dr. Umar Amiri (Morocco), Collective, *al-Mujtama* (since 1972) ed.: Ismail al-Shati	Large	Active (culturally politically) (Old)	Dubai Saudi Arabia Kuwait Bahrain Qatar U. A. E. Oman Syria	Kuwait
85. Ansar al-Dawah (Supporters of the Call)	Intellectuals, Arab and non-Arab	Medium	Sunni	Collective	Medium	Active (Old)	Pakistan India Gulf States	Gulf States

Organization	Membership		Sect	Leadership	Size	Status	Countries	
86. Jamaat al-Tabligh (Society of Transmission)	Indians, Arabs, Pakistanis and Lower-middle Workers	Low	Sunni	Collective	Medium	Active, spiritual (Old)	Gulf States Pakistan India Egypt	Gulf States
87. Hizb Allah (The Party of God)	Students, Intellectuals	High	Sunni	Charismatic, Zubayri: (founder), killed in 1965	Medium	Underground (New)	Saudi Arabia Gulf States W. Bank Europe	Yemen
88. Jabhat al-Islamiyyah Lil-Tahrir al-Bahrain (Islamic Front for Liberof Bahrain)	Middle, Lower-middle	High	Shiite	Charismatic, Mudarrisi	Medium	Suppressed, underground (New)	Iran Iraq Gulf States	Bahrain
89. Ittihad al-Islami (Islamic Union)	Students, Professionals	Medium	Sunni	Collective	Medium	Active, public (Old)	Europe Arab states	U. S. Arab world
90. Usrah al-Jihad (Family of Jihad)	Israeli Palestinians	High	Sunni	—	Small	Suppressed by Israel (New)	—	Israel (Galilee)
91. Ahl al-Hadith (People of the Hadith)	Students (abroad)	Medium	Sunni	Collective	Medium	Active (New)	Europe U. S.	Arab world Germany

191

Appendix II Glossary of Islamic Terms

abd: slave, servant (of God).

adhan: public call to prayer.

ada Allah wal-insan: enemies of Allah and man.

adl asas al-hukm: justice (righteousness) is the basis of authority.

ahd: covenant

ahd al-istidaf: era of weakness (Islamic)

ahl al-bayt: the Prophet's family.

ahl al-hadith: those who rely on Tradition *(sunnah)* i.e., jurists.

ahl al-hall wal aqd: those loose and bind; legislative assembly in an Islamic state.

ahl al-Kitab: the people of the Book—Christians and Jews; also called *dhimmi.*

ahli: popularly supported non-governmental mosques.

akh: brother (pl. *ikhwan*).

akhir al-zaman: at the end of time.

Alawi or Nusayri: Shiite sect in Syria, Turkey, and Iran.

alim: religious scholar, (pl. *ulama*).

amal: hope.

amir al-muminin: commander of the faithful; the caliph.

anqud: bunch of grapes (lit.); revolutionary cells.

aqidah: ideology.

asabiyyah: tribal or group solidarity.

asalah: genuineness.

asalib: modalities.

asayah: a cane.

asha: last prayers of day (evening).

Ashura: day of mourning sacred to Shiites, as anniversary of Husayn's martyrdom (10th of Muharram).

asl: source, root (pl. *usul*).
asliyyin: the original or the authentic ones (i.e., fundamentalists).
awqaf: religious endowments (sing. *waqf*).
ayatullah: "sign of God"; Shiite religious rank.

badu: bedouin tribesmen.
baraka: blessing.
batal al ubur: "Hero of the Crossing," referring to Sadat.
baath al-Islami: Islamic renaissance.
batini: esoteric.
bayah: oath of allegiance.
bidah: innovation; heretical doctrine or practice.

dar al-Islam: abode of Islam.
dar al-harb: abode of war; reference to non-Islamic lands.
dawah: propagation of the faith; religious propaganda.
dawlah: state.
dhal: straying from the right path.
dhimmi: Christians and Jews.
din: faith, religion.
Druze: a branch of Ismailis found in Syria, Lebanon, Jordan, and Israel.
duat: missionaries.

fajr: dawn (prayers).
fallahin: peasants (sing. *fallah*).
fann al-mawt: "the art of death"; martyrdom.
faqih: jurisconsult (pl. *fuqaha*).
fard: religious duty (pl. *furud*).
fard ayn: individual obligation.
fard kifayah: collective obligation.
fasad: moral corruption in society.
fath: conquest.
fatwa: legal opinion.
fikrah: ideology; thought.
fiqh: the jurisprudence of the *shariah*.
fitnah: situation of discord, strife and trial (pl. *fitan*); provocation.
fuqaha: (*faqih,* sing.) religious jurisconsult.
fuqara: the poor.

gallabiyyah: the traditional robe worn by men; also known as *thawb*.
ghaybah: the temporary occultation of the *imam* (Shiite).
ghulat: non-Twelver Shiite sects—Ismailis, Ali Ilahis, and Alawis.
ghutrah: a cloth worn over the head by men.

hadd: mandatory punishment (pl. *hudud*).
hadith: (pl. *ahadith*) compilations of the traditions of the Prophet.

hajj: pilgrimage or pilgrim.

hakimiyyah: reign of Allah's sovereignty on earth to end all sin, suffering, and repression.

halal: permissible, pure.

halaqat: chains.

haqq: right; truth; (pl. *huquq*).

haram: unlawful, illicit, impure.

Haramayn: the holy cities (Mecca and Medina).

hidayah: God-given guidance.

hijab: veil worn by women.

hijrah: the Prophet's migration, or escape from Mecca to Medina.

hizb: party.

hujar: plural of *hijrah*—migration; tribal settlements of puritanical warriors of Arabia.

hukm: rule, authority.

husayni: Shiite religious procession.

husayniyyah: Shiite center for religious education.

ibadah: submission to God; religious observance.

Ibadi: Kharijite sect dominant in Oman; also called Abadiyyah.

iftira: false accusation.

ihya al-Din: religious revival.

ijma: concensus.

ijtihad: independent and authoritative interpretation in Islamic law.

ikhwan: (sing. *akh*) brothers in a religious confraternity.

iktinaz: hoarding of goods and wealth.

imam: religious leader; for Shiites the "rightful" successors to Ali.

iman: faith.

imarah: see *majmuah* or *jamaah.*

infitah: Sadat's policy of economic liberalization—"opening" to the West.

iqal: Arab head dress.

islah: reform.

Islamiyyin: Islamists (i.e., fundamentalists).

Ismaili: Shiite sect (Severners).

ismah: infallibility.

isnad: the chain of transmission of a *hadith.*

Ithna ashariyyah: Twelver Shiites.

jabhah: front.

jahiliyyah: time of ignorance before Islam; in contemporary Islamist usage "a sinful society."

jamaah: society; also *imarah* or *majmuah.*

jamahiriyyah: mass democracy (i.e., Libya); or populist democracy.

jami: large mosque.

jamiyyah: association.

jazzabah: appeal, charm, charisma.

jizyah: levy imposed by an Islamic state on its non-Muslim subjects.
jihad: holy war.
jihad bil-sayf: striving by the sword.
jihaz al-qiyadi: leadership apparatus.
jihaz al-taqyim: supervisory apparatus.
jil al-dai: the lost generation.

Kaabah: A square structure built by Abraham in Mecca toward which Muslims
    turn to pray.
kabir al-ailah: head of family.
kafir: (pl. *kuffar*) irreligious, unbelieving, infidel.
Kalimah: article of Islamic faith. "There is no God but Allah; Muhammad is the
    messenger of Allah."
kashf: revelation.
khalifah: successor to the Prophet (Caliph).
Kharijite: Khawarij; assassins of Ali who opposed keeping the succession in
    the Prophet's lineage and who believed that any devout Muslim had the
    right to become caliph.
khatar: peril.
khimar: woman's face cover.
khurafah: superstition.
khutaba: (sing. *khatib*) preachers.
khutbah: sermon.
kuffar: unbelievers, sinners.
kufr: unbelief.

lihya: full beard.

madhhab: school of legal thought.
Maghrib: Arab West; North African Arab countries.
mahdi al-muntazir: the expected messiah.
majlis al-shura: consultative assembly.
majmuah: (imarah or *jamaah)* society; association.
makruh: abhorrence of impious conduct.
mal: property.
marifah: the comprehension and consciousness of Allah and his attributes.
marji: highest religious authority among Shiites.
marjiyyah: Shiite supreme religious authority.
marahil: stages.
masakin: the wretched.
Mashriq: Arab East.
masirah: (Shiite) mourning procession *(mawkib).*
masjid: small mosque.
maslahah: public interest.
mawkib: Shiite mourning procession *(masirah).*
mihnah: an inquisitional tribunal or trial.

minhaj: coherent program of action.
mufasilah al-shuuriyyah: spiritual separation.
mufsidun fil-ard: the corrupt on earth.
mufti: jurisprudent who issues fatwas.
muhaddith: scholar of hadith; traditionlist.
muhibbah: love.
mujaddid: one who undertakes and carries out *tajdid* (q.v.); renewer of faith.
mujahid: (pl. *mujahidin*) one who undertakes *jihad* (q.v.).
mujtahid fil-madhhab: independent legal interpreter of a school of law.
mulhid: apostate, heretic.
mulid: the birth of the Prophet (also *mawlid*).
mullah: mosque preacher or teacher.
mumin: Muslim believer (pl. *muminin*).
munadhdhir: theoretician.
munkar: reprehensible, disowned.
muraqib al-am: general supervisor.
murshid: guide.
murtadd: a Muslim who rejects Islam; an apostate.
mushaf: copy of the Quran.
Mushashain: Arab Shiite movement in Khuzistan.
mushrikin: idolaters; followers of *shirk* (q.v.)
mustadafin: the oppressed, the disinherited.
mustalahat: terminology.
mutaassib: (pl. *mutaassibin*) zealot, fanatic.
mutadayyin: (pl. *mutadayyinin*) pious, devout.
mutakallim: theologian.
mutatarrif: (pl. *mutatarrifin*) radical, extremist.
mutawatir: unbroken chain of authority in Islamic tradition *(ahadith)*.
Mutazilah: a rationalist theological-political movement in Islam.
Muwahhidin: Unitarians; followers of Abd al-Wahhab; known as Wahhabis.

nabi: prophet.
naib: deputy.
nashr al-dawah: propagation of the message.
nizam al-Islami: Islamic system (order).
Nusayri: Alawi; sect of Shiite Islam.

qadi: (pl. *qudat*) judge.
Qaramitah: Carmathians; Islamic insurrectionary movement.
qiblah: direction of Mecca.
qital: fighting.
Qiyadah al-Qutriyyah: Baathi Regional Command.
qiyas: reasoning by analogy.
Qizilbash: "red heads"; Shiite tribes of Eastern Anatolia which gave rise to the
    Safavid Dynasty.

Quran: Koran, holy book of Islam.
Quraysh: the Prophet's tribe.

rabbaniyyah: divinity, godship.
Rais al-mumin: the believer president (a reference to Sadat).
rakah: bowing and prostration during prayer.
Rashidin: the four "rightly guided" caliphs.
Rasul: messenger of God (Muhammad).
riba: interest, usury.
rububiyyah: divinity, godship.
ruh: spirit, soul.

sabr: patience.
sadaqah: charitable donation.
saff jadd: earnest believers.
Sahabah: Companions of the Prophet.
sahwah al-Islamiyyah: Islamic awakening.
Salaf: pious ancestors.
Salafiyyah: a movement of Islamic revival led by Abduh and Rida.
salat: prayers.
Sarayah al-Difa: defense squadrons (Syria).
sawm: fasting.
shahadah: profession of faith.
shahid: martyr.
shariah: Islamic Law.
shariyyah al-hukm: legitimate authority.
shaykh: tribal chief, religious teacher or respected elder.
shaytan: devil.
shiarat: slogans.
Shiat Ali: partisans of Ali.
shirk: polytheism.
shura: consultation.
sirat al-mustaqim: the correct path that inspired the first Muslims.
sufi: Islamic mystic.
sulb: toughness.
Sunni: a follower of sunnah; an "orthodox" Muslim.
sunnah: traditions of the Prophet as legally binding precedents; customs of
      orthodox Muslims.

taawun: solidarity, cooperation.
tabdhir: extravagance.
taghut: idolater; despot.
taghyir aqliyyah: a change of mentality or psycho-spiritual transformation.
taifiyyah: sectarianism.
tajdid: renewal of the true faith by a *mujaddid (q.v.).*

takfir: to charge someone with unbelief; excommunication; denouncement.
taliah: vanguard.
Taliah Muqatilah: combat vanguard.
tanzim: organization; regulation.
tanzim khayti: thread-like organization of cells.
taqashshuf: austereness; asceticism.
taqiyyah: dissimulation; hiding one's religious identity (i.e., *Shia*); also a cap.
taqlid: blind emulation in legal interpretation; opposite of *ijtihad.*
taqwa: God's fear, godliness.
tarif: special message.
tariqah: religious order.
tasbih: rosary.
tashih: rectification.
tawfiq: God-given success.
tawhid: the belief in the unity of Allah in opposition to *shirk*—the belief in ascribing "partners" to the godhead.
thawb: the traditional robe worn by a man; also known as the *gallabiyyah.*

ulama: (sing. *alim*) Islamic scholars.
uluhiyyah: divine power, sovereignty.
ummah: the Islamic polity.
usuliyyah al-Islamiyyah: Islamic fundamentalism.
usar: underground cells (lit. family).

Wahadat al-Khassah: Special Units (elite troops of Syria).
wakil: representative.
wala: allegiance.
walayah: friendship of God; possession of legitimacy.
wilayat al-faqih: guardianship of the jurisconsult (i.e., Iran).

zabibah: a black mark on forehead signifying piety.
zahir: exoteric.
zakat: compulsory almsgiving.
zalamah: injustice as referred to the deeds of the government, exploiting groups, or enemies.
zindiq: atheist.
ziyy al-Islami: Islamic attire.
zuama: leaders; notables; chieftains (sing. *zaim*).

Appendix III* Statistical Analysis and Summary of Islamist Groups

Objectives

An analysis of ninety-one Islamic fundamentalist groups and their organizational attributes (Appendix I) was undertaken to test the following hypotheses explicated in Chapter 5.

Islamic fundamentalist organizations follow two patterns of development:

1. New fundamentalist organizations are generally: (a) small in size; (b) high in militancy; (c) led by charismatic leaders; and (d) operate clandestinely.

2. Older, more established Islamic societies generally are: (a) large in size; (b) low in militancy; (c) led by bureaucratic leaders; and (d) operate openly.

Methodology

The data set contains five categories of attributes of ninety-one Islamic fundamentalist societies: militancy, leadership, size, legal status and organizational age. The qualitative nature of the data necessitated the use of a coding system to operationalize the variables (see Table 8). The lack of precise quantitative data on organizational age and size and the relatively judgmental nature of the data on status, militancy, and leadership limited the choice of em-

*The author wishes to acknowledge the efforts of Beth Ann Binns in performing the statistical analysis of this section.

Table 8
Coding System for Operationalization of Variables

Militancy—the ideological and activist orientation of each organization.
1. High
2. Medium
3. Low

Leadership—the leadership type of each society.
0. Bureaucratic
1. Charismatic

Size—the approximate size of each group.
1. Small
2. Medium
3. Large

Status—the degree of clandestineness of each society.
1. Underground
2. Semi-public
3. Public

Age—Duration of a group's existence; the mid-1960s are taken as the dividing point between "old" and "new" organizations.
0. Old
1. New

---

ployable statistical methodology. However, it was possible to utilize a coding system to rank the variables which were checked by three judges with area expertise.

Contingency table analysis was elected as the best method to analyze the data set and test the strength of the relationships between the attributes. When variables are measured at the nominal or ordinal level with few categories comprising the data set, then cross-tabulation provides an excellent means to study the frequency, percentages, and statistical significance of the data. In this study, three of the five variables were measured at the nominal level; the remaining two variables (militancy and size) were ordinally measured.

To identify patterns and associations between the five variables, ten cross-tabulation tables were constructed. The ten tables matched each variable controlled against the remaining four variables.

In addition, measures of association and correlation coefficients were calculated which were useful in indicating the strength of the relationship between any of the two categorical variables; these included: Phi, Cramer's V and Gamma (see Table 9). Cramer's V was selected as the best measure of association for this data set. Cramer's V is a chi-square measure of association for any size table. Its maximum value is less than 1.0 when row marginals are not identical to column marginals. V is identical to phi in a 2×2 case. A high value ($+1$) indicates a high degree of association.

Results

Contingency table analysis of the data yielded seven statistically significant measures of association for the Islamic groups (Table 10). All tables with a Cramer's V$\geq$ .5 are illustrated in Tables 10A—10G. The results measure the absolute frequency (the number of observations occurring in each matching), the row pct (the row percentage total) or the col pct (the column percentage total), and the percent of the total number of observations occuring in the row and column.

Table 10A Militancy × Age: Of the highly militant organizations, 88 percent are relatively new in age. Significantly, 100 percent of the societies with low militancy and 67 percent of the medium militant societies are old in age.

Table 10B Militancy × Status: 95 percent of the underground fundamentalist groups are highly militant. In addition, 86 percent of the semi-public and public societies are low to medium in militancy.

Table 10C Militancy × Leadership: 93 percent of the societies led by charismatics display high militancy. Conversely, 74 percent of the bureaucratically led societies possess medium to low levels of militancy.

Table 10D Leadership × Age: Of all the new Islamic societies, 79 percent are led by charismatics. Significantly, 81 percent of the older groups were led by bureaucratic types. Only 11 percent of the charismatically led groups have been in existence longer than fifteen years.

Table 10E Leadership × Status: 87 percent of the fundamentalist groups which were led by charismatics were clandestine. Only 4 percent of the publicly operating groups are led by charismatics.

Table 10F Leadership × Size: 90 percent of all of the societies con-

Table 9
List of Correlation Coefficients
(Cramer's V)

	Age	Status	Size	Leadership
Status	.55	X	—	—
Size	.47	.31	X	—
Leadership	.50	.58	.53	X
Militancy	.65	.64	.29	.70

*Cramer's V ≥ .5 represents a high degree of association

*All cross-tabulations where Cramer's V is ≥ .5 are illustrated in Tables 10A–10G.

Table 10
Contingency Table Analysis of Islamist Groups
(N-91)

10A: Militancy x Age

Age			
Frequency Row Pct	Old	New	Total
High	7	53	60
	12	88	69
Medium	14	7	21
	67	33	24
Low	6	0	6
	100	0	7
Total	27	60	87
Percent	31	69	100

10B: Militancy x Status

Status				
Frequency Col Pct	Underground	Semi-public	Public	Total
High	58	4	1	63
	95	31	6	69
Medium	3	9	10	22
	5	69	59	24
Low	0	0	6	6
	0	0	35	7
Total	61	13	17	91
Percent	67	14	19	100

10C: Militancy x Leadership

Frequency Col Pct	Leadership		
	Bureaucratic	Charismatic	Total
High	9	43	52
	26	93	65
Medium	19	3	22
	57	7	27
Low	6	0	6
	17	0	8
Total	34	46	80
Percent	42	58	100

10D: Leadership x Age

Frequency Col Pct	Age		
	Old	New	Total
Bureaucratic	21	11	32
	81	21	41
Charismatic	5	41	46
	19	79	59
Total	26	52	78
Percent	33	67	100

10E: Leadership x Status

Frequency Row Pct	Status			
	Underground	Semi-public	Public	Total
Bureaucratic	11	8	15	34
	32	24	44	43
Charismatic	40	4	2	46
	87	9	4	57
Total	51	12	17	80
Percent	64	15	21	100

10F: Leadership x Size

Frequency Col Pct	Size			
	Small	Medium	Large	Total
Bureaucratic	3	22	9	34
	10	63	64	43
Charismatic	28	13	5	46
	90	37	36	57
Total	31	35	14	80
Percent	39	44	17	100

10G: Status x Age

Frequency Row Pct	Age		
	Old	New	Total
Underground	10	48	58
	17	83	67
Semi-public	3	9	12
	25	75	13
Public	14	3	17
	82	18	20
Total	27	60	87
Percent	31	69	100

sidered "small" in size have charismatic leaders; 91 percent of the bureaucratically led societies were medium to large in size.

Table 10G Status × Age: 83 percent of the clandestine societies are relatively new in age. Conversely, 82 percent of the public societies have been in existence for several decades. Only 20 percent of the new fundamentalist groups enjoy semi-public or public status.

Conclusions

The foregoing analysis provides substantial support to hypotheses 1 and 2 above as explained in Chapter 5. Strong statistical correlations were found between five organizational attributes: (1) Duration of group's lifespan; (2) Type of leadership; (3) Level of militancy; (4) Group size; (5) Clandestineness. *The younger the society, the smaller its size, the higher its militancy, the higher the probabilities of leadership by charismatics and the likelihood of underground existence.*

This finding conforms to the general pattern which appears to characterize the evolution of religious and ideological movements. At its inception, the group is small, clandestine, militant, and led by a charismatic. In time, the group becomes a larger movement, operating openly, with a reduced level of militancy and led by bureaucratic types.

Notes

1—Islamic Resurgence in Modern Society

1. See R. Hrair Dekmejian, "The Anatomy of Islamic Rivival: Legitimacy Crisis, Ethnic Conflict and the Search for Islamic Alternatives," *Middle East Journal* 34, no. 1 (Winter 1980): 1–3. On the patterns of decline and resurgence see S. Abul Ala Maududi, *A Short History of the Revivalist Movement in Islam* (Lahore: Isalmic Publications, 1963).

2. For these terms see the incisive article by Hasan Hanafi, "Al-Harakah al-Islamiyyah al-Muasirah" [The Contemporary Islamic Movement], *Al-Watan,* November 20, 1982. Also useful is the French term *"intégrisme."*

3. Among the notable exceptions is Bernard Lewis, "The Return of Islam," *Commentary* 61 (January 1976): 39–49.

4. Dale W. Wimberley, "Socioeconomic Deprivation and Religious Salience: A Cognitive Behavioral Approach," *The Sociological Quarterly* 25 (Spring 1984): 223–24.

2—History of Islamist Movements: A Cyclical Pattern

1. R. H. Dekmejian, "The Anatomy of Islamic Revival," *Middle East Journal* 34, no. 1 (Winter 1980): 2–6; also R. H. Dekmejian, "The Islamic Revival in the Middle East and North Africa," *Current History* 78, no. 456 (April 1980): 169–74.

2. S. Abul Ala Maududi, *A Short History of the Revivalist Movement in Islam* (Lahore: Islamic Publications, 1963), pp. 45–50. According to Hitti, later generations regarded Umar II as a *mabuth*—one sent by God every century to renovate Islam. See Philip K. Hitti, *History of the Arabs,* 10th ed. (London: Macmillan, 1980), p. 222.

3. Bernard Lewis, *Islam in History* (New York: Library Press, 1973), pp. 245–49.

4. Hitti, *History,* pp. 399, 429. The ninth century also witnessed the writings and interpretations of other exponents of strict orthodoxy like Abu Dawud al-Sigistani

(b. 820) who wrote on *jihad,* and Ibn Muslim (b. 883), the compiler of "correct" *ahadith.* Both are cited as precedents by Mohammad Abdessalam Faraj, *Al-Jihad: The Forgotten Pillar* (Canada, no date), p. 37. For similar citations see Juhayman al-Utaybi, *Saba Rasail* [Seven Letters] (n.p., n.d.), pp. 25, 28, 65.

5. Note references to Ibn Hazm and Ibn Salamah in *The Forgotten Pillar,* p. 37, to justify violence.

6. Richard P. Mitchell, *The Society of the Muslim Brothers* (London: Oxford University Press, 1969), p. 3.

7. *Encyclopaedia of Islam,* Vol. 3 (Leiden: E. J. Brill, 1971), pp. 951–55.

8. Also important for present-day Islamist writers are Muhyi al-Din al-Nawawi, the pious *hadith* compiler of Damascus (b. 1253) and Ibn Hajar al-Asqalani (1372–1449), chief *qadi* of Cairo. See Chapter 4 for details.

9. Matti Moosa, "Ahwaz: an Arab Territory," *The Future of the Arab Gulf and the Strategy of Joint Arab Action* (Basrah, Iraq: Center for Arab Gulf Studies, 1981), pp. 17–20.

10. Nikki R. Keddie, *Iran: Religion, Politics and Society* (London: Frank Cass, 1980), pp. 90–91.

11. R. Stephen Humphreys, "The Contemporary Resurgence in the Context of Modern Islam," in *Islamic Resurgence in the Arab World* edited by Ali E. Hillal Dessouki (New York: Praeger, 1982), p. 74.

12. R. Hrair Dekmejian and M. J. Wyszomirski, "Charismatic Leadership in Islam: The Mahdi of the Sudan," *Comparative Studies in Society and History* 14, no. 2 (March 1972). Haim Shaked, *The Life of the Sudanese Mahdi* (New Brunswick, N.J.: Transaction, 1978), pp. 51–61, 204–207, 213–23.

13. For further details see Albert Hourani, *Arabic Thought in the Liberal Age 1798–1939* (London: Oxford University Press, 1970), pp. 231–32.

14. Fazlur Rahman, "Islam: Challenges and Opportunities," in *Islam: Past Influence and Present Challenge,* Alford T. Welch and Pierre Cachia, eds. (Edinburgh: Edinburgh University Press, 1979), pp. 318–23.

3—The Social-Psychological Bases of Islamic Revivalism

1. R. H. Dekmejian, "The Anatomy of Islamic Revival: Legitimacy Crisis, Ethnic Conflict and the Search for Islamic Alternatives," *Middle East Journal* 34, no. 1 (Winter 1980): 10.

2. For relevant theoretical foundation see Erik Erikson, *Young Man Luther* (New York: Norton, 1958); and *Identity, Youth and Crisis* (New York: Norton, 1968).

3. Emile Durkheim, *Suicide: A Study in Sociology* (Glencoe: Free Press, 1951), pp. 246–54. Also see Daniel Bell, "Sociodicy: A Guide to Modern Usage," *The American Scholar* 35, no. 4 (Autumn 1965): 700–01. On anomie in Egypt see Ali E. Hillal Dessouki, "The Resurgence of Islamic Organizations in Egypt: An Interpretation," in *Islam and Power,* edited by Alexander S. Cudsi and Ali E. Hillal Dessouki (Baltimore: Johns Hopkins University Press, 1981), p. 115.

4. On the Moroccan figures see *Le Monde Diplomatique* (January 1984): 8.

5. For details see R. Hrair Dekmejian, "The Dialectics of Islamic Revival," *Hellenic Review of International Relations* 1, no. 1 (1980). For a different point of view see

Daniel Pipes, " 'This World is Political!! The Islamic Revival of the Seventies," *Orbis* 24 (1980): 17–39.

6. Yvonne Yazbeck Haddad, *Contemporary Islam and the Challenge of History* (Albany, N.Y.: SUNY Press, 1982), pp. 33–45.

7. Shakir Mustafa, "Arab Cultural Crisis and the Impact of the Past," *The Jerusalem Quarterly* 11 (Spring 1979): 43–50 (reprinted in abridged form from *Al-Adab,* Beirut). On the interaction between the crises of identity, legitimacy, culture, and economy, see Jürgen Habermas, *The Legitimation Crisis* (Boston: Beacon Press, 1975), pp. 45–50, 18–20.

8. On the concept of "modal personality" see Gordon J. DiRenzo, *Personality and Politics* (Garden City, N.Y.: Anchor Press, 1974), p. 19.

9. Salim al-Bahnasawi, "Wara al-Ghudban Wulidu" [Born Behind Prison Bars], *Al-Arabi* (January 1982): 44–47.

10. Erik Erikson, *Childhood and Society* (New York: Norton, 1950), pp. 270–74.

11. Nazih N. M. Ayubi, "The Political Revival of Islam: The Case of Egypt," *IJMES* 12, no. 4 (December 1980): 491–96.

12. T. W. Adorno, et. al., *The Authoritarian Personality* (New York: Norton, 1950), pp. 228–29.

13. Yusuf al-Qaradawi, "Sit Alamat lil-Tatarruf al-Din" [Six Signs of Religious Extremism], *Al-Arabi* (January 1982): 32–36.

14. Ahmad Kamal Abu al-Majd, "Al-Tatarruf Ghayr al-Jarimah wal-Tashkhis al-Daqiq Matlub" [Extremism Is Not the Crime: A Precise Investigation Is Required], *Al-Arabi* (January 1982): 36–40.

15. Yusuf al-Qaradawi, *Al-Arabi* (January 1982): 32–36.

16. *Ibid.* Also, Muhammad Fathi Uthman, "Al-Qam Shabab lil-Tatarruf wa Laysa Ilajan Lahu" [Repression of Extremist Youth Is Not a Remedy], *Al-Arabi* (January 1982): 56–57.

17. Mohammad Abdessalam Faraj, *Al-Jihad: The Forgotten Pillar* (Canada: n.d.), pp. 35–55.

18. Muhammad al-Ghazali, "Hadar Min al-Din al-Makhshush" [Beware of the False Religion], *Al-Arabi* (January 1982). Also, Khalid Muhammad Khalid, *Al-Arabi* (January 1982).

19. Yusuf al-Qaradawi, *Al-Arabi* (January 1982): 32–36.

4—Islamist Ideology and Practice

1. On different types of *jihad* see Majid Khadduri, *War and Peace in the Law of Islam* (Baltimore: Johns Hopkins University Press, 1969), pp. 51–82. Also, Rudolph Peters, *Islam and Colonialism* (The Hague: Mouton, 1979).

2. These "pioneers" of Islamist thought are taken mainly from the writings of Hasan al-Banna, Sayyid Qutb, Mawdudi, Said Hawwa, Abd al-Salam Faraj, and Juhayman al-Utaybi.

3. Muhammad Abu Zahrah, *Tarikh al-Madhahib al-Islamiyyah* II [History of Islamic Schools of Law] (Cairo, n.d.), pp. 353–414.

4. Victor E. Makari, *Ibn Taymiyyah's Ethics* (Chico, Ca.: Scholars Press, 1983), pp. 113–14. Also see Abu Zahrah, *Tarikh,* pp. 421–76; and George Makdisi, "Hanbalite

Islam," in *Studies on Islam,* ed. and trans. by Merlin L. Swartz (New York: Oxford University Press, 1981), pp. 216–64.

5. Makari, *Ibn Taymiyyah's Ethics,* pp. 121, 11–12.

6. Henri Laoust, "L'influence d'Ibn Taymiyya" in *Islam: Past Influence and Present Challenge,* Alford T. Welch and Pierre Cachia, eds. (Edinburgh: Edinburgh University Press, 1979), pp. 18–19.

7. Makari, *Ibn Taymiyyah's Ethics,* p. 124. Of Ibn Taymiyyah's many writings, the *Siyasah al-Shariyyah* [The Politics of Legitimacy] is probably the most influential in present-day Islamist thought.

8. Laoust, "L'influence d'Ibn-Taymiyya," p. 25. Also, Awad Awadallah Jad Hijazi, *Ibn al-Qayyim wa Mawqifahu min al-Tafkir al-Islami* [Ibn al-Qayyim and His Position in Islamic Thought] (Cairo, 1973).

9. See Imad al-Din Ibn Kathir al-Dimashqi, *Kitab al-Ijtihad fi Talab al-Jihad* [The Book of Diligent Pursuit of Holy War] (Cairo, 1928).

10. Laoust, "L'Influence d'Ibn Taymiyya", pp. 29–30. On the extent of Ibn Abd al-Wahhab's reliance on Ibn Hanbal, Ibn Taymiyyah, Ibn al-Qayyim, Abu Dawud, and the six canonical books, see his *Kitab al-Tawhid* [Book of Unicity] (Beirut: The Holy Koran Publishing House, 1979). For an insightful overview of Islamic political thought see Charles E. Butterworth, "Prudence versus Legitimacy: The Persistent Theme in Islamic Political Thought," in *Islamic Resurgence in the Arab World,* edited by A. E. H. Dessouki (New York: Praeger, 1982), pp. 84–114.

11. For details see S. Abul Ala Maududi, *A Short History of the Revivalist Movement in Islam* (Lahore: Islamic Publications, 1963), p. 33.

12. *Ibid.,* pp. 38–39. For further analysis of Mawdudi's thought see, Charles J. Adams, "Mawdudi, and the Islamic State," in *Voices of Resurgent Islam,* edited by John L. Esposito (New York: Oxford University Press, 1983), pp. 99–133.

13. Mawdudi mentions the collections of *ahadith* by Muslim, Tirmidhi, Ibn Majah and the *Mustadrik,* as well as those given by Shatibi and Ismail Shahid.

14. P. M. Holt, *The Mahdist State in the Sudan 1881–1898* (Oxford: Clarendon Press, 1958), pp. 22. For an excellent collection of *ahadith* on Mahdism see *Themes of Islamic Civilization,* edited by John Alden Williams (Berkeley: University of California Press, 1971), pp. 191–251.

15. Maududi, *A Short History,* pp. 42–44.

16. Abd al-Qadir Awda, *Al-Islam wa Awdauna al-Siyasiyyah* [Islam and Our Political Positions] (Cairo, n.d.), pp. 55–63. Also Hasan al-Banna, *Mudhakkarat al-Dawah wal-Daiyyah* [Memoirs of the Call and the Caller] (n.p., 1951), pp. 102–3. For a cogent formulation of the fundamentalist position see Leonard Binder, *The Ideological Revolution in the Middle East* (New York: John Wiley, 1964), pp. 41–42.

17. Richard P. Mitchell, *The Society of the Muslim Brothers* (London: Oxford University Press, 1969), p. 234. On the Brotherhood's ideology see also Mahmud Abd al-Halim, *Al-Ikhwan al-Muslimun* (Alexandria, 1979), pp. 40–42.

18. Saad Eddin Ibrahim, "Anatomy of Egypt's Militant Islamic Groups," *IJMES* 12, no. 4 (December 1980): 430. Also, Said Hawwa, *Allahu Jalla Jalalahu* [God in His Exalted Majesty] (Beirut, 1975), pp. 9–20.

19. See teachings of Shukri Mustafa in Abd al-Rahman Abu al-Khayr, *Zikriyati Maa Jamaat al-Muslimin* [My Memories of the Muslim Society] (Kuwait, 1980), pp. 9–10.

20. Mitchell, *Society of Muslim Brothers,* p. 207. Also Juhayman al-Utaybi, *Saba Rasail* [Seven Letters] (n.p., n.d.), pp. 180–90.

21. Sayyid Qutb, *Milestones* (Kuwait: International Islamic Federation, 1978), pp. 110–18. While Qutb and Mawdudi seem to favor making *jihad* an obligation *(fard)*, Banna usually regarded it as a lesser duty or a communal obligation *(fard kifayah)*.

22. *Ibid.*, pp. 148–55, 129–30.

23. Sayyid Qutb, *Islam: The Religion of the Future* (Kuwait: International Islamic Federation, 1977).

24. Mitchell, *Society of Muslim Brothers*, pp. 252–53.

25. On Islamic Socialism, see Mustafa al-Sibai, *Ishtirakiyyah al-Islam* [Islamic Socialism] (Damascus, 1958). Abu Dharr is referred to as the first Muslim socialist or communist. One of Abu Dharr's modern followers was Sayyid Qutb; see *Al-Adalah al-Ijtimaiyyah fi al-Islam* [Social Justice in Islam] (Cairo, 1964). After Nasser's adoption of Arab socialism, Sayyid Qutb refrained from writing on socialism. Thus, the Nasserist cooptation of socialism, prompted Qutb to mute his own advocacy of socialism as an opponent of the regime.

26. Mohammad Abdessalam Faraj, *Al-Jihad: The Forgotten Pillar* (Canada, n.d.), pp. 15–19, 45–47. Also Mitchell, *Society of Muslim Brothers*, pp. 246–47.

27. Fadwa El Guindi, "Veiling Infitah with Muslim Ethic: Egypt's Contemporary Islamic Movements," *Social Problems* 28, no. 4 (April 1981): 474–75. Mitchell, *Society of Muslim Brothers*, p. 225.

28. See the emphasis on a "program" of action in Sayyid Qutb, *Maalim fi al-Tariq* [Signposts on the Road] (n.p., n.d.), pp. 7–8.

29. S. Abul Ala Maududi, *A Short History of the Revivalist Movement in Islam* (Lahore: Islamic Publications, 1963), pp. 31–34.

30. Muhammad Abu Zahrah, *Al-Dawah ila al-Islam* [The Call to Islam] (Cairo, 1973), p. 125.

31. Mitchell, *Society of Muslim Brothers*, p. 196. On Banna's instructions to the missionaries see Muhammad Shawqi Zaki, *Al-Ikhwan al-Muslimun wal-Mujtama al-Misri* [The Muslim Brothers and Egyptian Society] (Cairo, n.d.), pp. 132–34.

32. Al-Bahi al-Khuli, *Tafkirat al-Duat* [Thoughts on Missionaries] (Cairo, 1953), *passim*.

33. During the mid-forties the Brethren supervised 35 mosques in Cairo and Giza. See Zaki, *Al-Ikhwan*, pp. 132–34.

34. Saad Eddin Ibrahim, "Anatomy of Egypt's Militant Islamic Groups," *IJMES* 12, no. 4 (December 1980): 437–40. Also see *Al-Dawah* (December 1982): 42–43. On the attraction of the youth to Islamist groups, see Tariq al-Bishri, "Sayabqa al-Ghulu Ma Baqiyah al-Taghrib" [Extremism will Remain as Long as there is Westernization], *Al-Arabi* (January 1982): 58–61.

35. It is reported that in Egypt the recruits come from the rural middle- and lower-middle classes. See Saad Eddin Ibrahim, "Anatomy of Militant Groups," p. 439.

36. Hasan Hanafi, *Al-Watan* (November 28, 1982).

37. Fred H. Lawson, "Social Bases of the Hama Revolt," *MERIP Reports* (November/December 1982): 224–28.

38. Zouhaier Dhaouadi, "Islamismes et Politique en Tunisie," *Peuples Méditerranéens* 21 (October-December, 1982): 158.

39. El Guindi, "Veiling," pp. 465–85. On the behavioral attributes of the activists see Ahmad Kamal Abu al-Majd, *Al-Arabi* (January 1982): 36–40.

40. Hasan Hanafi, "Wa Kanat al-Naksah Nuqtah Tahawwul" [The Defeat Was a Turning Point], *Al-Watan* 5 (November 20, 1982).

41. Mitchell, *Society of Muslim Brothers*, pp. 193–94.

5—Taxonomy of Islamist Societies and State Responses

1. For a list of over thirty religious authorities on Mahdiship see *Crescent International* (October 1–5, 1980).

2. Charles L. Montesquieu, "Consideration sur les causes de la grandeur des Romains et de leur decadance," *Œuvres Complètes de Montesquieu* (Paris, 1951), p. 70. On Weber see R. Hrair Dekmejian, *Egypt Under Nasir* (Albany: SUNY Press, 1971), pp. 14–15.

3. For a similar classification see Ernest Gellner, *Muslim Society* (Cambridge: Cambridge University Press, 1981), p. 69.

4. An excellent exposition of Qadhafi's views are found in Ann Elizabeth Mayer, "Islamic Resurgence or New Prophethood: The Role of Islam in Qahdafi's Ideology," in Ali E. Hillal Dessouki, ed., *Islamic Resurgence in the Arab World* (New York: Praeger, 1982), p. 207.

5. Mayer, "Islamic Resurgence," p. 201.

6. *Le Monde Diplomatique* (January 1984).

7. Al-Sadiq Al-Mahdi, "Islam—Society and Change," in *Voices of Resurgent Islam,* edited by John L. Esposito (New York: Oxford University Press, 1983), pp. 239–40.

8. Jean-Claude Vatin, "Revival in the Maghreb: Islam as an Alternate Political Language," in Dessouki, *Islamic Resurgence in the Arab World,* pp. 238–42. Also, Peter von Sivers, "Work, Leisure and Religion: The Social Roots of the Revival of Fundamentalist Islam in North Africa," in *Islam et Politique au Maghreb,* edited by Ernest Gellner and Jean-Claude Vatin (Paris, 1981), pp. 368–70.

9. *Le Monde* (January 5, 1984).

10. Vatin, "Revival in the Maghreb," p. 236.

11. Fred Halliday, "The Yemens: Conflict and Coexistence," *The World Today* (August–September 1984): 359.

12. Robert W. Stookey, "Religion and Politics in South Arabia," in *Religion and Politics in the Middle East,* edited by Michael Curtis (Boulder, Co.: Westview, 1981), pp. 356, 360–61.

13. Augustus Richard Norton, "Making Enemies in South Lebanon: Harakat Amal, The IDF, and South Lebanon," *Middle East Insight* (January–February, 1984): 13–20.

6—Egypt: Cradle of Islamic Fundamentalism

1. On Banna's personality see Rifat al-Said, *Hasan al-Banna* (Cairo, 1979), pp. 46–59. Also Ishak Musa Husaini, *The Moslem Brethren* (Beirut: Khayat's, 1956), pp. 25–38. On charisma, see Max Weber, *The Theory of Social and Economic Organization* (New York: Oxford University Press, 1947).

2. See *Five Tracts of Hasan al-Banna (1906–1949),* transl. and annotated by Charles Wendell (Berkeley: University of California Press, 1978), pp. 100, 149, 150, 160, 161.

3. Richard P. Mitchell, *The Society of the Muslim Brothers* (London: Oxford University Press, 1969), p. 30. For further sources on the Brethren see Zakariyya Sulayman Bayyumi, *Al-Ikhwan al-Muslimin* [The Muslim Brethren] (Cairo, 1979).

4. R. H. Dekmejian, *Egypt Under Nasir* (Albany: SUNY Press, 1971), p. 25.

5. *Ibid.*, pp. 32–33. For a detailed account of the persecution of the Brotherhood see Jabir Rizq, *Madhabih al-Ikhwan fi Sujun Nasser* [The Killing of the Brothers in Nasser's Prisons] (Cairo, 1977).

6. There is no direct evidence that Sadat's presence on the Tribunal was the primary reason for his murder.

7. Dekmejian, *Egypt Under Nasir,* p. 257.

8. Rizq, *Madhabih, passim.* Also Saad Eddin Ibrahim, "Anatomy of Egypt's Militant Islamic Groups," *IJMES* 12, no. 4 (December 1980): 434–35.

9. Dekmejian, *Egypt Under Nasir,* p. 257.

10. Hasan Hanafi, "Wa Kanat al-Naksah Nuqtah Tahawwul" [The Defeat was a Turning Point], *Al-Watan* (November 20, 1982).

11. *Ibid.*

12. R. H. Dekmejian, "Egypt and Turkey: The Military in the Background," in *Soldiers, Peasants and Bureaucrats,* edited by R. Kolkowicz and A. Korbonski (London: George Allan and Unwin, 1982), pp. 37–40.

13. On the Brotherhood's attacks on Sadat's internal and external policies, see for example, *Al-Dawah* (February 1977): 2–16, and *Al-Itisam* (April–May 1981): 28–29. On the passage of *shariah* legislation on apostasy, see Philippe Rochot, *La Grande Fievre du Monde Musulman* (Paris, 1981), pp. 143–45.

14. See Hasan Hanafi's series of incisive articles in *Al-Watan,* beginning on November 20, 1982. In 1980, the government promised to build about 1,000 mosques; see Rochot, *La Grande Fievre,* pp. 143–45.

15. *Ibid.;* also see Hassan Hanafi, "The Relevance of the Islamic Alternative in Egypt," *Arab Studies Quarterly* 4, nos. 1 and 2 (Spring 1982): 62–63.

16. Nazih N. M. Ayubi, "The Political Revival of Islam: The Case of Egypt," *IJMES* 12, no.4 (December 1980): 492.

17. See the direct threat issued to President Mubarak in *Al-Mujtama* (Kuwait) (May 19, 1982): 44. This is the official organ of the Social Reform Society of Kuwait. Also an assassination attempt against Mubarak was reported on April 25, 1982; see *Al-Mujtama* (May 11, 1982).

18. Hasan Ismail al-Hudaybi, *Duah la Qudah* [Proselytizers not Judges] (Cairo, 1977), pp. 63–65.

19. Sayyid Qutb, *Maalim fil-Tariq* [Signposts on the Road] (n.p., 1970), pp. 8–10, 83–96.

20. *Ibid.*, pp. 66–82. On "permanent" *jihad* see Sayyid Qutb, *Al-Salam al-Alami wal-Islam* [World Peace and Islam] (Cairo: n.d.), p. 151.

21. Qutb, *Maalim,* pp. 9–10.

22. *Ibid.*, pp. 8, 25, 35.

23. See the criticism by the Brotherhood's former Supreme Guide Hasan al-Hudaybi, *Duah la Qudah,* pp. 63–65.

24. Sayyid Qutb, *Khasais al-Tasawwur al-Islami wa Muqawwamatuhu* [Characteristics of the Islamic Vision and its Components] (Cairo, 1965), p. 49. For details see Sayyid Qutb, *Fi Zilal al-Quran* [Under the Shadows of the Quran] Vol. 4, Parts 12–18 (Beirut: Dar al-Shuruq, 1974), pp. 2011–13.

25. Salim Ali al-Bahnasawi, *Al-Hukm wal-Qadiyyah Takfir al-Muslim* [The Government and the Cause of the Accusation of Muslims] (Kuwait, 1981), p. 48.

26. See particularly Sayyid Qutb, *Fi Zilal al-Quran* [Under the Shadows of the Quran] Vol. 4 Part 10, (n.p., 1966), pp. 65–67.

27. Bahnasawi, *Al-Hukm,* pp. 127–33. Also, Bahnasawi, *Al-Arabi* (January 10, 1982).

28. Abd al-Rahman Abu al-Khayr, *Zikriyati maa Jamaat al-Muslimin* [My Recollections of the Society of Muslims] (Cairo, 1980), p. 19.

29. *Ibid.,* p. 137.

30. *Ibid.,* pp. 138–39.

31. For an insightful comparative study see Saad Eddin Ibrahim, "Anatomy," pp. 423–53.

32. Salim al-Bahnasawi, *Al-Arabi* (January 10, 1982).

33. Ibrahim, "Anatomy," pp. 432–35.

34. Bahnasawi, *Al-Hukm,* pp. 34–37.

35. *Ibid.,* pp. 36–38.

36. Abu al-Khayr, *Zikriyati,* p. 10.

37. Ibrahim, "Anatomy," pp. 435–36.

38. Bahnasawi, *Al-Arabi* (January 10, 1982).

39. Ibrahim, "Anatomy," p. 437.

40. Israel Altman, "Islamic Movements in Egypt," *The Jerusalem Quarterly* (Winter 1979): 101.

41. Ibrahim, "Anatomy," pp. 436–39.

42. *Ibid.,* p. 441.

43. Ahmad Kamal Abu al-Majd, "Al-Tatarruf Ghayr al-Jarimah wal-Tashkhis al-Daqiq Matlub" [Extremism is not the Crime: A Precise Investigation is Required], *Al-Arabi* (January 1982): 36–40; and Abu al-Khayr, *Zikriyati,* pp. 9–13.

44. Abu al-Khayr, *Zikriyati,* p. 61. *Al-Musawwar* (May 4, 1984): 20–25.

45. On details see *Al-Jihad* (December 31, 1982): 22; Mohamed Heikal, *Autumn of Fury* (London: André Deutsch, 1983), pp. 242–55. Also, see the series of insightful articles by Hasan Hanafi, "Al-Harakah al-Muasirah al-Islamiyyah," *Al-Watan* (November 20–December 12, 1982).

46. This similarity is noted by Nazih N. M. Ayubi, "Militant Islamic Movements," *Journal of International Affairs* 36, no. 2 (Fall/Winter 1982–83): 279.

47. Hanafi, *Al-Watan* (December 8, 1982).

48. Heikal, *Autumn,* pp. 246–47, 249.

49. *Ibid.,* p. 246.

50. Muhammad Abd al-Salam Faraj, *Al-Faridah al-Ghaibah* [The Absent Obligation] (n.p., n.d.)

51. For some unknown reason Sadat's name appears only in the English translation. See Faraj, *Al-Jihad: The Forgotten Pillar* (Canada, n.d.), p. 19.

52. See *Al-Mujtama* (October 13, 1982): 21; also *Al-Mujtama* (December 14, 1982).

53. Examples of these self-help societies are: Jamiah al-Shariyyah; Ansar al-Sunna al-Muhammadiyyah; Jamaah al-Hidayah; al-Waz wal-Irshad; al-Amr bil-Maruf wal-Nahya an al-Munkar.

54. See Abu Khalid (pen name), "Al-Harakah al-Islamiyyah wa Nizam Husni Mubarak" [The Islamic Movement and the Regime of Husni Mubarak], *Al-Mujtama* (October 13, 1982).

55. *Al-Akhbar* (May 9, 1982).

56. For further discussion, see Amr H. Ibrahim, "Légitimité et Révolution en Islam," *Peuples Méditerranéens* no. 21 (October–December 1982): 81–101. Also *Al-Ahram* (November 21, 1981).

[A Preliminary Juristical Glance at the Draft of the Constitution of the Islamic Republic in Iran] (Qum, 1979), pp. 18–35.

11. Muhammad Baqir al-Sadr, *Khilafat al-Insan wa Shihadat al-Anbiya* [Caliphate of Men and Testimony of Prophets] (Qum, 1979), pp. 21–27, 49–55.

12. *Tariq al-Haq* (April 1982): 3, 20–21.

13. Batatu, "Iraq's Underground," pp. 590–91.

14. Philippe Rochot, *La Grande Fièvre du Monde Musulman* (Paris: Sycomore, 1981), p. 62.

15. Batatu, "Iraq's Underground," pp. 591–92.

16. *Ibid.*, p. 594.

17. Rochot, *La Grande Fièvre,* p. 62. Also see *Sawt al-Rafidayn* (December 1982): 5–9.

18. Batatu, "Iraq's Underground," p. 578.

19. *Ibid.*, p. 593.

20. *Sawt al-Rafidayn* (December 1982): 5–9.

21. *Ibid.*, pp. 2–4.

22. *Al-Jihad* (September 1982): 6.

23. *Al-Tawheed (May 1983): 3. Al-Mustaqbal* (April 7, 1984): 55–56.

24. See the undated letter sent to Tilmisani by Hujjat al-Islam Sayyid Hadi Khusru Shahi.

9—Saudi Arabia: Sunni and Shiite Militancy Against an Islamic State

1. For details see H. St. John Philby, *Saudi Arabia* (New York: Praeger, 1955). Most Saudi followers of Abd al-Wahhab resent being called Wahhabis since they associate themselves with the School of Ibn Hanbal.On ideological foundations see Shaykh Muhammad Ibn Abd al-Wahhab, *Kitab al-Tawhid* [Book of Unicity], translated by Ismail Raji al-Faruqi (Beirut: The Holy Koran Publishing House, 1979).

2. James P. Piscatori, "The Role of Islam in Saudi Arabia's Political Development," in *Islam and Development,* edited by John L. Esposito (Syracuse: Syracuse University Press, 1980), p. 125.

3. For a comprehensive analysis see the underground publication authored under the pen name of Abu Dharr, *Al-Ikhwan Madiyan wa Hadiran* [The Brethren in the Past and the Present] (n.p., 1980), pp. 243–52. Note that Abu Dharr was the Prophet's "communist" companion, which reflects the identity of the leftist coalition that opposes the Saudi regime with its publication series under the title of *Sawt al-Talia* [Voice of the Vanguard].

4. Abu Dharr, *Al-Ikhwan,* pp. 246–47.

5. Farouk A. Sankari, "Islam and Politics in Saudi Arabia," in Ali E. Hillal Dessouki, ed., *Islamic Resurgence in the Arab World* (New York: Praeger, 1982), pp. 186–88.

6. *Ibid.,* pp. 184–85.

7. Piscatori, "The Role of Islam," p. 135.

8. Over 30,000 Americans were reported to be living in Saudi Arabia in the late 1970s. See George Linabury, "The Creation of Saudi Arabia and the Erosion of Wahhabi Conservatism," in Michael Curtis ed., *Religion and Politics in the Middle East* (Boulder, Co.: Westview, 1981), p. 282.

9. Abu Dharr, *Al-Ikhwan,* pp. 248–52.

10. William Ochsenwald, "Saudi Arabia and the Islamic Revival," *International Journal of Middle East Studies* 13, no. 3 (August 1981): 274.

11. Juhayman ibn al-Saif al-Utaybi, *Saba Rasail* [Seven Letters] (n.p., n.d.), p. 145.

12. Anonymous, "Ahdath al-Haram Bayn al-Haqaiq wal-Abatil" [The Events of the Grand Mosque between Truth and Lies], *Sawt al-Talia* (May 1980): 120–22.

13. Utaybi, *Saba Rasail,* pp. 3–31, 35–51, 133–90.

14. *Ibid.;* and *Sawt al-Talia* (May 1980): 22–29, 144–48.

15. There is wide disagreement on the number of insurgents; see *Sawt al-Taliah* (May 1980): 42–45.

16. Abu Dharr, *Al-Ikhwan,* pp. 250–52.

17. *Le Point* (Paris, January 28, 1980). Some sources have mentioned Jordanian participation in crushing the Grand Mosque revolt. See *Al-Safir* (Beirut, December 9, 1979). Reportedly, five French anti-insurgency experts were brought in to direct the attack by use of television.

18. *Sawt al-Talia* (May 1980): 128–29. Rochot, *La Grande Fièvre,* p. 92.

19. See "La Révolution dans la Présqu'île en 1400 H. Étude de la Lutte Populaire avant le Soulèvement de la Présqu'île Arabe," *Peuples Méditerranéens* 21 (Paris, October–December 1982): 60–71.

20. Documents Arabie Séoudite, "L'Islamisme en Effervescence," *Peuples Méditerranéens* 21 (Paris, October–December 1982): 63.

21. *Ibid.,* also see *Sawt al-Taliah* (March 1974): 66–70.

22. Fred Halliday, "The Shifting Sands Beneath the House of Saud," *The Progressive* (March 1980): 39.

23. This was the thrust of interviews conducted with a dozen Saudi university students in May 1983.

24. Piscatori, "The Role of Islam," p. 127.

25. Documents, pp. 168–69.

26. *The Washington Post* (June 16, 1983).

10—Islamic Fundamentalism in the Gulf

1. James A. Bill, "Islam, Politics and Shiism in The Gulf," *Middle East Insight* 3, no. 3 (January/February 1984): 7.

2. Tawfic E. Farah, "Politics and Religion in Kuwait," in Ali E. Hillal Dessouki, ed., *Islamic Resurgence in the Arab World* (New York: Praeger, 1982), pp. 171, 176.

3. See *Al-Muslim al-Muasir* and *Al-Wayi al-Islami.*

4. *Al-Mujtama* (May 19, 1982): 44.

5. *Al-Mujtama* (August 4, 1982): 12.

6. *Al-Mustaqbal* (December 17, 1983): 16–18.

7. *Facts on File* (1982), p. 58.

8. *Ibid.*

9. *Ibid.,* pp. 58, 398. *Al-Dustur* (January 11, 1982): 26–27.

10. Philip Hitti, *History of the Arabs* (London: Macmillan, 1980), pp. 246–47.

11. Nabil M. Kaylani, "Politics and Religion in Uman: A Historical Overview," *International Journal of Middle East Studies* 10, no. 4 (November 1979): 574.

12. See *MERIP Reports* (January 1980): 19–22.

13. The percentage of the Arab natives in the U. A. E. is 22 percent. See *MERIP Reports* (January 1980): 21.

14. *Iran Times* (June 18, 1982): 2.

15. *MERIP Reports* (January 1980): 19–22, 25.

11—Prognostic Factors in Crisis Environments

1. See Abu Khalid (pen name), in *Al-Mujtama* (July 27, 1982).

2. On the causal relationship between fundamentalism and the Arab-Israeli conflict see R. H. Dekmejian, "Islamic Revival and the Arab-Israeli Conflict," *New Outlook* (November–December 1980).

3. Nabil Abd al-Hadi, "Al-Islam wal-Ilam al-Misri" [Islam and the Egyptian Mass Media] *Al-Jihad* (Tehran, December 31, 1982): 20.

4. For a similar approach based on the work of Gellner and others see Michael M. J. Fisher, "Islam and the Revolt of the Petit Bourgeoisie," *Daedalus* (Winter 1982): 110–20.

5. On the persistence of revivalism as a cultural vocabulary see Ira M. Lapidus, *Contemporary Islamic Movements in Historical Perspective* (Berkeley: University of California Press, 1983), pp. 62–63.

Bibliography

Books

Abdalati, Hammudah. *Islam in Focus.* Kuwait: The International Islamic Federation of Student Organizations, 1978.

Abd-Allah, Umar F. *The Islamic Struggle in Syria.* Berkeley, Ca.: Mizan Press, 1983.

Abd al-Halim, Mahmud. *Al-Ikhwan al-Muslimun* [The Muslim Brothers]. Alexandria, 1979.

Abdel-Malek, Anouar. *Egypt: Military Society.* New York: Random House, 1968.

Abrahamian, Ervand. *Iran Between Two Revolutions.* Princeton: Princeton University Press, 1982.

Abu al-Khayr, Abd al-Rahman. *Zikriyati Maa Jamaat al-Muslimin: Al Takfir wal-Hijrah* [My Memoirs of the Society of Muslims]. Kuwait, 1980.

Abu al-Majd, Ahmad Kamal. *Al-Tatarruf* [Extremism]. Cairo, n.d.

Adorno, T. W. *et al. The Authoritarian Personality.* New York: Norton, 1982.

Anbar, Muhammad Abd al-Rahim. *Nahwa Thawrah Islamiyyah* [Toward an Islamic Revolution]. Cairo, 1979.

Anonymous. *Al-Muslimun fi Suriya wal-Irhab al-Nusayri* [The Muslims in Syria and Nusayri Terror]. n.p., n.d.

Antonious, George. *The Arab Awakening.* New York: Capricorn Books, 1965.

Arberry, A. J., ed. *Religion in the Middle East.* Cambridge, U.K.: Cambridge University Press, 1969.

Awda, Abd al-Qadir. *Al-Islam wa Awdauna al-Siyasiyyah* [Islam and Our Political Positions]. Cairo, n.d.

Ayoob, Mohammed, ed. *The Politics of Islamic Reassertion.* London: St. Martin's. 1981.

Badawi, Abd al-Rahman. *Madhahib al-Islamiyyah al-Hadith* [Modern Islamic Schools of Law]. Cairo, 1964.

al-Bahnasawi, Salim Ali. *Al-Hukm wal-Qadiyyah Takfir al-Muslim* [The Authority and the Cause of the Muslim Accusation of Unbelief]. Kuwait, 1981.

al-Banna, Hasan. *Mudhakkarat al-Dawah wal-Daiyyah* [Memoirs of the Call and the Caller]. 1951.

Bayyumi, Zakariyya Sulayman. *Al-Ikhwan al-Muslimin* [The Muslim Brethren]. Cairo, 1979.

Bin Nabi, Malik. *Mushkilat al-Afkar fil-Alam al-Islami* [The Problem of Ideas in the Muslim World]. Cairo, 1971.

———. *Al-Muslim fi Alam al-Iqtisad* [The Muslim in the Economic World]. Beirut, n.d.

———. *Al-Zahirah al-Quraniyyah* [An Essay on Quranic Theory]. n.p., n.d.

Binder, Leonard. *The Ideological Revolution in the Middle East.* New York: John Wiley and Sons, 1964.

———. *In a Moment of Enthusiasm.* Chicago: University of Chicago Press, 1978.

Cudsi, S. Alexander, and Dessouki, A. E. H., eds. *Islam and Power.* Baltimore: The Johns Hopkins University Press, 1981.

Curtis, Michael, ed. *Religion and Politics in the Middle East.* Boulder, Co.: Westview, 1981.

Dekmejian, R. Hrair. *Egypt Under Nasir.* Albany, N.Y.: SUNY Press, 1971.

———. *Patterns of Political Leadership: Egypt, Israel & Lebanon.* Albany, N.Y.: SUNY Press, 1975.

Dessouki, Ali E. Hillal, ed. *Islamic Resurgence in the Arab World.* New York: Praeger, 1982.

Devlin, John F. *Syria: Modern State in an Ancient Land.* Boulder, Co.: Westview, 1982.

Dhar, Abu (pseud.). *Al-Ikhwan Madiyan wa Hadiran* [The Brethren in the Past and in the Present]. n.p., 1980.

Direnzo, Gordon, J. *Personality and Politics.* Garden City, N.Y.: Anchor Press/ Doubleday, 1974.

Donohue, John, and Esposito, J. L., eds. *Islam in Transition: Religion and Sociopolitical Change.* New York: Oxford University Press, 1982.

Durkheim, Emile. *Suicide: A Study in Sociology.* Glencoe, Il.: Free Press, 1951.

Enayat, Hamid. *Modern Islamic Political Thought.* Austin: University of STexas Press, 1982.

Encyclopaedia of Islam. Vol. 3. Leiden: E. J. Brill, 1971.

Erikson, Erik. *Young Man Luther.* New York: Norton, 1958.

———. *Identity, Youth and Crisis.* New York: Norton, 1968.

———. *Childhood and Society.* New York: Norton, 1950.

Esposito, John L., ed. *Islam and Development: Religion and Sociopolitical Change.* Syracuse, N.Y.: Syracuse University Press, 1980.

Fadlallah, Muhammad Husayn. *Al-Islam wa Mantiq al-Quwwah* [Islam and the Sphere of Power]. n.p., 1979.

Faraj, Mohammad Abdessalam. *Al-Jihad: The Forgotten Pillar.* Ontario, Canada: n.p., n.d.

———. *Al-Faridah al-Ghaibah* [The Absent Obligation]. N.p. N.d.

Fischer, Michael M. J. *Iran, from Religious Dispute to Revolution.* Cambridge, Ma.: Harvard University Press, 1980.

Gellner, Ernest. *Muslim Society.* Cambridge: Cambridge University Press, 1981.

Gibb, Hamilton A. R. *Modern Trends in Islam.* Chicago: University of Chicago Press, 1947.

———. *Studies on the Civilization of Islam.* Boston, Ma.: Beacon Press, 1962.

Gilsenan, Michael. *Recognizing Islam.* London: Pantheon, 1983.

Guillaume, Alfred. *Islam.* New York: Penguin, 1954.

Habermas, Jürgen. *The Legitimation Crisis.* Boston: Beacon Press, 1975.

Haddad, Yvonne Yazbeck. *Contemporary Islam and the Challenge of History.* Albany, N.Y.: SUNY Press, 1982.

al-Hajjaji, Ahmad Anis. *Al-Rajul alladhi Ashal-Thawrah* [The Man Who Sparked the Revolution]. Cairo, 1952.

Hamad, Muhammad Abu al-Qasim Hajj. *Al-Sudan.* Beirut, 1980.

Hawwa, Said. *Allahu Jalla Jalalahu* [God in His Exalted Majesty]. Beirut, 1975.

———. *Jawalat fil-Fiqhayn al-Kabir wal-Akbar* [Excursions on Two Fiqhs—The Great and The Greatest]. Alexandria, Egypt, 1980.

———. *Min Ajl Khatwah ila al-Amam ala Tariq al-Jihad al-Mubarak* [To Take a Step Forward on the Road to Blessed Jihad]. Beirut, 1979.

Heikal, Mohamed. *Autumn of Fury: The Assassination of Sadat.* London: André Deutsch, 1983.

Hijazi, Awad Awadallah Jad. *Ibn al-Qayyim wa Mawqifahu min al-Takfir al-Islami* [Ibn al-Qayyim and His Position in Islamic Thought]. Cairo, 1973.

Hitti, Philip K. *History of the Arabs.* London: Macmillan, 1980.

Hodgson, Marshall. *The Venture of Islam.* Chicago: University of Chicago Press, 1977.

Holt, P. M. *The Mahdist State in the Sudan 1881–1898.* Oxford: Clarendon Press, 1958.

Hourani, Albert. *Arabic Thought in the Liberal Age, 1798–1939.* London: Oxford University Press, 1970.

al-Hudaybi, Hasan. *Duah la Qudah* [Proselytizers Not Judges]. Cairo, 1977.

Hudson, Michael C. *Arab Politics: The Search for Legitimacy.* New Haven, Ct.: Yale University Press, 1979.

Husaini, Ishak Musa. *The Moslem Brethren.* Beirut: Khayat's, 1956.

Ibn Abd al-Wahhab, Shaykh Muhammad. *Kitab al-Tawhid* [Book of Unicity]. Translated by Ismail Raji al-Faruqi. Beirut: The Holy Koran Publishing House, 1979.

Ibn Kathir al-Dimashqi, Imad al-Din. *Kitab al-Ijtihad fi Talab al-Jihad* [The Book of Diligent Pursuit of Holy War]. Cairo, 1928.

Ibn Taymiyyah, Taqi al-Din Ahmad. *Al-Siyasah al-Shariyyah* [The Politics of Legitimacy]. Beirut, 1966.

Imara, Muhammad. *Al-Islam wa Falsafat al-Hukm* [Islam and the Philosophy of Government]. Beirut, 1979.

——. *Muslimun Thuwwar* [Revolutionary Muslims]. Cairo, 1972.

——. *Al-Islam wal-Thawrah* [Islam and Revolution]. Cairo, 1979.

Iskandar, Amir. *Saddam Husayn*. Paris: Hachette, 1980.

Jansen, G. H. *Militant Islam*. New York: Harper and Row, 1980.

Jawzi, Bandali. *Min Tarikh al-Harakat al-Fikri fil-Islam* [A History of Intellectual Movements in Islam]. n.p., 1981.

Kazim, Fuad. *Arqam wa Ara Hawl Nizam al-Baath fi al-Iraq* [Numbers and Opinions Regarding Baath Rule in Iraq]. Tehran, 1982.

Keddie, Nikki R. *Iran: Religion, Politics, and Society*. London: Frank Cass, 1980.

Kerr, Malcolm H. *The Arab Cold War, 1958–1967: A Study of Ideology in Politics*. London: Oxford University Press, 1971.

——. *Islamic Reform*. Berkeley, Ca.: University of California Press, 1966.

Khadduri, Majid. *Political Trends in the Arab World: The Role of Ideas and Ideals in Politics*. Baltimore: Johns Hopkins University Press, 1970.

——. *Independent Iraq 1932–1958*. London: Oxford University Press, 1960.

——. *War and Peace in the Law of Islam*. Baltimore: Johns Hopkins University Press, 1955.

al-Khuli, al-Bahi. *Tafkirat al-Duat* [Thoughts on Missionary Work]. Cairo, 1953.

al-Khumayni, Ayatullah. *Al-Hukumah al-Islamiyyah* [The Islamic Government]. Beirut, 1979.

Lacey, Robert. *The Kingdom*. New York: Harcourt Brace Jovanovich, 1981.

Lapidus, Ira M. *Contemporary Islamic Movements in Historical Perspective*. Berkeley: University of California Press, 1983.

Lewis, Bernard. *The Arabs in History*. New York: Harper and Row, 1980.

——. *Islam in History*. New York: The Library Press, 1973.

Mahdi, al-Sadiq, Al. *Al-Mahdiyyah* [The Mahdiyyah]. Beirut, 1975.

Makari, Victor E. *Ibn Taymiyyah's Ethics*. Chico, Ca.: Scholars Press, 1983.

Malefijt, Anemarie De Waal. *Religion and Culture*. New York: Macmillan, 1968.

Maududi, S. Abul Ala. *A Short History of the Revivalist Movement in Islam*. Lahore, Pakistan: Islamic Publications, 1963.

al-Mawdudi, Abu al-Ala. *Nadhariyyah al-Islam wa Hadiyyah fi al-Siyasah wal-Qanun al-Dusturi* [Islamic Theory and Guidance in Politics, Law, and Constitution]. Beirut, 1975.

Mitchell, Richard P. *The Society of the Muslim Brothers*. London: Oxford University Press, 1969.

Montesquieu, Charles L. "Considération sur les causes de la Grandeur des

Romains et de leur Décadance," *Oeuvres Complètes de Montesquieu.* Paris, 1951.

Penrose, E. F. and Edith. *Iraq.* Boulder, Co.: Westview Press, 1978.

Peretz, Don; Moench, Richard U.; and Mohsen, Safia. *Islam: Legacy of the Past, Challenge of the Future.* North River Press, 1984.

Peters, Rudolph. *Islam and Colonialism.* The Hague: Mouton, 1979.

Philby, St. John. *Saudi Arabia.* New York: Praeger, 1955.

al-Qadiri, Abu Bakr. *Fi Sabil Wayi al-Islami* [In the Path of Islamic Spirit]. 1977.

Qasim, Awn al-Sharif. *Al-Islam wal-Baath al-Qawmi* [Islam and the National Renaissance]. Beirut, 1980.

———. *Al-Islam wal-Thawrah al-Hadariyyah* [Islam and the Revolution of Civilization]. Cairo, 1965.

Qutb, Muhammad. *Al-Insan Bayna al-Maddiyyah wal-Islam* [Man between Materialism and Islam]. Cairo, 1965.

Qutb, Sayyid. *Al-Adala Al-Ijtimaiyyah fi al-Islam* [Social Justice in Islam]. Cairo, 1964.

———. *Dirasat Islamiyyah* [Studies on Islam]. Jeddah, 1967.

———. *Fi Zilal al-Quran* [Under the Shadows of the Quran]. Vol. 4, 12–18. Beirut: Dar al-Shuruq, 1974.

———. *Fi Zilal al-Quran* [Under the Shadows of the Quran]. Vol. 4, 10. N.p., 1966.

———. *Hadha al-Din* [This is the Religion]. Cairo. N.d.

———. *Islam: The Religion of the Future.* Kuwait: New Era Publishers, 1977.

———. *Khasais al-Tasawwur al-Islami wa Muqawwamatuhu* [Characteristics of the Islamic Vision and its Components]. Cairo, 1965.

———. *Maalim fil-Tariq* [Milestones]. Beirut, 1968.

———. *Milestones.* Kuwait: New Era Publishers, 1978.

———. *Al-Salam al-Alami wal-Islam* [World Peace and Islam]. Cairo, n.d.

———. *Social Justice in Islam.* Washington, D.C.: American Council of Learned Societies, 1953.

———. *This Religion of Islam.* Kuwait: New Era Publishers, 1977.

Rahman, Fazlur. *Islam.* Chicago: University of Chicago Press, 1979.

Rizq, Jabir. *Madhabih al-Ikhwan fi Sujun Abd al-Nasser* [The Killing of the Brothers in Nasser's Prisons]. Cairo, 1977.

Rochot, Philippe. *La Grande Fièvre du Monde Musulman.* Paris: Sycomore, 1981.

Rodinson, Maxime. *Mohammed.* New York: Vintage Books, 1974.

Rosenthal, Franz, trans. *The Muqaddimah: An Introduction to History.* Princeton: Princeton University Press, 1958.

al-Sadr, Muhammad Baqir. *Al-Bank al-Laribawi fil-Islam* [The Non-Usurious Bank in Islam]. Kuwait, n.d.

———. *Contemporary Man and Social Problems.* Tehran, 1980.

———. *Falsafatuna* [Our Philosophy]. Beirut, 1962.

———. *Khilafat al-Insan wa Shihadat al-Anbiya* [Caliphate of Men and Testimony of Prophets]. Qum, 1979.

———. *Lamhah Fiqhiyyah Tamhidiyyah an Mushru Dustur al-Jumhuriyyat al-Islamiyyah fi Iran* [A Preliminary Glance at the Draft of the Constitution of the Islamic Republic in Iran]. Qum, 1979.

Safran, Nadav. *Egypt in Search of Political Community 1804–1952.* Cambridge, Ma.: Harvard University Press, 1961.

al-Said, Rifat. *Hasan al-Banna.* Cairo, 1979.

Shaked, Haim. *The Life of the Sudanese Mahdi.* New Brunswick, N.J., Transaction, 1978.

Saqr, Abd al-Hadi. *Kayfa Nadu al-Nas* [How do We Summon the People]. Cairo, 1976.

Shalabi, Rauf. *Al-Shaykh Hasan al-Banna* [The Shaykh Hasan al-Banna]. Cairo, 1978.

Shariati, Ali. *Intizar . . . Madhabi Itiraz* [Awaiting . . . The Religion of Protest]. Tehran, 1971.

al-Sharqawi, Abd al-Rahman. *Qiraat fil-Fikr al-Islami* [Readings in Islamic Thought]. Beirut, 1975.

al-Sibai, Mustafa. *Ishtirakiyyah al-Islam* [Islamic Socialism]. Damascus, 1958.

Smith, Wilfred Cantwell. *Islam in Modern History.* Princeton: Princeton University Press, 1957.

Stoddard, Philip; Cuthell, D. C.; and Sullivan, M. W., eds. *Change and the Muslim World.* Syracuse, N.Y.: Syracuse University Press, 1981.

al-Tahtawi, Muhammad Ismail. *Fil-Dawah ila al-Islam* [Invitation to Islam]. Cairo, 1979.

Tarbush, Mohammad A. *The Role of the Military in Politics: A Case Study of Iraq to 1941.* London: Routledge and Kegan Paul, 1982.

al-Utaybi, Juhayman Ibn Saif. *Saba' Rasa'il* [Seven Letters]. N.p., N.d.

Van Dam, Nikolaos. *The Struggle for Power in Syria,* 2nd ed. London: Croom Helm, 1981.

Voll, John Obert. *Islam: Continuity and Change in the Modern World.* Boulder, Co: Westview, 1982.

Von Grunebaum, G. E. *Medieval Islam.* Chicago: University of Chicago Press, 1947.

Weber, Max. *The Theory of Social and Economic Organization.* New York: Oxford University Press, 1947.

Wendell, Charles, ed. *Five Tracts of Hasan al-Banna.* Berkeley, Ca., 1978.

Williams, John Alden, ed. *Themes of Islamic Civilization.* Berkeley: University of California Press, 1971.

Wise, George S., and Issawi, Charles, eds. *Middle East Perspectives: The Next Twenty Years.* Princeton: Princeton University Press, 1981.

Zahrah, Muhammad Abu. *Al-Dawah Ila al-Islam* [The Call to Islam]. N.p., 1973.

———. *Tarikh al-Madhahib al-Islamiyyah II:* [History of Islamic Schools of Law]. Cairo, n.d.

Zaki, Muhammad Shawqi. *Al-Ikhwan al-Muslimun wal-Mujtama al-Misri* [The Muslim Brethren and Egyptian Society]. N.p. N.d.

Zeine, N. Zeine. *The Struggle for Arab Independence*. Delmar, N.Y.: Caravan Books, 1977.

Journals and Newspapers (Arabic)

Al-Mujtama [The Society]	Kuwait
Al-Arabi [The Arabian]	Kuwait
Al-Watan [The Fatherland]	Kuwait
Sawt al-Talia [Voice of the Vanguard]	Saudi Arabia
Al-Mustaqbal al-Arabi [The Arab Future]	Lebanon
Al-Dawah [The Call]	Saudi Arabia, Egypt/Austria
Al-Itisam [Preservation]	Lebanon/Egypt
Al-Ahram [The Pyramid]	Egypt
Al-Ahali [The People]	Egypt
Al-Nadhir [The Warner]	Syria/Austria
Al-Minbar [The Pulpit]	Geneva
Tariq al-Haq [The Way of Truth]	USA
Al-Akhbar [The News]	Egypt
Sawt al-Rafidayn [Voice of Mesopotamia]	USA
Al-Jihad [Holy Struggle]	Iran
Al-Tawheed [Unity of God]	USA
Al-Safir [The Ambassador]	Beirut
Al-Baath [The Renaissance]	Syria
Al-Muslim al-Muasir [The Contemporary Muslim]	Kuwait
Al-Tasawwuf al-Islami [Islamic Sufism]	Kuwait
Manar al-Islam [Lighthouse of Islam]	Kuwait/Egypt
Al-Wayi al-Islami [Islamic Consciousness]	Kuwait/Egypt
Minbar al-Islam [Islamic Pulpit]	Egypt
Al-Hidayah [The Gift]	Bahrain
Al-Ummah [The Community]	Qatar
Liwa al-Islam [Flock of Islam]	Egypt

Articles (Non-Arabic)

Abrahamian, E. "Structural Causes of the Iranian Revolution." *MERIP Reports* 10, no. 4: 1980.

Ajami, Fouad. "The End of Pan-Arabism." *Foreign Affairs* (Winter 1979).

Altman, Israel. "Islamic Movements in Egypt." *The Jerusalem Quarterly* 10: 1979.

Ayubi, Nazih N. M. "The Political Revival of Islam: The Case of Egypt." *IJMES* 12, no. 4 (December 1980).

———. "Militant Islamic Movements." *Journal of International Affairs* 36, no. 2 (Fall/Winter 1982–83).

Batatu, Hanna. "Iraq's Underground Shi'a Movements: Characteristics, Causes and Prospects." *Middle East Journal* 35, no. 4 (Autumn 1981).

———. "Some Observations on the Social Roots of Syria's Ruling Military Group and the Causes for its Dominance." *Middle East Journal* 35, no. 3 (Summer 1981).

———. "Syria's Muslim Brethren." *MERIP Reports* (November–December 1982).

Bell, Daniel. "Sociodicy: A Guide to Modern Usage." *The American Scholar* 35, no. 4 (Autumn 1965).

Bello, Iysa Ade. "The Society of Muslim Brethren: An Ideological Study." *Islamic Studies* 20, no. 2: 1981.

Bill, James A. "Islam, Politics, and Shiism in the Gulf." *Middle East Insight* 3, no. 3 (January–February 1984).

Butterworth, Charles E. "Prudence Versus Legitimacy: The Persistent Theme in Islamic Political Thought." In *Islamic Resurgence in the Arab World* edited by Ali E. Hillal Dessouki. New York: Praeger, 1982.

Cantori, Louis J. "Religion and Politics in Egypt." In M. Curtis, ed. *Religion and Politics in the Middle East.* Boulder, Co.: Westview, 1981.

Dekmejian, R. Hrair. "The Anatomy of Islamic Revival: Legitimacy Crisis, Ethnic Conflict and the Search for Islamic Alternatives." *Middle East Journal* 34, no. 1 (Winter 1980).

———. "Egypt and Turkey: The Military in the Background." In *Soldiers, Peasants and Bureaucrats,* edited by R. Kolkowicz and A. Korbonski. London: George Allen and Unwin, 1982.

———. "The Islamic Revival in the Middle East and North Africa." *Current History* 78, no. 456 (April 1980).

———. "Islamic Revival and the Arab-Israeli Conflict." *New Outlook* 23 (November 1980).

———. "Political Thought: Quest for an Ideology." In *The Middle East: Its Governments and Politics,* edited by Abid al-Marayati. Belmont, Ca.: Duxbury, 1972.

———. "The Dialectics of Islamic Revival." *Hellenic Review of International Relations* 1, no. 1 (1980).

Dekmejian, R. Hrair, and M. J. Wyszomirski. "Charismatic Leadership in Islam: The Mahdi of the Sudan." *Comparative Studies in Society and History* 14, no. 2 (March 1972).

Dessouki, Ali E. Hillal. "The Islamic Resurgence: Sources, Dynamics and Implications." In *Islamic Resurgence in the Arab World,* edited by A. E. H. Dessouki. New York: Praeger, 1982.

———. "The Resurgence of Islamic Organizations in Egypt: An Interpretation." In *Islam and Power,* edited by A. S. Cudsi and A. E. H. Dessouki. Baltimore: Johns Hopkins University Press, 1981.

Dhaouadi, Zouhaier. "Islamismes et Politique en Tunisie." *Peuples Méditerranéens* 21 (October–December 1982).

Drysdale, Alasdair. "The Asad Regime and its Troubles." *MERIP Reports* 12, 9 (September 1982).

Enayat, Hamid. "The Resurgence of Islam: The Background." *History Today* 30 (February 1980).

Farah, Tawfic E. "Politics and Religion in Kuwait." In *Islamic Resurgence in the Arab World,* edited by A. E. H. Dessouki. New York: Praeger, 1982.

Fischer, Michael M. J. "Islam and the Revolt of the Petit Bourgeoisie." *Daedalus* (Winter 1982).

Goldberg, E. "Bases of Traditional Reaction: A look at the Muslim Brothers." *Peuples Méditerranéens* 14 (1981).

El-Guindi, Fadwa. "Veiling Infitah with Muslim Ethic: Egypt's Contemporary Islamic Movements." *Social Problems* 28, no. 4 (April 1981).

———. "Is There an Islamic Alternative? The Case of Egypt's Contemporary Islamic Movement." *International Insight* 1, no. 6 (July–August 1981).

———. "Religious Revival and Islamic Survival in Egypt." *International Insight* 1, no. 2 (1980).

Habiby, Raymond N. "Mu'amar Qadhafi's New Islamic Scientific Socialist Society." *Middle East Review* 11, no. 4 (1979).

Haddad, Yvonne. "The Arab-Israeli Wars, Nasserism and the Affirmation of Islamic Identity." In *Islam and Development,* edited by John L. Esposito. Syracuse, N.Y.: Syracuse University Press, 1980.

Hanafi, Hasan. "Des Idéologies Modernistes à l'Islam Révolutionnaire." *Peuples Méditerranéens* 21 (October–December 1982).

———. "The Relevance of the Islamic Alternative in Egypt." *Arab Studies Quarterly* 4, nos. 1 and 2 (1982).

Halliday, Fred. "The Shifting Sands Beneath the House of Saud." *The Progressive* (March 1980).

———. "The Yemens: Conflict and Coexistence." *The World Today* (August–September 1984).

Hassan, Ibrahim. "La Syrie de La Guerre Civile." *Peuples Méditerranéens* 21 (October–December 1982).

Hinnebusch, Raymond A. "The Islamic Movement in Syria: Sectarian Conflict and Urban Rebellion in an Authoritarian-Populist Regime." In *Islamic Resurgence in the Arab World,* edited by A. E. H. Dessouki. New York: Praeger, 1982.

Hodgkin, Thomas. "The Revolutionary Tradition in Islam." *Race and Class* 21, no. 3 (1980).

Hudson, Michael C. "Islam and Political Development." In *Islam and Development,* edited by John L. Esposito. Syracuse, N.Y.: Syracuse University Press, 1980.

Humphreys, R. Stephen. "Islam and Political Values in Saudi Arabia, Egypt and Syria." In *Religion and Politics in the Middle East,* edited by Michael Curtis. Boulder, Co.: Westview, 1981.

———. "The Contemporary Resurgence in the Context of Modern Islam." In *Islamic Resurgence in the Arab World,* edited by A. E. H. Dessouki. New York: Praeger, 1982.

Ibrahim, Amr. H. "Légitimité et Révolution en Islam: Le Débat Ouvert par l'Obligation Absente. *Peuples Méditerranéens* 21 (October–December 1982).

Ibrahim, Saad Eddin. "Anatomy of Egypt's Militant Islamic Groups: Methodological Note and Preliminary Findings." *IJMES* 12, no. 4 (December 1980).

———. "An Islamic Alternative in Egypt: The Muslim Brotherhood and Sadat." *Arab Studies Quarterly* 4, nos. 1 and 2 (Spring 1982).

———. "Islamic Militancy as a Social Movement: The Case of Two Groups in Egypt." In *Islamic Resurgence in the Arab World,* edited by A. E. H. Dessouki. New York: Praeger, 1982.

Israeli, R. "The New Wave of Islam." *International Journal* 34, no. 3 (1979).

Kaylani, Nabil M. "Politics and Religion in Uman: A Historical Overview." *IJMES* 10, no. 4 (November 1979).

Laoust, Henri. "L'influence d'Ibn Taymiyya." In *Islam: Past Influence and Present Challenge,* edited by Alford T. Welch and Pierre Cachia. Edinburgh: Edinburgh University Press, 1979.

Lawson, Fred H. "Social Bases of the Hamah Revolt." *MERIP Reports* (November/December 1982).

Lerman, E. "Mawdudi's Concept of Islam." *Middle East Studies* 17, no. 4 (October 1981).

Lewis, Bernard. "The Return of Islam." *Commentary* 1 (January 1976).

Linabury, George. "The Creation of Saudi Arabia and the Erosion of Wahhabi Conservatism." In *Religion and Politics in the Middle East,* edited by Michael Curtis. Boulder, Co: Westview, 1981.

Mahdi, Al-Sadiq Al. "Islam—Society and Change." In *Voices of Resurgent Islam,* edited by John L. Esposito. New York: Oxford University Press, 1983.

Makdisi, George. "Hanbalite Islam." In *Studies on Islam,* edited and trans. by Merlin L. Swartz. New York: Oxford University Press, 1981.

Marshall, Susan E. "Islamic Revival in the Maghreb: The Utility of Tradition for Modernizing Elites." *Studies in Comparative International Development* 14, no. 2 (Summer 1979).

Mayer, Ann Elizabeth. "Islamic Resurgence or New Prophethood: The Role of Islam in Qadhafi's Ideology." In *Islamic Resurgence in the Arab World,* edited by A. E. H. Dessouki. New York: Praeger, 1982.

Moosa, Matti. "Ahwaz: an Arab Territory." *The Future of the Arab Gulf and the Strategy of Joint Arab Action.* Iraq, 1981.

Mustafa, Shakir. "Arab Cultural Crisis and the Impact of the Past." *The*

Jerusalem Quarterly 11 (Spring 1979). (Reprinted in abridged form from *Al-Adab,* Beirut).

Norton, Richard Augustus. "Making Enemies in South Lebanon: Harakat Amal, The IDF, and South Lebanon." *Middle East Insight* (January–February 1984).

Ochsenwald, W. "Saudi Arabia and the Islamic Revival." *IJMES* 13, no. 3 (August 1981).

Picard, Elisabeth. "La Syrie de 1946 à 1979." In *La Syrie d'Aujourd'hui,* edited by André Raymond. Paris, 1980.

Pipes, Daniel. "'This World is Political!!' The Islamic Revival of the Seventies." *Orbis* 24 (1980).

———. "Oil Wealth and Islamic Resurgence." In *Islamic Resurgence in the Arab World,* edited by A. E. H. Dessouki. New York: Praeger, 1982.

Piscatori, James P. "The Roles of Islam in Saudi Arabia's Political Development." In *Islam and Development,* edited by John L. Esposito. Syracuse: Syracuse University Press, 1980.

Rabinovich, Itamar. "The Islamic Wave." *Washington Quarterly* 1 (1979).

Rahman, Fazlur. "Islam: Challenges and Opportunities." In *Islam: Past Influence and Present Challenge,* edited by Alford T. Welch and Pierre Cachia. Edinburgh: Edinburgh University Press, 1979.

———. "Roots of Islamic Neo-Fundamentalism." In *Change and the Muslim World,* edited by P. Stoddard et al. Syracuse: Syracuse University Press, 1981.

Reed III, Stanley. "Dateline Syria: Fin de Régime?" *Foreign Policy* (Summer 1980).

Roussillon, Alain. "Science Moderne, Islam et Stratégie de Légitimation." *Peuples Méditerranéens* no. 21 (October–December 1982).

Sankari, Farouk A. "Islam and Politics in Saudi Arabia." In *Islamic Resurgence in the Arab World,* edited by A. E. H. Dessouki. New York: Praeger, 1982.

Serageldin, Ismail. "Individual Identity, Group Dynamics and Islamic Resurgence." In *Islamic Resurgence in the Arab World,* edited by A. E. H. Dessouki. New York: Praeger, 1982.

Shuta, Sharif M. "Islamic Revolution in Iran and its Impact on Iraq." *Islamic Studies* 19, no. 3 (1980).

Sivan, Emmanuel. "How Fares Islam?" *Jerusalem Quarterly* 13 (1979).

Springborg, Robert. "Egypt, Syria and Iraq." In *The Politics of Islamic Reassertion,* edited by M. Ayoob. London: Croom Helm, 1981.

Stevens, R. "Sudan's Republican Brothers and Islamic Reform." *Journal of Arab Affairs* 1, no. 1 (October 1981).

Stookey, Robert W. "Religion and Politics in South Arabia." In *Religion and Politics in the Middle East,* edited by M. Curtis. Boulder, Co.: Westview Press, 1981.

Vatin, Jean-Claude. "Revival in the Maghreb: Islam as an Alternative Political Language." In *Islamic Resurgence in the Arab World,* edited by A. E. H. Dessouki. New York: Praeger, 1982.

————. "Religious Resistance and State Power in Algeria." In *Islam and Power,* edited by A. S. Cudsi and A. E. H. Dessouki. Baltimore: Johns Hopkins University Press, 1981.

Vieille, Paul, and Z. Dhaouadi. "Pour Une Approche Anthropologique de l'Islamisme." *Peuples Méditerranéens* 21 (October–December 1982).

Voll, John. "The Islamic Past and the Present Resurgence." *Current History* 78, no. 456 (1980).

————. "Wahhabism and Mahdism: Alternative Styles of Islamic Renewals." *Arab Studies Quarterly* 4, nos. 1 and 2 (1982).

von Sivers, Peter. "Work, Leisure and Religion: The Social Roots of the Revival of Fundamentalist Islam in North Africa." In *Islam et Politique au Maghreb,* edited by Ernest Gellner and Jean-Claude Vatin. Paris, 1981.

Wimberley, Dale W. "Socioeconomic Deprivation and Religious Salience: A Cognitive Behavioral Approach." *Sociological Quarterly* 255 (Spring 1984).

Documents

Bayan al-Thawrah al-Islamiyyah fi Suriyya wa Minhajiha [Declaration and Program of the Islamic Revolution in Syria]. Damascus, November 9, 1980.

"Declaration and Program of the Islamic Revolution in Syria" (in English). Issued in Damascus, on November 9, 1980, by the Higher Command of the Islamic Revolution in Syria.

"Documents Arabie Séoudite, L'Islamisme en Effervescence." *Peuples Méditerranéens* 21 Paris. October–December, 1982.

Istishhad al-Imam Muhammad Baqir al-Sadr min Manzur Hadari [The Martyrdom of Imam Muhammad Baqir al-Sadr from a Civilizational Perspective]. Lebanon, 1981.

"La Révolution dans la présqu'île arabe: Étude de la lutte avant le soulèvement de la présqu'île en 1400 H" (text in French; original in Arabic). Issued by The Organization of the Revolution in the Arabian Peninsula, dated July 9, 1980.

Journals and Newspapers in English and French

Le Monde
Le Monde Diplomatique
The Washington Post

Crescent International
Arab Studies Quarterly
International Journal of Middle East Studies
Current History
New Outlook
Middle East Review
Comparative Studies in Society and History
Hellenic Review of International Relations
The Jerusalem Quarterly
Journal of International Affairs
Iran Times
Peuples Méditerranéens
Al-Nadhir (in English)
El-Nazir (in French)
Le Point
The Progressive
Facts on File
The Middle East Journal
Iran Times
The Washington Post
The New York Times

Index

ISLAM IN REVOLUTION

was composed in 10-point Mergenthaler Linotron 202 Times Roman and leaded
2 points by Coghill Book Typesetting Co., Inc.,
with display type in Chevalier by Eastern Graphics;
printed by sheet-fed offset on 50-pound, acid-free Glatfelter Antique Cream,
Smythe-sewn, and bound over binder's boards in Joanna Arrestox B,
also adhesive bound with paper covers, by Maple-Vail Book Manufacturing Group, Inc.;
and published by

SYRACUSE UNIVERSITY PRESS
Syracuse, New York 13210